Knowledge and Skepticism

Knowledge
and Skepticism

EDITED BY

Marjorie Clay

Bloomsburg University of Pennsylvania

AND

Keith Lehrer

University of Arizona

Westview Press

BOULDER • SAN FRANCISCO • LONDON

Copyright © 1989 by Westview Press, Inc.

Published in 1989 in the United States of America by Westview Press, Inc., 5500 Central Avenue, Boulder, Colorado 80301, and in the United Kingdom by Westview Press, Inc., 13 Brunswick Centre, London WC1N 1AF, England

Library of Congress Cataloging-in-Publication Data
Knowledge and skepticism / edited by Marjorie Clay and Keith Lehrer.
    p.   cm.
  Includes bibliographies.
  Contents: A "doxastic practice" approach to epistemology / William P. Alston—Understanding human knowledge in general / Barry Stroud—The skeptic's appeal / Ernest Sosa—Précis and update of Epistemology and cognition / Alvin I. Goldman—The need to know / Fred Dretske—Convention, confirmation, and credibility / Henry E. Kyburg, Jr.—Probability in the theory of knowledge / Roderick Chisholm—Knowledge reconsidered / Keith Lehrer—Knowledge representation and the interrogative model of inquiry / Jaakko Hintikka.
    ISBN 0-8133-0778-3   ISBN 0-8133-0777-5 (pbk.)
    1. Knowledge, Theory of. I. Clay, Marjorie. II. Lehrer, Keith.
BD161.K59   1989
121—dc20   89-33827
                                                                                   CIP

Printed and bound in the United States of America

The paper used in this publication meets the requirements of the American National Standard for Permanence of Paper for Printed Library Materials Z39.48-1984.

10   9   8   7   6   5   4   3   2   1

To the lecturers and participants of the 1986
Summer Institute on Theory of Knowledge,
Boulder, Colorado

Contents

Introduction

We present this collection of essays as characteristic of philosophical writing in the theory of knowledge. The articles contain a number of major themes: skepticism, externalism, reliabilism, probability, and justification. Many of the articles articulate the relationship among these notions. The majority of them concern themselves one way or another with a problem raised by some form of skepticism and answered by some form of reliabilism. The articles by Alston, Stroud, Sosa, Dretske, and Lehrer belong in this category. Skepticism arises from the risk of error. The risk of error is, however, compatible with a high probability of truth, which may suffice for knowledge. Chisholm offers an explication of probability. Kyburg builds an account of knowledge on epistemic probability and an interest in minimizing error. The probability of truth may, however, be the result of the reliability of the processes generating our beliefs as Goldman, Dretske, and Alston argue, or of our trustworthiness in the quest for truth as Lehrer proposes.

Whether the skeptic prevails depends on the justification we have for rejecting skeptical hypotheses — those concerning dreams, hallucinations, deceptions, and other skeptical favorites. The question of the justification of what we believe is considered by Goldman and Lehrer and, indirectly, by Chisholm. Replying to the skeptic depends on finding access to information that will answer the questions raised. Hintikka provides an interrogative model to explicate how the game we play with some internal or external source of information provides us with knowledge. Though not all of the authors conceive of their problem as that of answering skepticism, we believe that the skeptic provides a useful heuristic device for understanding our various authors and the connections between their work. So let us embrace the skeptic, not so much as an opponent to be vanquished but as a source of enlightenment.

How should we think of the skeptic? That depends on what the skeptic affirms, or, more exactly, on what the skeptic denies. The skeptic denies that we know some things that we think we know. In this way, all of us are skeptics about some things on some occasions, and wisely so. We do not always know as much as we think we do. That provides an opening for the skeptic. If we sometimes are in error when we think we know something, and, indeed, in error in just those circumstances in which we think there is little or no chance that this is so, then we must admit that in all matters of the same sort we are fallible and may fall into error. So we are fallible. Does that mean that knowledge is an illusion? Should we declare, as some have suggested, that epistemology is dead because we are fallible and may err?

There are many replies. Some think and argue that there is no satisfactory reply to the skeptic and, therefore, that the traditional attempt to construct an epistemology that will answer the skeptic is a failure. Stroud belongs to this group. Sosa opposes it. Kyburg argues, contrary to the skeptic, that we are infallible in our reports simply because they are reports, and that the rest of the things we know result from convention — indeed, from conventions depending on the risk of error. There are those, however, who think the challenge of the skeptic may be answered. Alston, Goldman, and Dretske contend that we attain knowledge when our beliefs are generated in a reliable way. Some have denied that this is a necessary condition of knowledge, and others that it suffices. But suppose Alston, Goldman, and Dretske are right. Suppose that reliably generated true beliefs *are* knowledge. Would that send the skeptic packing? Perhaps, but it will be a long, mind-bending farewell.

The foregoing argument against skepticism has been formulated in terms of what is called externalism, a position that, though variously defined, is based on the idea that the relationship between belief and truth that converts true beliefs into knowledge may be one of which the knower herself is completely ignorant. The relationship is external in that the knower may have no idea that the relationship holds. In other words, some external person may know that the relationship holds while the knower herself does not. My belief that I see a computer may be the product of some reliable belief-forming process, though I am ignorant of this fact. Indeed, on this account, children and animals — the family dog, for example — who have no conception of reliable belief-forming processes or, for that matter, of truth or error, have knowledge nonetheless when their beliefs result from such processes. The dog believes that meat is near. His trusty nose makes the generation of his belief reliable. He is rarely wrong about meat. The knowledge of the dog suffices to refute the skeptic. It also shows that we do not need to be able to refute the skeptic in order to have knowledge. Fido knows, but he is unable to refute anyone. Is this line of thought to be taken seriously? Qualifications might be added. One might hold that knowledge is reliably generated true belief but reject the thesis that dogs have beliefs of the requisite kind. The same might be said of children. In fact, however, reliabilists such as Dretske and Goldman take pride in ascribing knowledge to children and animals, and they regard this as an advantage of their theory.

Before considering a skeptical reply, we should note that the main feature of reliabilism — the claim that knowledge may result from something of which we are ignorant, namely, the appropriate relationship between belief and truth — is also a feature of a traditionally opposed epistemology, to wit, foundationalism. A foundationalist may hold that beliefs of a specified sort, foundational beliefs, are justified in themselves because of some intrinsic quality — that of being an introspective, perceptual, or memory belief of a securely circumscribed sort, for example — even though the subject is ignorant of the existence of this intrinsic quality. Chisholm once suggested, for example, that all sensible perceptual takings were evident, where a *sensible* taking was one having a certain sort of internal content. If that principle were correct, then my taking something to be red would be evident for me, even if I were ignorant of the intrinsic feature, that is, even if I had no idea that my taking was a sensible taking. This sort of foundationalism might be called *internal* foundationalism. It holds that some internal feature of beliefs is what converts basic beliefs to knowledge, rather than some relationship between the belief and what makes it true. But this sort of foundationalism shares with reliabilism a common reply to the skeptic, namely, that we may have no idea of the feature of belief that converts true belief to knowledge. Other sorts of theories, including some coherence theories that define coherence in terms of internal relations between beliefs, might employ a similar reply, to wit, that what converts true belief to knowledge is coherence among one's beliefs even if one is ignorant of such coherence.

What might we say on behalf of the skeptic? It would be best to let her speak for herself. "You claim that beliefs have a feature that converts them to knowledge even if the subject is ignorant of them. Is this something you claim to know? If so, you must show me how you know it. If not, for all you know, beliefs might be true and reliably generated, or they might be true and sensible takings, which are not knowledge." In short, to refute a skeptic, you must show that we have knowledge, and, to do that, you must proceed from premises you can show to be true. If you do not, then, though the skeptic may be in error, you may know as you say you do, but you will not have shown that the skeptic is in error. If you concede that you have not shown the skeptic to be in error but insist nonetheless that she *is* in error, you have abandoned epistemology for the dogmatism of the vulgar.

The paper by Alston is directly relevant to these issues. Alston has argued in earlier work that if beliefs are reliably formed, then they are justified, whether or not we know they are reliable. In this paper, however, he notes that the "if" contained in the claim provides the basis for a skeptical challenge. How can we show that the beliefs are reliably formed? Any attempt to do so appears to lead to epistemic circularity. Is there any escape from such circularity? After detailed consideration of the problem, Alston proposes, following Wittgenstein, that it is a consequence of our social practices pertaining to epistemic matters that it is rational to judge certain beliefs to be reliably formed. This consequence raises the question, he notes, of whether the practices can be shown to yield reliably formed beliefs, and he notes that the attempt to establish this connection appears again to be circular. He contends that not all kinds of circularity are vicious, but the major defense of our judgments of reliability based on a social practice must be based on some features of the practice. The question that he seeks to answer is what renders one practice superior to another. We leave it to the reader to discover the answer in the last section of his article.

Stroud agrees with Alston that the challenge of skepticism is not met by the appeal to externalism and, more specifically, to reliabilism. Again, assuming the externalist principle — if our beliefs are reliably formed, then they are justified — it follows that we might have justified beliefs and even knowledge without knowing that the principle is true. Such an account might give us the conditions under which sense experience yields knowledge, but it does not provide any general explanation of how knowledge is possible. We can, of course, explain how we know some specific thing, but we will be at a loss to explain how we can know anything at all. The latter problem arises when we attempt to explain how our knowledge in one domain — our knowledge of the data of sense, for example — could give us knowledge in a wider domain, knowledge of external objects, for example. To explain this, we must be able to account for the connection between the one sort of knowledge and the other, or our explanation of how we know the latter will be incomplete. But then, contrary to the externalist, we must know what the connection is and how it holds. For otherwise we shall fail to explain how we have the wider knowledge. But the problem is that to know that such a connection holds, we must already have knowledge of the things in the wider domain, which is what we were seeking to explain. So, though we may, contrary to affirmations of the skeptic, know some of the things she denies we know, she remains correct in saying that we can offer no epistemology to explain how we know. In other words, we cannot have a completely general understanding of how we know.

Sosa offers a critical account of skepticism that he considers important to providing not only an account of knowledge and other epistemic concepts but also, contrary to Stroud, a general understanding of the conditions under which we have knowledge. Sosa's current paper focuses on a detailed critique of skeptical argumentation. Such argumentation may involve principles of deductive closure (that we know what we deduce from what we know), principles of reasonable belief (that we know only what we have some reasons to believe), or principles of verification (that we do not know something until we have verified the consequences of it). Skeptical argumentation, when precisely formulated, rests on principles we may reasonably reject. It is, however, one thing to find specific arguments of the skeptic to be defective. It is another to explain why she is, in general, incorrect.

Maybe there is no proof of skepticism. Might it not be reasonable to accept skepticism, even total skepticism, without proof? If, however, the total skeptic goes so far as to deny that there is any such thing as reasonable belief, and advocates suspension of judgment, she falls victim to refutation. For she can have no basis for suspension of belief for her kind of intellectual suicide. To be justified, she must have some reasonable basis, and that is precluded by her repudiation of the notion of reasonable belief. Even a more moderate skeptic, one who rejects the idea of reasonable belief, must fall into some sort of incoherence, namely, the incoherence of acting as though something were true while denying that it is reasonable to believe that it is true. With some qualification, therefore, we may say that skepticism leads to a kind of vital incoherence, that is, an incoherence in action. In this way, acting in a certain way presupposes that certain beliefs are reasonable and, in that sense, justified.

The aforementioned articles have alleged that reliabilism falls short of meeting the skeptical challenge. Though other authors in the volume have insisted on the importance of reliability or trustworthiness, the most radical defenders of reliabilism are Goldman and Dretske. Both have maintained the importance of the connection between epistemology and cognitive science. Goldman's article contains a previously unpublished summary of his major work on reliabilism, with an update reflecting subsequent modifications of his theory. Goldman and Dretske differ fundamentally over the importance of justified belief in the theory of knowledge, however. Goldman is, in this respect, insisting on the centrality of justified belief to an analysis of knowledge. He contends that justified belief, which is a condition of knowledge, is belief permitted by a right system of rules, which he calls J-rules. What makes the system of rules right is simply the consequences to which they lead, the verific consequences of producing beliefs that are true. Hence, as in his earlier articles, justified belief is the product of a reliable belief-forming mechanism.

Does Goldman's account provide a reply to the skeptic? It has been objected that on his view, belief would turn out not to be justified under conditions of systematic and unavoidable deception occasioned by powerful demons or scientists who render our system of rules productive of error instead of truth. Goldman replies to the objection by appeal to a modified account of justification. Suppose, however, that we are not deceived. Do we then have a reply to the skeptic? We could say this much on Goldman's account. Justified belief is permitted belief. If the rules of our system do not prohibit our believing that those rules are reliable, then, assuming we are not deceived and the rules produce true beliefs, our belief that our rules are reliable would be justified. Is this reply to the skeptic adequate? This is the question raised and answered by Alston and Stroud above. We leave it to the reader to study Goldman's theory of naturalized reliabilism articulated in his article to determine whether it contains the resources to meet the skeptical objections raised by the other authors.

Dretske has a different sort of reliabilist view that, though it shares with Goldman an emphasis on the processes that form belief to account for the acquisition of knowledge, rejects the proposal that justification is what converts true belief to knowledge. Knowledge, according to Dretske, is just true belief that originates in a special way, that is, originates from receiving information from the senses. Dretske has a special twist on reliabilism that gives a special kind of reply to the skeptic, resulting from his attempt to provide a unified reliabilist theory of both representation and knowledge. Some source supplies us with information. The way in which we receive that information accounts both for what we believe (i.e., the representation we have of the world) and for what we know. The skeptic asks how we know that our beliefs are generated in a reliable manner. Dretske asks how we know what we believe, what the content of our beliefs is. In answering the latter question, we may obtain an answer to the skeptic, Dretske claims, because we may assign just that sort of representational content to our beliefs that is consistent with the claim that the processes that generate those beliefs are reliable. In determining the representational content of our beliefs, we assume that the mechanism generating those beliefs is the outcome of an evolutionary process that would enable the organism to adapt and survive. The best explanation we could give of why organisms with such belief-forming mechanisms survive while others do not is that those mechanisms produce true beliefs. Hence the best overall account will be one in which we assign content to our beliefs in a way that is consistent with supposing the generating mechanisms of our beliefs to be reliable. The reply to the skeptic's question of how we can show that our beliefs result from a reliable mechanism is that it would be bad science to interpret the beliefs in a way inconsistent with the assumption that the mechanism is reliable.

Kyburg's account, like Dretske's, is based on strict empiricism. Unlike Dretske's empiricism, however, Kyburg's view is based on the assumption that the information we receive may be erroneous. If the empirical information we receive may, and often is, erroneous, then we confront the problem of what it is reasonable to accept based on probability instead of certainty. Even at the level of observation, error is possible. We need some convention to decide whether to attribute error to observation reports. Dretske raises the question of how to assign content to our basic beliefs, those of perception. Kyburg raises the question of how to assign error to our basic beliefs, those of observation. The convention he proposes is that we adopt an overall system that minimizes the attribution of error and distributes the error we must attribute as evenly as possible. This treatment of error, which acknowledges the ubiquity of our fallibility, provides us with a system of rational acceptance of observation and, when combined with Kyburg's formally articulated theory of objective epistemic probability, of the acceptance of quantified statements as well. Can we extract a reply to the skeptic from Kyburg's account? How, on his account, can we meet the skeptic's challenge to show us that what we rationally accept is the result of a reliable process? Extrapolating considerably from what he says, we might answer as follows. There is no avoiding a conventional element in our system of rational acceptance. Given the convention concerning treatment of error, however, all that we rationally accept will be objectively probable. In that sense, what we rationally accept by the rules he advances will be productive of truth. To the skeptical query concerning the conventions, Kyburg would answer that he has shown that they are inescapable. Convention is inescapable, but once a convention is adopted, the skeptic is answered. Without accepting some convention, no one can be answered.

The conception of epistemic probability, which becomes central in any confrontation with skepticism, is the focus of Chisholm's essay. Chisholm sets out to define an essentially epistemic, as opposed to a logical or a statistical, notion of probability. This is the sense of probability in which we say that something is probable for some person. According to Chisholm, this is equivalent by definition to saying that the person is more justified in believing the thing in question than in believing the negation of it. Thus the notion of probability is epistemic in the sense that some epistemic notion, that of being more *justified* in believing one thing than another, is used to define probability. This comparative epistemic locution may, as Chisholm shows, be used to define other epistemic notions, most notably those of being evident and being certain. To further clarify the nature of epistemic probability, Chisholm undertakes the explication of the notion of one thing tending to make another probable, of such a tendency being defeated, and of the notion of total evidence. Though Chisholm himself in other works has made only modest claims concerning the capacity of his approach to deal with skepticism, it seems to us to provide the basis for an internalist reply. Suppose a skeptic claims that any attempt to show that anything is probable will involve reasoning in a circle, because we would first need to show that things of this kind are frequently true, or, at least, more often true than false, which would presuppose knowledge of such matters. We might, if we adopt Chisholm's account of probability, claim that probability does not depend on such frequencies, and, therefore, that our knowledge that something is probable does not require knowledge of such frequencies. Chisholm is an internalist concerning the application of epistemic notions, and, therefore, he believes that our being more justified in believing one thing than another does not depend upon the external frequency with which such things turn out to be true. The skeptic might yet persist and inquire how we can show that we are better justified in believing one thing than another, but the answer to that question, which for an internalist would be based on substantive epistemic principles, avoids the skeptic's circularity argument that an externalist inevitably confronts.

Lehrer's essay follows Chisholm's lead in taking a comparative epistemic notion, that of one thing being more reasonable for a person to accept than another, as primitive, though he advocates a coherence theory of knowledge as opposed to Chisholm's foundationalism. The coherence theory of knowledge he presents is based on a notion of personal justification, which in turn is based on what a person accepts, which, if undefeated, converts into knowledge. Personal justification is defined as coherence with what the person accepts, her acceptance system. Coherence is defined as the beating or neutralizing of competitors on the basis of such a system. Such justification is undefeated just in case the personal justification would be sustained when error in the acceptance system was removed or replaced with the acceptance of the denial of what was erroneously accepted.

Lehrer argues, moreover, that personal justification depends on what we accept about our trustworthiness in accepting what is true and avoiding accepting what is false. If we accept that we are trustworthy, and we are right in this, knowledge may be our reward. If we are untrustworthy, on the other hand, we are also ignorant. Thus, we must, on this theory, concede to the skeptic that if we are not trustworthy in what we accept in our quest to obtain truth and avoid error, then the skeptic wins the day. The powerful demon or scientist can render us untrustworthy in spite of our best efforts. We may be epistemically faultless in our endeavors in such a situation, but we are doomed to ignorance nonetheless.

The theory contains a reply to the skeptic. Suppose we are trustworthy, as we suppose. We are personally justified in accepting that we are not deceived, and, if we are correct in this, our justification is undefeated. We have knowledge. Moreover, we can show that we are personally justified, for that is an internal matter which depends only on what we accept. Can we show that our personal justification is undefeated? We can give no argument beyond appealing to what we accept, but the demand that we go beyond what we accept in the quest for anti-skeptical premises is incoherent. So whether the skeptic is wrong, and, indeed, has been shown to be wrong by our argumentation from what we accept, will depend on whether we are trustworthy in the ways we take ourselves to be. If we are trustworthy, our argument against the skeptic succeeds; if not, we are in no position to establish anything.

Hintikka presents us with an interrogative model of inquiry. On this model, an inquirer seeking knowledge is conceived of as an ideal inquirer trying to prove some conclusion on the basis of some initial information articulated as a premise, using as additional premises answers obtained from some source of information. Thus, the quest for knowledge is conceived of as a question-and-answer game played with some source of information. The rules of the game specify the conditions under which an answer may be obtained. Though there is some similarity between this approach and that of Dretske — both conceive of knowledge in terms of information received from a source of information — Hintikka's model differs from Dretske's in suggesting that the acquisition of information will result from a game in which the inquirer is given an active role in formulating questions to present to nature or some other source of information.

The focus of Hintikka's present essay is tacit knowledge, the sort of knowledge that is implicit within us, and potential knowledge, the sort of knowledge the boy in the *Meno* had of the Pythagorean theorem. Tacit knowledge provides us with a simple case for considering the interrogative model because here the source of information is internal. The game is to make tacit knowledge explicit. It is clear that in this game what one recovers from one's internal base of information will depend on what question one poses. If one asks whether a given statement is true or false, for example, one may obtain the answer. Thus, in this game one starts with a disjunction of the statement and its negation, a simple tautology, as a premise. This use of the tautology is equivalent to directing attention to a specific statement in the question-and-answer game.

How is the model relevant to the demands of the skeptic? Hintikka does not deal with this question in his essay, but it provides us with the basis for an interesting reply to the skeptic. If the skeptic asks us to show that some conclusion or belief is justified, we reply by explaining how the conclusion is an answer obtained from a source of information, nature, for example, according to the rules of the game. If the skeptic persists and asks whether the source is reliable, that question is simply a question to be answered, as with any other question, by applying the interrogative model. If, on the other hand, the skeptic rejects the question-and-answer game, then no answer to any query is possible, and the skeptical game is up.

We have used skepticism and the skeptic for our own expository purposes. The philosophical importance of skepticism is not merely heuristic, of course. As the history of philosophy has taught us, however, many central features of an epistemological theory become apparent when one asks how one would reply to the challenges of the skeptic in terms of the theory. There are, nevertheless, important questions concerning the nature of knowledge, probability, justification, and reliability that go beyond the questions raised by the skeptic. These articles represent diverse attempts to answer these questions. They exhibit, we believe, the creativity of contemporary work in the theory of knowledge in this country. Though connected with the past, they reveal the novelty and vitality characteristic of present-day research in epistemology, resulting from confronting the traditional skeptic, on one side, and the cognitive scientist, on the other. The intersection is a crossroad of intellectual ferment and innovation.

We should like to conclude with some explanation of our choice of contributors. They were all lecturers at a Summer Institute in the Theory of Knowledge, directed by Alvin Goldman and Keith Lehrer, and funded by the National Endowment for the Humanities under the auspices of the Council for Philosophical Studies in the summer of 1986. We found a great deal of interest in what had transpired at the summer institute among those who had not been present, and a desire to receive copies of the lectures that were presented at the institute. In addition, a book, *Teaching Theory of Knowledge*, edited by Clay and published by the Council for Philosophical Studies, was prepared by the participants of the institute, and the interest in this book further supported the idea that presenting the results of the institute to a wider audience would be useful. To that end, we invited the lecturers from the institute to contribute to the present volume. Some did not choose to contribute, but the present collection is a good sample of the most recent research of the lecturers. This will explain why the work of other important writers on the subject is missing from the collection. To those whose work is contained herein, we should like to express our gratitude for their cooperation in the construction of this volume. Finally, we should like to express our gratitude to the National Endowment for the Humanities for providing the funding from which it all began.

Marjorie Clay
Keith Lehrer

1
A 'Doxastic Practice' Approach to Epistemology

William P. Alston

I

How can we determine which epistemic principles are correct, valid, or adequate? One way to motivate concern with this issue is to consider controversial principles. What does it take to be justified in perceptual beliefs about the physical environment? Can I be justified in believing that there is a tree in front of me just by virtue of that belief's stemming, in a certain way, from a certain kind of visual experience? Or do I also need reasons, in the form of what I know about my visual experience or about the circumstances of that perception? How do we tell what set of conditions is sufficient for the justification of such beliefs? Another and more usual way to motivate concern with the issue is to raise the specter of skepticism. Why suppose that *any* set of conditions we can realize is sufficient? No matter what experiences and beliefs I have, couldn't they have been produced directly by an omnipotent being that sees to it that there is no physical world at all and that all my perceptual beliefs are false? That being the case, why should we suppose that our sensory experience justifies us in holding any beliefs about the physical world?

As the above paragraph suggests, the epistemic principles I will be thinking of lay down conditions under which one is justified in holding beliefs of a certain kind. I shall be using the justification of perceptual beliefs as my chief example. For a more specific focus, you can take your favorite principle of justification for perceptual beliefs. Following my own injunction, I will focus on my favorite, which runs as follows.

I. — S is *prima facie* justified in perceptually believing that x is P iff S has the kind of sensory experience that would normally be taken as x appearing to S as P, and S's belief that x is P stems from that experience in the normal way.

If we were interested in this principle for its own sake, much more would have to be done by way of elucidation. Here I will just say that the justification is only *prima facie* because it can be overridden by sufficient reason to suppose that x is not P or that the experience in this case is not sufficiently indicative of x's being P. I present this particular principle only to have something fairly definite to work with. Our concerns in this paper lie elsewhere. Nothing will hang on the specific character of I.

What it takes to be justified in accepting a principle of justification depends on what justification is. I have discussed this matter at some length elsewhere.[1] Here I must confine myself to laying it down that epistemic justification is essentially "truth conducive." That is, to be justified in believing that p is to believe that p in such a way that it is at least quite likely that one's belief is true.[2] One way of developing this idea is to say that S is justified in believing that p only if that belief was acquired in a reliable manner. This is not to *identify* justification with reliability; the 'only if' principle leaves room for other necessary conditions. I shall be thinking of justification as subject to a "reliability constraint." If this is distasteful to you, you can take the chapter as having to do with the epistemic status of principles of reliability, and leave justification out of the picture altogether.

So to determine which of the competing principles of the justification of perceptual beliefs is correct, if any, we have to determine, *inter alia*, which of them, if any, specify a reliable mode of belief-formation. And to show, against the skeptic, that perception is a source of justified belief (knowledge), we have to show that some mode of forming perceptual beliefs is reliable. But how to do this? Let's take a particular principle that specifies a mode of perceptual belief-formation, e.g., I., and consider what it would take to show that the mode so specified is reliable. The main difficulty is that there seems to be no otherwise effective way of showing this that does not depend on sense perception for some or most of its premises. Take the popular argument that sense perception proves its veridicality by the fact that when we trust our senses and build up systems of belief on that basis we have remarkable success in predicting and controlling the course of events. That sounds like a strong argument until we ask how we know that we have been successful at prediction and control. The answer is, obviously, that we know this only by relying on sense perception. Somebody has to take a look to see whether what we predicted did come to pass and whether our attempts at control were successful. Though I have no time to argue the point here, I suggest that any argument for the reliability of perception that is not otherwise disqualified will at some point(s) rely on perception itself. I shall assume this in what follows.[3]

What I have just been pointing to is a certain kind of circularity, one that consists in assuming the reliability of a source of belief in arguing for the reliability of that source. That assumption does not appear as a premise in the argument, but it is only by making the assumption that we consider ourselves entitled to use some or all of the premises. Let's call this *epistemic circularity*. In a recent essay I argue that, contrary to what one might suppose, epistemic circularity does not render an argument useless for justifying or establishing its conclusion.[4] Provided that I can *be* justified in certain perceptual beliefs without already being *justified* in supposing sense perception to be reliable,[5] I can legitimately use perceptual beliefs in an argument for the reliability of sense perception.

However, this is not the end of the matter. What I take myself to have shown in "Epistemic Circularity" is that epistemic circularity does not prevent one from showing, on the basis of empirical premises that are ultimately based on sense perception, that sense perception is reliable. But whether one actually does succeed in this depends on one's being justified in those perceptual premises, and that in turn, according to our assumptions about justification, depends on sense perception being a reliable source of belief. In other words, *if* (and only if) sense perception is reliable, we can show it to be reliable.[6] But how can we cancel out that *if*?

Here is another way of posing the problem. If we are entitled to use beliefs from a certain source in showing that source to be reliable, then any source can be validated. If all else fails, we can simply use each belief twice over, once as testee and once as tester. Consider crystal ball gazing. Gazing into the crystal ball, the seer makes a series of pronouncements: p, q, r, s. . . Is this a reliable mode of belief-formation? Yes. That can be shown as follows. The gazer forms the belief that p, and, using the same procedure, ascertains that p. By running through a series of beliefs in this way, we discover that the accuracy of this mode of belief-formation is 100%! If some of the beliefs contradict others, that will reduce the accuracy somewhat, but in the absence of massive internal contradiction the percentage of verified beliefs will still be quite high. Thus, if we allow the use of mode of belief-formation M to determine whether the beliefs formed by M are true, M is sure to get a clean bill of health. But a line of argument that will validate any mode of belief-formation, no matter how irresponsible, is not what we are looking for. We want, and need, something much more discriminating. Hence the fact that the reliability of sense perception can be established by relying on sense perception does not solve our problem.[7]

II

This is where the "doxastic practice" approach of the title comes into the picture. For help on the problem of the first section, I am going to look to two philosophers separated by almost two hundred years, Thomas Reid and Ludwig Wittgenstein. Both were centrally concerned with our problem, albeit in somewhat different guises. Since within the limits of this paper I am simply drawing inspiration from these figures, mining their work for ideas that I will develop in my own way, I will not attempt to present their views in anything like an adequate fashion.

First Wittgenstein. In *On Certainty*[8] Wittgenstein is concerned with the epistemic status of propositions of the sort G. E. Moore highlighted in his "Defence of Common Sense" and "Proof of an External World" — such propositions as *This is my hand*, *The earth has existed for many years*, and *There are people in this room*. The gist of Wittgenstein's position is that the acceptance of such propositions is partially *constitutive* of participation in one or another fundamental "language-game."[9] To doubt or question such a proposition is to question the whole language-game of which it is a keystone. There is no provision within that language-game for raising such doubts. In fact, there is no provision within the language-game for justifying such beliefs, exhibiting evidence for them, or showing that we know such matters, as Moore tried to do. Hence we cannot even say that we know or are certain of such matters. They are too fundamental for that. By accepting these and other "anchors" of the game we are thereby enabled to question, doubt, establish, refute, or justify less fundamental propositions. Nor can we step outside the language-game in which they figure as anchors and critically assess them from some other perspective. They have their meaning only within the game in which they play a foundational role; we cannot give sense to any dealings with them outside this context.

Thus, if we ask why we should suppose that some particular language-game is a reliable source of belief, Wittgenstein responds by denying the meaningfulness of the question. The concept of a trans- or inter-language-game dimension of truth or falsity is ruled out on verificationist grounds. We can address issues of truth and falsity only *within* a language-game, by employing its criteria and procedures to investigate issues that are within its scope. Hence there is no room for raising and answering questions about the reliability of a language-game as a whole. To be sure, language-games are not sacrosanct or fixed in cement. It is conceivable that they should be abandoned and new ones arise in their place. But even if we should have some choice in the matter, something that Wittgenstein seems to deny, the issue would be a practical, not a theoretical, one. It would be a choice as to what sort of activity to engage in, not a choice as to whether some proposition is true or false.[10] The foundation of the language-game is action, not intuition, belief, or reasoning.

Applying this to the problem raised in section I, Wittgenstein's view is that no sensible question can be raised concerning the reliability of the language-game that involves forming beliefs on the basis of sense-perception. There is no perspective from which the question can be intelligibly raised. This is a sphere of activity in which we are deeply involved; "this language-game is played."[11] We could try to opt out, but even if, *per impossible,* we could do so, that would have been a practical decision; and what possible reason could we have for such a decision? If, as is in fact the case, we continue to be a whole-hearted participant, we are simply engaged in (perhaps unconscious) duplicity in pretending to question, doubt, or justify the practice.

Now I do not accept for a moment Wittgenstein's verificationist restrictions on what assertions, questions, and doubts are intelligible. There is no time here for an attack on verificationism. I will simply testify that I can perfectly well understand the propositions that sense perception is (is not) reliable, that physical objects do (do not) exist, and that the earth has (has not) been in existence for more than a year, whether or not I or anyone else has any idea of how to go about determining whether one of these propositions is true. This confidence reflects a realistic concept of truth, on which a proposition's being true is *not* a matter of anyone's actual or possible epistemic position vis-à-vis the proposition. Hence I cannot accept Wittgenstein's solution to skepticism about perception and his answer to the question of the epistemic status of epistemic principles, the solution that seeks to dissolve the problem by undercutting the supposition that it can be meaningfully posed.

But then how can I look to Wittgenstein for inspiration? I shall explain. First a terminological note. Because I am concentrating on ways of forming and critically evaluating beliefs, I shall use the term 'doxastic practice,' instead of 'language-game.' The term 'practice' will be misleading if it is taken to be restricted to voluntary activity; for I do not take belief-formation to be voluntary. I am using 'practice' in such a way that it stretches over, e.g., psychological processes such as perception, thought, fantasy, and belief-formation, as well as voluntary action. A doxastic practice can be thought of as a system or constellation of *dispositions* or habits, or, to use a currently fashionable term, *mechanisms*, each of which yields a belief as output that is related in a certain way to an "input." The sense perceptual doxastic practice (hereinafter SPP) is a constellation of habits of forming beliefs in a certain way on the basis of inputs that consist of sense experiences.

Let me now set out the basic features of the view of doxastic practices I have arrived at, partly inspired by Wittgenstein. Some of these features are not stressed by Wittgenstein and some are only hinted at. But I believe that all of them are in the spirit of his approach.

1. We engage in a plurality of doxastic practices, each with its own sources of belief, its own conditions of justification, its own fundamental beliefs, and, in some cases, its own subject matter, its own conceptual framework, and its own repertoire of possible "overriders." There is no one unique source of justification or knowledge, such as Descartes and many others have dreamed of. However, this point needs to be handled carefully. What it is natural to count as distinct doxastic practices are by no means

wholly independent. We have to rely on the output of memory and reasoning for the overriders of perceptual beliefs. Apart from what is stored in memory, and used in reasoning, concerning the physical world and our perceptual interactions therewith, we would have nothing to go on in determining when sensory deliverances are and are not to be trusted. Reasoning is beholden to other belief-forming practices for its premises. We can, of course, reason from the output of previous reasoning, but somewhere back along the line we must have reasoned from beliefs otherwise obtained.[12] Thus we must avoid any suggestion that these practices can be engaged in separately.

We need to distinguish between what we may call "generational" and "transformational" practices. Generational practices produce beliefs from non-doxastic inputs; transformational practices transform belief inputs into belief outputs.[13] Generational practices *could* be used without reliance on other practices, as in forming perceptual beliefs without any provision for a second, "censor" stage that filters out some beliefs as incompatible with what we already firmly believe. This would be a more primitive kind of practice than we actually have in mature human beings, but it is possible, and may well be actual in very young children and lower animals. Moreover, our mature "introspective" practice is of this independent sort if, as seems likely, beliefs about one's current conscious states do not regularly pass any test of compatibility with what we believe otherwise. Transformational practices, on the other hand, cannot be carried on in any form without dependence on other practices. We have to acquire beliefs from some other source in order to get reasoning started.

Each of the generational practices has its own distinctive subject matter and conceptual scheme. SPP is a practice of forming beliefs about the current physical environment of the subject, using the common sense "physical object" conceptual scheme. Introspective practice is a practice of forming beliefs about the subject's own current conscious states, using the "conscious state" conceptual scheme, whereas beliefs formed by reasoning and by memory can be about anything whatever and can use any concepts whatever.

Then is there anything common to all doxastic practices, other than the fact that each is a regular systematic way of forming beliefs? Yes. In the initial statement I said that each practice has its own "sources of belief" and its own "conditions of justification." These are two sides of the same coin. We may take the former as our fundamental criterion for distinctness of doxastic practices. The practices we have distinguished differ in the kind of belief-forming "mechanism" involved. Such a mechanism consists of a "function" that yields a certain belief as output, given a certain input. This means that belief-forming mechanisms differ as to the sorts of inputs involved and as to the way in which inputs map onto belief outputs. There will be as many (possible) deductive inference belief-forming mechanisms as there are forms of deductive inference.[14] And perceptual belief-forming mechanisms will differ as to the type of sensory experience inputs, and as to the way in which beliefs about environmental states of affairs are extracted from a certain kind of sensory experience. The conditions of justification for each practice simply amount to an epistemic version of the psychological notion of a belief-forming mechanism.[15] Thus the criteria of justification built into SPP have to do with the way a perceptual belief is standardly based on sense experience. The criteria of justification built into an inferential practice have to do with the way a belief is based on the kind of inference that constitutes the basic source for that practice.[16]

Thus we can translate our basic issue concerning the reliability of belief sources, or modes of belief-formation, into an issue concerning the reliability of doxastic practices. A practice is reliable *iff* its distinctive belief-forming mechanisms (modes of belief-formation) are reliable. And we can similarly restate the "reliability constraint" on principles of justification in these terms. A (general enough) principle of justification, e.g., I., will be true (valid, acceptable. . .) only if the doxastic practice in which we form beliefs in the way specified in that principle is reliable. From now on we will be thinking of reliability as attaching to doxastic practices.

We have also spoken of each practice as possessing its own distinctive set of foundational presuppositions. This is an idea that bulks large in *On Certainty*. I feel that Wittgenstein is much too generous in according this status to beliefs. It seems clear to me that *This is my hand* and *The earth has existed for more than a year* are propositions for the truth of which I have a great deal of empirical evidence *within* SPP (or rather within some combination of that with memory and reasoning of various sorts), rather than a basic presupposition of the practice. However, I do recognize this latter category. The existence of physical objects and the general reliability of sense perception are basic presuppositions of SPP; we couldn't engage in it wholeheartedly without at least tacitly accepting those propositions. Similarly, the reality of the past and the reliability of memory are basic presuppositions of the practice of forming memory beliefs.

2. These practices are acquired and engaged in well before one is explicitly aware of them and critically reflects on them. When one arrives at the age of reflection, one finds oneself ineluctably involved in their exercise. Here especially, the owl of Minerva flies only at the gathering of the dusk. Philosophical reflection and criticism build on the *practical* mastery of doxastic practices. Practice precedes theory; and the latter would be impossible without the former. This is a recurrent theme in *On Certainty*. If we hadn't learned to *engage* in inference, we could never develop a system of logic; we would have nothing either to reflect *on* or to reflect *with*. If we had not learned to form perceptual beliefs, we would have no resources

for formulating the philosophical problems of the existence of the external world and of the epistemic status of perceptual beliefs.

3. Practices of *belief-formation*, on which we have been concentrating, are set in the context of wider spheres of practice. We learn to form perceptual beliefs along with, and as a part of, learning to deal with perceived objects in the pursuit of our ends. Our practice of forming beliefs about other persons is intimately connected with interpersonal behavior, treating persons as persons and forming typically interpersonal relations with them.

4. These practices are thoroughly *social*: socially established by socially monitored learning, and socially shared. We learn to form perceptual beliefs about the environment in terms of the conceptual scheme we acquire from our society. This is not to deny that innate mechanisms and tendencies play a role here. We still have much to learn about the relative contributions of innate structures and social learning in the development of doxastic practices. Reid places more stress on the former, Wittgenstein on the latter. But whatever the details, both have a role to play; and the final outcome is socially organized, reinforced, monitored, and shared.

At the beginning of this section I said that I was going to develop an approach to epistemology that was inspired by Reid and Wittgenstein. So far nothing has been said about the former. But only the name has been absent. The conception of doxastic practices just outlined is, in its essentials, the view of Reid, even though the terminology is different.[17] Where I speak of various doxastic practices Reid speaks of various kinds of "evidence": "the evidence of sense, the evidence of memory, the evidence of consciousness, the evidence of testimony, the evidence of axioms, the evidence of reasoning."[18] "We give the name of evidence to whatever is a ground of belief."[19] Alternatively, he speaks of "general principles of the human mind" by which we form beliefs of certain sorts under certain conditions.[20] Reid stresses the plurality of these principles or sorts of evidence, and the impossibility of reducing them to a single supreme principle. ". . .I am not able to find any common nature to which they may all be reduced. They seem to me to agree only in this, that they are all fitted by nature to produce belief in the human mind. . ."[21] Again, Reid often stresses the point that we utilize these principles in practice long before we are explicitly aware of them as such. As mentioned above, he stresses the contribution of innate structure, whereas Wittgenstein stresses social learning, but in both cases there is emphasis on the point that we have them and use them before we reflect on them. Reid, much more than Wittgenstein, goes into the way in which belief-forming dispositions, once established, can be modified by experience.[22] On the other hand, Reid does not stress the way in which cognitive practices are set in the context of practices of overt dealings with the environment. Reid's perspective is that of a purely cognitive, mentalistic psychology. Finally, I should mention the point that one reason my account is closer to Reid's is that Reid had the advantage of philosophizing before the advent of verificationist and other anti-realist philosophies. Reid never suggests that there is anything unintelligible about the idea that, e.g., sense perception is or is not reliable, or that we cannot meaningfully raise the question of whether this is so, however difficult it may be to find a way to answer the question. As we shall see, this leaves Reid, and me, free to look for ways of evaluating basic doxastic practices.[23]

III

But how does my Reidian view of doxastic practices provide us with a solution of our central problem, viz., how we can determine, with respect to a particular practice such as SPP, whether it is reliable? Thus far I have presented my view as what we might call "cognitive social psychology," an account of how it is in fact with our activities of belief-formation. I believe that there can be no doubt that this account is correct, at least in its general outlines. But so far this is just psychology. What bearing does it have on our central epistemological question? How does it help us to determine which practices are reliable ones?

I am not going to tackle this question head on. Instead I am going to shift ground in this section and the next, and consider what resources our approach gives us for determining whether a given practice is *rationally* accepted (engaged in). Having completed that task, I shall turn, in section V, to the question of what bearing all this has on our central issues of the reliability of practices and the assessment of principles of justification.

Our two role models seek to make epistemological hay out of their psychology in different fashions. In a word, Wittgenstein draws linguistic conclusions from the psychology (while not admitting for a moment that it is psychology) and then applies these linguistic points to epistemology, while Reid tries to move more directly from the psychology to the epistemological position, if indeed he does clearly distinguish the two. Wittgenstein's linguistic solution, as already pointed out, is that no meaning can be given to a question as to the truth or justifiability of beliefs that are constitutive of a practice. We can't address such questions in the practice itself, nor can we address them in any other practice. The only meaningful questions are those for the investigation of which a practice makes provision; and no such provision is made for questions as to the fundamental presuppositions of a practice or as to its own reliability. I have already made clear that I do not accept the verificationist assumptions that underlie Wittgenstein's restrictions on meaningfulness, and hence I cannot avail myself of his solution. Reid's response is hazier and more difficult to summarize neatly, at least insofar as it goes beyond reminding the skeptic that he is deeply involved in practices the presuppositions and outputs of which he is questioning; and despite the popular picture of Reid, it is clear that his response does go beyond this, however difficult it may be to say in exactly what way.[24] Since my aims in this paper are not historical, I shall state in my own way what I take to be essentially a Reidian response.

Consider a typical reaction of a contemporary American epistemologist to my suggestion that a study of social cognitive psychology can throw light on our epistemic question about the rationality of a practice. "What does all this have to do with epistemology? The fact that a given practice is socially established cuts no ice whatever epistemologically. The function of the epistemologist is to subject any such practice to critical standards, bring it before the bar of reason, playing no favorites on grounds of familiarity, general acceptance, practical indispensability, irresistibility, innateness, or commonsense plausibility."[25]

Let's term this position "Autonomism." It holds that epistemology is autonomous vis-à-vis psychology and other sciences dealing with cognition. It holds that epistemology is essentially a normative or evaluative enterprise, and that here as elsewhere values are not determined by fact.

But this non-naturalist philippic inevitably provokes a naturalist rejoinder. "You say that the province of epistemology, so far as it is concerned with doxastic practices, is to carry out a rational assessment of such practices. Well and good. But where is the epistemologist to obtain the standards by which that evaluation will be carried out? I doubt that there is any such special epistemological procedure for setting standards. Certainly there is none that is utilized by all or most epistemologists; or if there is, its employment does not yield general agreement. I suggest that when an epistemologist propounds principles of justification, these utterances, no matter how solemn the intonation, are rooted in one or another of the established practices we have been discussing. Does the epistemologist claim to be proceeding on the basis of self-evident principles of evaluation? Well then, he is participating in the well-established practice of forming beliefs on the basis of their appearing to be obviously true just on consideration. Even if this enables him to pass judgment on other practices, these judgments are worth only as much as the credentials of the practice within which they were pronounced. And if his epistemological judgments are made on some other basis, e.g., coherence or argument to the best explanation, he is still *presupposing* the acceptability of that mode of forming beliefs, in passing judgment on other practices. And he can't critically evaluate that mode in the same way without falling into epistemic circularity. Thus the autonomist, however lordly his pretensions, cannot, in the end, avoid reliance on one or more of the doxastic practices from which he was seeking to distance himself. He avoids a wholesale commitment to established doxastic practices only by taking one or more uncritically so as to have a platform from which to judge others. We cannot avoid dependence on the doxastic practices in which we find ourselves engaged when we begin to reflect. At most, we can restrict ourselves to one or two as the only ones we will accept without rational warrant, subjecting the others to the standards of these chosen few. Thus, on closer scrutiny, the autonomist turns out to be a selective heteronomist. And this is arbitrary partiality. It can have no rational justification. What justification can there be for accepting the pretensions of, e.g., rational intuition or introspection without critical scrutiny, while refusing the same privilege to sense perception?[26] If the epistemologist is to escape such arbitrariness, he must content himself with delineating the contours of established doxastic practices, perhaps neating them up a bit and rendering them more internally coherent and more consonant with each other. He must give up pretensions to an Archimedean point from which he can carry out an impartial rational evaluation of *all* practices."

Let's call the position suggested by the last two sentences of this retort, "Heteronomism." We may think of Autonomism and Heteronomism as constituting an antinomy. Our present task is to resolve this antinomy.

The first step in that resolution is to point out that neither side of the antinomy does full justice to the epistemological enterprise. As for the autonomist, his opponent has already made explicit where he falls short. The autonomist, since he eschews implicit trust in established doxastic practices, needs some other source and warrant of his critical standards, and what could that be? But this criticism can be pushed further by pointing out that the practice of epistemology reveals, at several points, an uncritical reliance on the practices we acquired with our mothers' milk. If we look at attempts to formulate and establish principles of justification, we will find the protagonists engaged in two sorts of activities. First, they put forward various principles as plausible, reasonable, sensible, or evident. Second, they test these principles by confronting them with various examples of justified and unjustified beliefs. Now where do they get these principles, and what is the source of their plausibility? Why is it that I. and its many near relatives seem so reasonable? A plausible answer is that such principles formulate, or come close to formulating, the principles of belief-formation and assessment built into our familiar practice of forming perceptual beliefs. Why else should these principles make a strong claim on our assent? Is it that we have some special access to a realm of being known as "epistemic justification"? That seems unlikely. *Nous n' avons pas besoin de cette hypothese.* When we encounter a formulation of some deeply embedded practice of ours, it naturally makes a strong appeal. As for examples of justified and of unjustified beliefs, why do they evoke such widespread concurrence? Again, the most reasonable hypothesis is that the judgments are being made from within widely shared doxastic practices. Thus Chisholm *et al.* are, much of the time, doing just what the heteronomist says they should do, viz., making explicit the structure of one or another common doxastic practice.

But the heteronomist doesn't have the whole story either. In seeking to make the delineation and refinement of established practices the whole task of epistemology, she neglects the fact that making judgments on absolutely general questions, and deciding between opposing positions on such questions, is constitutive of the philosophical enterprise, in epistemology as elsewhere. How can the epistemologist fail to ask about the rationality of forming beliefs in one or another way, without violating her Socratic oath? The unexamined practice is not worth engaging in, at least not once it has been dragged into the light and made a possible subject of philosophical criticism. It is absolutely fundamental to the philosophical enterprise to subject all the basic features of our life to rational criticism, and not the least of these is the set of belief-forming tendencies with which we are endowed, or saddled as the case may be. Any "naturalism" that spurns this task is unworthy of the name of philosophy.

So where does this leave us? If epistemology is confined to the deline-ation of existing doxastic practices, it will thereby renounce its most sacred charge — to carry out a rational criticism of all claims to knowledge and justification. And yet how can it assess any particular doxastic practice without making use of some other in order to do so? And in that case, how can it subject all epistemic claims to rational scrutiny? Even if epistemology had a distinctive epistemic practice all its own, what would give this practice a licence to set itself up in judgment over its fellows? Don't the Reidian charges of arbitrary partiality come back to haunt us?

I think we can find a way out of this thicket by attending to the distinc-tion between a more or less tightly structured *practice* with more or less fixed rules, criteria, and standards on the one hand, and a relatively free, unstructured "improvisational" activity on the other. When we engage in an organized practice, whether it is a doxastic practice, a game, a traditional craft such as carpentry, or speaking a language, our activity is more or less narrowly confined by antecedent rules and procedures, which themselves constitute the substance of the practice. This is not to say that all the details are laid down in advance. There will be room for free variation, and the degree of this will vary. When a carpenter puts together a wall of a room from plans and blueprints, his activity is fairly well predetermined in its gross outlines, though no set of plans specifies exactly how many hammer strokes are to be given to each nail. The rules of a language determine what combinations are acceptable and what ways there are to express a given meaning, but they do not dictate just what one is to say at a given stage of an extended conversation.

In contrast to these highly circumscribed forms of activity, there are others that call for the exercise of "judgment," where no established rules or criteria put tight constraints on what judgment is to be made in a particular situation. Familiar examples are found in aesthetics, religion, and science. When it is a question of the comparative worth of two works of art, or of what makes a particular work of art so striking, there are no formulable canons that the critic can consult to determine what the verdict should be. The critic must use her sensitivity, experience, familiarity with the field, and "intuition" to arrive at a considered judgment. And that judgment can in turn be validated or challenged only by the use of similar resources. From the sphere of religion a similar story is to be told concerning, e.g., the spirituality of a particular person. No generally accepted checklist of observable features will settle the matter. What is required is trained judgment and sensitivity. Finally, in science, although many things are to be done by following definite rules, e.g., the preparation of chemical solutions, competing high-level theories are to be evaluated in terms of their relative fecundity, explanatory power, simplicity, and the like; and for the determination of these matters there is no calculus. Again trained judgment is called for.[27]

Where philosophy is concerned with ultimate questions it falls, I suggest, on the latter side of our contrast. It is distinctive of philosophy, in epistemology and elsewhere, to be operating at a level deeper than those spheres of intellectual activity for which there are established rules. In philosophy *everything* is up for grabs. If anyone suggests a set of rules, methods, or procedures for philosophy, that itself immediately becomes a matter of controversy. Just think of the historically prominent attempts to provide effective decision procedures for philosophical problems, from Descartes' *Rules for the Direction of Mind*, through Locke's *Essay*, Kant's *Critique of Pure Reason*, Russell's *Our Knowledge of the External World as a Field for Scientific Method in Philosophy*, and the Vienna Circle. Each proposed methodology, instead of setting philosophy onto the secure path of science, simply becomes an additional disputed claim. So far from being susceptible of regularization, philosophy is, rather, *inter alia*, the activity of subjecting proposed methodologies to reflective examination. The philosopher must search for the best way of answering questions, as well as search for the answers. The philosopher must arrive at whatever *judgment* best recommends itself after careful reflection, rather than proceed according to rules that are constitutive of the enterprise. That is what makes philosophy so uncomfortable, so unsettling, and at the same time so exciting and challenging. One can never rest secure in the realization that one has a bedrock from which to proceed further. One is always dangling in the air from a rope that isn't tied down anywhere. Or, to pile on still another metaphor, epistemology is, like the rest of philosophy, largely a "seat of the pants" enterprise.

All this suggests that we resolve the antinomy of Autonomism and Heteronomism by distinguishing two aspects of the epistemological enterprise. First, as the heteronomist points out, the epistemologist makes explicit the structure of one or another established doxastic practice. This is an activity with fairly definite criteria and procedures, in which one can be shown to be correct or incorrect, although it is much less firmly regularized than, say, census taking or chemical engineering. The final appeal is always to one's implicit acquaintance with the doxastic practice in question. However, this is sufficiently widespread and sufficiently retrievable to provide a usable touchstone.

But, second, as the autonomist points out, the epistemologist is called on to make judgments on the acceptability of one or another such practice, especially those which are not universally engaged in, such as practices of religious belief-formation as well as judgments on how to settle conflicts between practices. Here, for reasons we have already rehearsed, no set of rules or criteria can be appealed to. If the question is whether SPP (the sense perceptual doxastic practice) is rationally engaged in, we cannot make use of SPP in answering the question; and if we try to use the criteria of some other practice(s), we throw ourselves open to the Reidian charge of arbitrary partiality. Hence, when doing this more ultimate sort of epistemology, one is forced into the wilderness, outside settled territory with its laws and regulations. Thus the epistemologist in her critical function is not, or need not be, arbitrarily setting up one established practice in judgment over another, because she is not operating within any established practice at all. She is improvising, seeking to reach a *judgment* on the basis of what commends itself to her on due reflection as decisive for the question at hand.

This, then, is the resolution of our perplexity. The epistemologist, in seeking to carry out a rational evaluation of one or another doxastic practice, is not working from within a particular such practice. Nor need she be proposing to establish a novel practice, the specifications of which she has drawn up herself in her study. On the other hand, she need not abjure everything, or anything, she has learned from the various practices she has mastered. She makes use of her doxastic skills and tendencies, not by following the relatively fixed rules and procedures of some particular practice, but by using all this in a freer fashion. In that way an epistemologist can carry out the traditional philosophical function of critical evaluation without chauvinistically picking one or more practices to set in judgment over the others.

IV

But how far will this free "exercise of judgment" take us? If we eschew reliance on the criteria and standards of any established practice, how firm a judgment can we rationally pass on a given practice? What considerations will commend themselves to us as relevant when we confront the question of the rationality of SPP? And will those considerations be sufficient to justify a definite answer?

I will address these questions by practicing what I have been preaching, i.e., by engaging in the improvisational activity of which I have been speaking. At least I will give you the meta-theory thereof, reflecting on what considerations are relevantly adduced in such an evaluation, while avoiding both epistemic circularity and chauvinism.

But first I should warn you not to get carried away by the rhetoric of the last few paragraphs into an expectation of more unanimity here than we find on other fundamental philosophical issues. As we have seen, the exercise of judgment is not subject to rules or criteria by appeal to which it can be definitively established that a particular judgment is correct. Hence it is to be expected that different persons, with different backgrounds, orientations, sensitivities, and experience will sometimes arrive at different judgments. This is not to say that no reasonable argument is possible, but only that we should not expect such argument to always produce agreement. These facts of life are, no doubt, excessively familiar to readers of this essay.

To turn, then, to the principles of my "seat of the pants" critical epistemology, I will begin by reminding you of an earlier point. If we eschew epistemically circular support, we will not be able to establish the reliability of any of our basic practices.

This being the case, what is the most rational attitude to take toward established fundamental practices? Disallowing epistemically circular arguments, none can be shown to be reliable; and if we admit such arguments, an airtight case can be made for each of them, as pointed out in section I. Hence as far as proofs of reliability are concerned, they are all on a par. Is there any other basis for distinguishing between them as candidates for rational acceptance? A number of candidates suggest themselves. Some may be more essential for the conduct of life than others; some may yield greater payoffs in the way of prediction and control; and so on. However, we can't establish any of this either without falling into epistemic circularity. How, for example, can we show that the formation of perceptual beliefs is necessary for the conduct of life without relying on what we learn from perception to do so? To be sure, we might be able to show one or another practice to be unreliable. However, since a large part of our resources for doing this involves using the outputs of one practice to discredit those of another, this enterprise is best considered at a second stage, after we already have a number of *prima facie* acceptable practices to work with. Therefore, apart from reasons for unreliability and at a first stage of evaluation, it would be arbitrary to distinguish between established basic practices; reason dictates that they all be accepted as rational or all be rejected as irrational. Is the latter option a live one? Clearly, abstention from all doxastic practices is not a real possibility; therefore, we could brand them all as irrational only at the price of a severe split between theory and practice, a state of affairs I take to be rationally unacceptable.[28] Hence the only rational alternative open to us is to regard all established doxastic practices as rationally engaged in, pending sufficient reasons to take any of them as unreliable, and pending any other sufficient disqualifying considerations, if any. In other words, the only rational course is to take all established basic practices to be *prima facie* rational. This is a sort of "negative coherentism"[29] with respect to established practices; each such practice is innocent until proved guilty. Note that I am not endorsing negative coherence with respect to *beliefs*; I take a belief to require positive support in the form of adequate grounds on which it is based.[30]

It might be contended that we should restrict our *prima facie* acceptance to practices that are not only socially established but also *universally* engaged in, at least by all normal adult human beings. This would cut out, e.g., such religious belief-forming practices as we find in established religions such as Christianity and Hinduism. But I find this exclusion unwarranted. Why suppose that the outputs of a practice are unworthy of *prima facie* acceptance just because it is engaged in by only a part of the normal adult population? Why this predilection for egalitarianism in the epistemic sphere, where its credentials are much less impressive than in the political sphere? Of course, in taking non-universal established practices to be *prima facie* acceptable, the possibility is left open of taking non-universality as a sufficient disqualifying consideration.[31]

My judgment may also be assailed as not permissive enough. "Why not take *all* practices to be *prima facie* acceptable, not just socially established ones? Why this prejudice against the idiosyncratic? If Cedric has developed a practice of consulting sundried tomatoes to determine the future of the stock market, why not take that as reliable too unless we have something against it?" Now in fact, I think that we will almost always have something decisive against idiosyncratic doxastic practices; and so it would perhaps do no harm to let all of them in as *prima facie* acceptable, knocking them out at a second stage by sufficient reasons to the contrary. Nevertheless, there is a significant reason for doing it my way. When a doxastic practice has persisted over a number of generations, it has earned a right to be considered seriously in a way that Cedric's consultation of sundried tomatoes has not. It is a reasonable supposition that a practice would not have persisted over large segments of the population unless it was putting people into effective touch with some aspect(s) of reality and proving itself as such by its fruits. But there are no such grounds for presumption in the case of idiosyncratic practices. Hence we will proceed more reasonably, as well as more efficiently,[32] by giving initial, ungrounded credence only to the socially established practices. Newcomers will have to prove themselves.

If all established practices are *prima facie* acceptable, the remaining question concerns what sorts of disqualifying considerations, what sorts of "reasons to the contrary," can be identified, from the free swinging, non-rule-bound perspective that is appropriate for radical epistemological criticism. Before presenting my choices, let me emphasize the point that we must avoid holding one practice subject to the special requirements of another, unless we have sufficient reason for taking those requirements to be universally applicable. We must avoid, *pace* Plato and Descartes, supposing that SPP is disqualified by failing to come up to mathematical standards of precision and determinateness; and we must likewise avoid supposing, *pace* Hume, that induction is disqualified for failing to come up to the standards of deduction. In the papers cited in note 31, I have argued in like fashion that it is illegitimate to fault the practice of forming beliefs about God on the basis of religious experience for failing to satisfy constraints of predictability and checkability that are laid down by SPP for beliefs in its domain.

My first suggestion is that a practice is disqualified by persistent and irremediable inconsistency in its output. Consistency is a requirement of unrestricted generality just because its violation frustrates the most basic cognitive aim: to believe what is true and not to believe what is false. Massive internal inconsistency guarantees that a significant proportion of one's beliefs are false. But note that I am taking only a "persistent and irremediable" inconsistency to be disqualifying. Some degree of inconsistency pops up in all practices, and it is undoubtedly healthy that it should. Since it is often not crystal clear which side of a contradiction is true, it is well that different practitioners should be free to explore different sides.[33] If a practice should persistently deliver large numbers of mutually inconsistent beliefs, without any tendency over time to reduce their incidence, that would be a disqualification.

Second, and for the same reason, a massive and persistent inconsistency between the outputs of two different practices is a good reason for disqualifying at least one of them. This principle, of course, does not tell us which of the contenders to eliminate; and I don't see how to lay down any decision procedure for this from the standpoint of radical epistemological criticism. The only principle that suggests itself to me as both unchauvinistic and eminently plausible is the conservative principle that one should give preference to the more firmly established practice. What does being more firmly established amount to? I don't have a precise definition, but it involves such components as (a) being more widely accepted, (b) having a more definite structure, (c) being more important in our lives, (d) having more of an innate basis, (e) being more difficult to abstain from, and (f) its principles seeming more obviously true. But mightn't it be the case in a particular conflict that the less firmly established practice is the more reliable? Of course that is conceivable. Nevertheless, in the absence of anything else to go on, it seems the part of wisdom to go with the more firmly established. It would be absurd to make the opposite choice; that would saddle us with all sorts of bizarre beliefs.

It is easy to suppose that this principle can be illustrated by the way in which religious beliefs have progressively given way to scientific beliefs in the last few centuries. However, we must be careful to distinguish a choice between doxastic practices and a choice between particular beliefs (outputs of doxastic practices). When *some* religious beliefs contradict *some* scientific beliefs, the less firmly established practice can be preserved by sacrificing some of its beliefs and/or by modifying its belief-forming procedures. This is what has happened in our culture over the last few centuries. What we may term the "Christian doxastic practice" has been modified by, e.g., changes in Biblical interpretation, so that it no longer generates a belief structure that is massively inconsistent with the belief structure generated by the "scientific doxastic practice." Thus the former is modified, not abandoned. To be sure, as this example indicates, our principle favoring the more firmly established could also be applied to choices between inconsistent beliefs, but that is not our present concern.

My final suggestion for a disqualifying consideration has to do not with a ground for definitive rejection, but with something that will strengthen or weaken the *prima facie* acceptability. The point is this. A practice's claim to acceptance is strengthened by significant "self-support," and the claim is weakened by the absence of such.

But how can self support enter into the picture if we are eschewing epistemically circular considerations? To answer this question we must distinguish different sorts of self-support. The reasons given earlier for not taking just any epistemically circular support to establish the credentials of a practice was that this was too easy, so easy that it would result in validating any practice whatever, no matter how absurd. For any practice can be conclusively self-supported if we allow ourselves to use each doxastic output twice, once as testee and once as tester. But we were too hasty in supposing that any self-support would be equally trivial. Consider the following ways in which SPP supports its own claims. (1) By engaging in SPP and allied memory and inferential practices we are enabled to make predictions, many of which turn out to be correct, and thereby we are able to anticipate and control, to some considerable extent, the course of events. (2) By relying on SPP and associated practices we are able to establish facts about the operation of sense perception that show both that it is a reliable source of belief and why it is reliable. These results are by no means trivial. It cannot be taken for granted that any practice whatever will yield comparable fruits. It is quite conceivable that we should not have attained this kind or degree of success at prediction and control by relying on the output of SPP; and it is equally conceivable that this output should not have put us in a position to acquire sufficient understanding of the workings of perception to see why it can be relied on. To be sure, an argument from these fruits to the reliability of SPP is still infected with epistemic circularity; apart from reliance on SPP we have no way of knowing the outcome of our attempts at prediction and control, and no way of confirming our suppositions about the workings of perception. Nevertheless, this is not the trivial epistemically circular support that necessarily extends to every practice. Many practices cannot show anything analogous; crystal ball gazing and the reading of entrails cannot. Since SPP supports itself in ways it conceivably might not, and in ways other practices do not, its *prima facie* claims to acceptance are thereby strengthened; and if crystal ball gazing lacks any non-trivial self support, its claims suffer by comparison.

We must be careful not to take up another chauvinistic stance, that of supposing that a practice can be non-trivially self supported only in the SPP way. The acceptability of rational intuition or deductive reasoning is not weakened by the fact that reliance on the outputs of these practices does not lead to achievements in prediction and control. The point is that they are, by their very nature, unsuitable for this use; they are not "designed" to give us information that could serve as the basis for such results. Since they do not purport to provide information about the physical environment, it would be unreasonable in the extreme to condemn them for not providing us with an evidential basis for predictive hypotheses. Similarly, I have argued in the articles cited in note 31 that it is equally inappropriate to expect predictive efficacy from the practice of forming beliefs about God on the basis of religious experience, and equally misguided to consider the claims of that practice to be weakened by its failure to contribute to achievements of this ilk. On the other hand, we can consider whether these other practices yield fruits that are appropriate to their character and aims. And it would seem that the combination of rational intuition and deduction yields impressive and fairly stable abstract systems, while the religious experiential practice mentioned earlier provides effective guidance to spiritual development.

Much more could and should be said about the ways in which the *prima facie* acceptability of one or another doxastic practice can be strengthened or weakened. But perhaps the above will suffice to indicate that it is possible, without falling into reprehensible chauvinism, to carry out a rational assessment of doxastic practices. But again we must be careful not to expect too much from this activity. The most we can hope from radical epistemic criticism is that some of the *prima facie* acceptable doxastic practices may be weeded out, and the claims of some strengthened and of others weakened, so that we may have a rank ordering of preferability to use when massive conflicts arise. For the most part, then, the epistemologist's proper and distinctive work will be that delineated by the heteronomist: to make explicit the structure of various established doxastic practices.

V

In the last two sections we have departed from our original issues concerning the epistemic status of principles of justification and concerning the *reliability* of doxastic practices, and have instead been considering how we could determine whether it is *rational* to engage in a certain practice. It is now time to return to the question of reliability and see what our conclusions concerning rationality have to tell us about that. I have suggested that the epistemologist, in her critical function, can make a sound (valid, acceptable. . .) judgment to the effect that it is rational to engage in SPP and other established doxastic practices. What implications does that have for the reliability of SPP? It might seem to have none. First of all, it is clear that the rationality of a practice does not *entail* its reliability. At least this is clear if the notion of a rational doxastic practice works at all as we have been assuming. We have supported the *prima facie* rationality of engaging in established doxastic practices without producing any evidence in support of a reliability claim. Instead, our main point was that all such practices are on a par with respect to the crucial issue of evidence for reliability, so that, as far as that is concerned, they all stand or fall together. Since abstaining from all doxastic practices is not a live option, the only reasonable course is to regard them all as rationally engaged in, pending sufficient disqualifying reasons. It is clear that all this could be the case, and hence that we are rational in engaging in, e.g., SPP, even if it were in fact unreliable. Moreover, the rationality of SPP does not even provide non-deductive but sufficient grounds for supposing it to be reliable. That follows from our initial assumption that there can be no adequate non-epistemically-circular argument for the reliability of SPP and other fundamental doxastic practices. But then it looks as if the judgment that the practice is "rationally" engaged in has no bearing on the likelihood that it will yield truths; rationality has no "truth-conductivity" force. And so that judgment will not advance our original aim of determining how principles of justification are to be established, by determining how the reliability of modes of belief-formation is to be ascertained.

Before responding to this challenge, let's digress long enough to note that the above claim that rationality does not entail reliability may seem to conflict with our earlier claim that a principle of justification is correct only if the mode of belief-formation it takes to be sufficient for justification is reliable. This would seem to be true only if justification entails reliability. But now we are denying that the rationality of a practice entails its reliability. There are several ways in which one might argue that there is no real conflict here. (1) There's a difference between justification and rationality. (2) There's a difference between the justification (rationality) of *beliefs* and the justification (rationality) of *practices*. (3) However, I feel that the real explanation for the seeming discrepancy is that I have been speaking of the justification of *beliefs* in an objective, "externalist" sense of 'justification,' while speaking of the rationality of *practices* in a more subjective or "internalist" sense of 'rationality.'[34] In the externalist sense, a belief is justified (rational) only if it was formed in what is in fact a reliable way; and similarly a practice is rational (justified) only if it is in fact reliable. Whereas in the sort of internalist sense in question here, a belief is justified (rational) if it is more reasonable, all things considered, to adopt it than not to do so; and similarly a practice is rational (justified) if, all things considered, it is more reasonable to engage in it than to refrain from doing so. It would be a long story to explain fully my proceeding in this way (an externalist concept of the justification of beliefs and an internalist concept of the rationality of practices), and to defend that choice. The short story is this. I have tried to be objectivist as long as possible. But the difficulties in establishing justification (rationality) for beliefs in an objectivist sense drives us (sooner or later, and why make it any later?) to appeal to an internalist rationality for practices. If one still wonders why we couldn't have used an internalist conception of justification for beliefs in the first place and saved ourselves this extended treatment of practices, that issue will be addressed a few paragraphs down the road.

But, to return to the contention that a judgment of the rationality of a practice has no bearing on the question of the reliability of the practice, this is an illusion, born of a confusion of the most basic way of *establishing* a reliability claim with the *import* of that claim, another manifestation of that many-headed monster, verificationism. The fact that we cannot give a conclusive deductive or inductive argument for the reliability of SPP does *not* show that we are not *judging* that practice to be reliable when, as a critical epistemologist, we judge it be rational. How could we judge it to be rationally engaged in without judging it to be reliable? To accept some doxastic practice, like SPP, as rational is to judge that it is rational to take it as a way of finding out what (some aspect of) the world is like; it is to judge that to form beliefs in accordance with this practice is to reflect the character of some stretch of reality. That means that to judge SPP to be rational is to judge that it is a reliable mode of belief-formation; for the beliefs thus formed could not be an accurate reflection of the facts without being generally true. Hence in explaining how one can form a sound, defensible judgment to the effect that SPP is rational, we have explained how one can arrive at a sound judgment that SPP is reliable.

It may seem that if a judgment of the rationality of SPP carries with it a judgment of its reliability, this can only be because rationality entails reliability, contrary to what I have said. But entailment of q by p is only one way in which judging that p amounts to judging that q. There is also pragmatic implication, as when in judging that I believe that p I thereby judge that p is true or, perhaps better, commit myself to the truth of p. And, closer to home, when I take myself to be rational or justified in believing that p, or take it that p is adequately supported by all relevant evidence, I thereby take p to be true. And in none of these cases is the truth of p entailed by what I explicitly judge. It could be the case that I believe that p, that p is justifiably or rationally believed, and that p is adequately supported by all relevant evidence, and still not be the case that p is true. Likewise in our case. In taking SPP to be rationally engaged in, I thereby commit myself to regarding it as reliable; so that I cannot, if I know what I am about, affirm the one and deny the other. But that is because of what I am committing myself to in making the judgment of rationality, not because of an entailment, or other species of logical support, that obtains between the proposition that SPP is rational and the proposition that SPP is reliable.

Let's approach the whole matter from another angle. We have seen (at least I have laid it down) that a basic practice like SPP cannot be shown to be reliable in what we may call a "direct" fashion. That is, we cannot exhibit the proposition *SPP is reliable* as the conclusion of a deductive or inductive argument that meets the epistemic conditions for establishing the truth of the conclusion (non-circularity, premises knowable without already accepting the conclusion, and so on). That means that if we are to have any basis at all for making a judgment as to the reliability of SPP, we will have to take a more roundabout approach. More specifically, we need to consider the higher-level question as to whether the proposition *SPP is reliable* is justifiably or rationally accepted. Blocked from giving direct support to the proposition, we are led to seek support for a proposition about its epistemic status. This will provide indirect support to the proposition itself; for it is certainly a recommendation of a proposition that it is rational to accept it. This is just what we have been doing in indicating how one could make a sound judgment to the effect that it is rational to engage in SPP, and thereby a sound judgment to the effect that SPP is reliable. No doubt, it would be much more satisfying to produce a direct demonstration of the truth of the proposition that *SPP is reliable*. But since that is impossible, the next best thing is to show that it is reasonable to believe that SPP is reliable.[35]

Now for the question: "Is this detour through doxastic practices necessary?" If we are unable to give a straightforward argument for the reliability of ordinary perceptual beliefs, and are thereby unable to provide a straightforward defense of an externalist principle of justification for perceptual beliefs, why shouldn't we simply defend an internalist principle of justification for perceptual beliefs, rather than erect an elaborate framework of doxastic practices, and then defend an internalist principle of justification (rationality) for the *practice* of forming perceptual beliefs in the usual way? If we must retreat from externalist to internalist judgments of rationality, why not execute the maneuver on the field of beliefs rather than move into an entirely different sector?

A good question. But the answer is quite simple. So long as we consider beliefs in isolation, we have no sufficient basis for an internalist judgment of rationality. Take my present perceptual belief that there is a squirrel on the telephone wire outside my window. Recall that I cannot give a non-epistemically-circular argument for its being formed in a reliable manner, and hence am debarred from arguing directly for its being justified in an externalist sense. How can I support the thesis that it is, nevertheless, reasonable for me to believe this in the present situation? If I am unable to ascertain that it is formed in a reliable fashion, what other epistemically relevant recommendation can I give to this particular belief? I am at a loss to say. Hence the switch to something more general: the general mode of forming perceptual beliefs of which this is an instance. By focusing on this general *way* of forming beliefs, we may have a hope of finding some basis for an internalist judgment of (*prima facie*) reasonableness for all beliefs so formed. But how does the move to generality help us? We are still unable to carry out a direct demonstration of reliability. Well, I don't think generalization is a help, so long as we think of the mode of belief-formation abstractly, as a possible input-output device, or as the function that defines the device. Why is it more rational to instantiate one such function than another? We come onto something really helpful only when we take the mode of belief-formation *concretely*, as an aspect of a practice that is socially established and that plays a central role in human life. Then, and only then, do we find reasons for a judgment that it is reasonable to engage in the practice. Those reasons essentially depend on the fact that this practice, and other fundamental practices, are thoroughly entrenched in our lives, to such an extent that we can hardly, if at all, imagine life without them. It is against this background that we find the most reasonable judgment to be that any such way of forming beliefs is rationally employed, in the absence of sufficient disqualifying considerations. Hence the "detour" through practices is essential to the line of argument of this paper.

VI

How is the "doxastic practice approach" to epistemology presented in this paper related to the most prominent issues in epistemology and the most prominent positions on those issues? Is it foundationalist or coherentist? Is it internalist or externalist? What position does it take, or dictate, on the nature of knowledge, the nature of justification, and their interrelation? For that matter, how is this "approach" related to positions I have taken in recent publications?[36] Is this an about-face on my part, or does it simply continue and extend my recent work?

The key to answering these questions lies in the distinction between meta-epistemology and substantive epistemology, parallel to the more familiar distinction between meta-ethics and normative ethics. My doxastic practice approach is, most centrally, a position on the nature of epistemology: what its central problems and tasks are; how to go about those tasks; what sort of success it is reasonable to expect in this enterprise. This is meta-epistemology — a view about epistemology, its nature, conduct, methodology, and prospects — rather than a position developed in the prosecution of the discipline itself. Therefore, we should not expect this paper to present any position on those central issues mentioned in the last paragraph. And that is what we find. The *approach* developed here tells us that epistemology is primarily a reflection, both descriptive and critical, on established doxastic practices. But it doesn't tell us what that reflection will uncover. It doesn't tell us what practices there are, how they are structured, what criteria of justification or rationality are built into them, or how resistant to criticism those criteria are. We need to go about doing epistemology along these lines in order to resolve those issues. The meta-epistemology won't do that for us.

Nevertheless, just as with the relation between meta-ethics and normative ethics, the compartments are not hermetically sealed. Being an intuitionist or a naturalist in meta-ethics is going to put some constraints on the positions that can reasonably be taken in normative ethics. And so it is here. Thus, in conclusion, I will give a sketchy presentation of the major respects in which my doxastic practice approach does and does not carry commitments in substantive epistemology.

First, in taking epistemology to be centrally concerned with doxastic practices we commit ourselves to the view that the source of a belief is crucial for its epistemic status. Thus this approach rules out those views that take rationality or justification to be determined by, e.g., the evidence a person *has* for a belief, regardless of what the belief was based on; and it definitely aligns itself with views that see a close connection between the psychology of belief-formation and epistemology. Second, the approach rules out what we might call "universalism" in epistemology, any view that, like classical forms of both foundationalism and coherentism, suppose that one's knowledge or justified belief forms a single unified structure, so that the epistemic credentials of any belief is to be determined by locating it within that unique structure. On this approach, by contrast, pluralism reigns; there is no common measure for all beliefs. The epistemic status of a particular belief depends on the doxastic practice(s) from which it sprang; it depends on whether the belief conforms to the requirement of that practice, and, of course, on whether that practice itself is acceptable. There is no single, all-inclusive system by reference to which the credentials of any belief is to be assessed.[37] Third, the approach carries a strong prejudice toward an emphasis on reliability. This is largely because of the first commitment, to the epistemic relevance of the psychological source of beliefs. Once we take that step, it is almost inevitable that the reliability of the source will be a major factor in epistemic evaluation. If the most important thing to determine about a belief, from an epistemic point of view, is its mode of origin, then, given the acquisition of truth and the avoidance of error as the defining aim of the epistemic point of view, it can hardly be denied that the epistemically most important feature of a source is the reliability with which it yields true beliefs.[38]

Finally, there are more complicated relations with coherentism. There is a definite antipathy to coherentism, but it is multifaceted and qualified. For one thing, coherentism is typically universalist in character and so falls under the ban on universalist theories. But this doesn't show the approach to be more antithetical to coherentism than to classical foundationalism. For another thing, coherentism in its more plausible forms rejects source relevance. A source-relevant form of coherentism would have it that a belief is justified only if it is formed on the basis of its coherence with the total system of one's beliefs; and since beliefs are rarely, if ever, so formed, it would turn out that practically no beliefs are justified. Finally, the argument that attempts to establish the reliability of basic doxastic practices are infected with epistemic circularity, and therefore don't do the desired job, an argument that is basic to this whole approach, presupposes the inadequacy of coherentism. For a classical coherentism wouldn't worry about that circularity. Reliability claims for basic sources can, for such a theorist, be justified in the way any other belief can, by its coherence with one's total system of beliefs.

These, then, are the major respects in which this approach makes commitments, positive and negative, in substantive epistemology. Now, finally, we turn to some of the major issues it leaves open. First, it carries no implications for the complete analysis of the major epistemological concepts, such as knowledge, justification, rationality; though, as we have seen, it does provide some constraints on such analyses, particularly with respect to justification and rationality. Second, the approach itself does not prejudge the fundamental questions of the structure of one or another doxastic practice. In keeping with its pluralist thrust, it does not assume that they all have the same structure. With respect to any one, it does not assume that the criteria of justification or rationality involved are internalist or externalist, in any of the many understandings of those notions, nor does it prejudge the question of the relative mix of foundationalist and coherentist elements in that structure. And, of course, it leaves wide open the question of what it takes for a ground of a belief to be *adequate*. Thus it is firmly committed to full employment for substantive epistemologists. [39]

NOTES

1. "Concepts of Epistemic Justification," *The Monist*, Vol. 68, No. 1 (January, 1985); "An Internalist Externalism," *Synthese*, Vol. 74 (1988), pp. 265-283.

2. For some defense of this position see, e.g., my "Concepts of Epistemic Justification" and Laurence Bonjour, *The Structure of Empirical Knowledge* (Cambridge, Mass.: Harvard U. Press, 1985), Ch. I.

3. Note that this thesis is plausible only for the whole of one of our major sources of belief, sense perception, memory, introspection, inductive reasoning, etc. If we were asking about some partial source, e.g., vision, or, still more partial, thermometers, we could easily find non-circular support by using other sense modalities or other instruments.

4. "Epistemic Circularity," *Philosophy and Phenomenological Research*, Vol. 47, No. 1, September, 1986.

5. Note that I., and many other widely accepted principles of the justification of perceptual beliefs, implies that this is possible. For I. lays down sufficient conditions of the justification of perceptual beliefs that do not require S to be justified in believing sense perception to be reliable.

6. It may be that 'show' is most properly used as a "success" word, so that one shows that p only if it is the case that p. If so, then the previous sentence simply makes explicit a conceptual truth about 'show' and has no special bearing on the problem of showing a source of belief to be reliable. But I mean to be using 'show' in a weaker sense in which it is synonymous with 'present adequate reasons in support of.' (If the English word 'show' cannot properly be used in this way, just take it that I am using 'show' as an abbreviation for the phrase just quoted.) Given that use of 'show,' it will still be true that we can show sense perception to be reliable only if it is reliable, even though it is not generally true that one can show that p only if p.

7. Later we shall see that some forms of self-support are of greater value than others.

8. *On Certainty*, ed., G. E. M. Anscombe and G. H. von Wright, tr., D. Paul and G. E. M. Anscombe (Oxford: Basil Blackwell, 1969).

9. What Wittgenstein called a "language-game" is something much more inclusive than the term would suggest. It involves modes of belief-formation and assessment (the aspect we shall be concentrating on under the rubric "doxastic practice"), characteristic attitudes and feelings and modes of behavior toward certain sorts of things, as well as ways of talking. The Wittgensteinian term, "form of life," is better suited to suggest the richness of the concept.

10. There is a striking similarity here to Rudolf Carnap's distinction between questions that are internal to a conceptual framework and hence theoretical, and questions that are external to a conceptual framework and hence practical. See his "Empiricism, Semantics, and Ontology," *Revue Internationale de Philosophie*, 11 (1950).

11. *Philosophical Investigations*, tr., G. E. M. Anscombe (Oxford: Basil Blackwell, 1953) I, 654.

12. This is a psychological rather than an epistemic regress argument. See Robert Audi, "Psychological Foundationalism," *The Monist*, Vol. 62, No. 4 (1978).

13. See Alvin I. Goldman, "What Is Justified Belief?" in G. S. Pappas, ed., *Justification and Knowledge* (Dordrecht: D. Reidel Pub. Co., 1979). It is not clear just where to put memory in this classification. If it is possible to form beliefs for the first time about a remembered scene, then memory can sometimes be generational, though it will usually operate on previously acquired beliefs. When it does, it should perhaps be termed "preservative" rather than "transformational," since it is a way of storing and retrieving the same belief that constitutes the input, unless we wish to rule that whereas the previously held belief was, e.g., that one *does* have a stomachache, the memory belief is that one *did* have a stomachache.

14. We might think of the input to an inferential belief-forming mechanism as the beliefs that constitute the premises, leaving the inferential part to the operation of the mechanism. Or we might think of the input as the "realization" (conscious or unconscious) that the conclusion follows (deductively or in some other way) from the premises, thereby, in effect, absorbing the inferential link into the input. In either case, the output is the belief in the conclusion. In this paper I will employ the second alternative.

15. At least this is the case on the "source-relevant" and "truth-conducive" concept of justification we are employing in this chapter. On a "source-irrelevant" conception of justification, according to which it is enough for justification that the subject *have* adequate grounds for the belief, whether the belief was based on them or not, a different verdict would be forthcoming.

16. Thus far we are simply talking about what criteria of justification are inherent in a given practice, what a practitioner *takes* to be sufficient for justification. Whether this amounts to "real justification" is something we will be taking up later.

17. For a discussion of Reid that stresses this point, see Nicholas Wolterstorff, "Thomas Reid on Rationality," in *Rationality in the Calvinian Tradition*, ed., H. Hart, J. Vanderhoeven, and N. Wolterstorff (Lanham, Md.: University Press of America, 1983).

18. *Essays on the Intellectual Powers of Man* (Cambridge, Mass.: MIT Press, 1969), Essay II, Ch. 20, p. 291.

19. *Ibid.*

20. See, e.g., *An Inquiry into the Human Mind* (Chicago: U. of Chicago Press, 1970), Ch. 6, section xxiv.

21. *Essays*, II, 20, pp. 291-292.

22. See *Inquiry*, Ch. 6, sec. xxiv.

23. As should be clear from the above, my theory of doxastic practices differs radically from the various non-realist, verificationist, and relativistic versions of

Sprachspielism now current, represented by such writers as D. Z. Phillips and Richard Rorty, and by such rumblings as deconstructionism that emanate from the continent of Europe. I am far from supposing, with many of these writers, that each "language-game," "conceptual scheme," "discourse," or what have you, carries with it its own special concept of truth and reality, that each defines a distinct "world," or that truth is to be construed as "what one's linguistic peers will let one get away with" (Rorty). My theory of doxastic practices is firmly realistic, recognizing a single reality that is what it is, regardless of how we think or talk about it. The doxastic practice is a source of criteria of justification and rationality; it does not determine truth or reality. Another way of putting this is to say that for me doxastic practices are crucial epistemologically, not metaphysically.

24. For one attempt to formulate Reid's response, see my "Thomas Reid on Epistemic Principles," *History of Philosophy Quarterly*, Vol. 2, No. 4 (October, 1985).

25. These are all considerations Reid adduces with respect to what he calls "first principles," which include claims to the reliability of our basic doxastic practices. See my article listed in the last note.

26. This is a point stressed by Reid. See my "Thomas Reid on Epistemic Principles" for details.

27. This last contrast is well exemplified by the Kuhnian distinction between "normal science," subject to fairly definite standards and procedures, and "scientific revolutions," in which the previously accepted standards and procedures are thrown into question, and it is everyone for himself.

28. A defence of this judgment would be difficult and tortuous, and this is not the place for it. I will only point to the great importance of this issue and its pervasive neglect. Note that even if universal abstention were a live possibility, it would still be the case that we are firmly entrenched in these practices; hence the burden of proof would seem to fall on the proponent of abandonment rather than on the proponent of continuance.

29. For this term see John Pollock, "A Plethora of Epistemological Theories," in G. S. Pappas, ed., *Justification and Knowledge* (Dordrecht: D. Reidel Pub. Co., 1979), p. 101.

30. For a development of this view about the justification of belief see my "An Internalist Externalism."

31. I have argued against taking non-universality to be disqualifying in "Religious Experience and Religious Belief," *Nous*, Vol. 16 (1982), and in "Christian Experience and Christian Belief," in *Faith and Rationality*, ed., A. Plantinga and N. Wolterstorff (Notre Dame, Ind.: U. of Notre Dame Press, 1983).

32. As for efficiency, contrast the procedure of accepting all applicants to a graduate program and then flunking out the unqualified ones, with the procedure of carefully screening the applicants and accepting only those whose record grounds a *prima facie* presumption of success.

33. For other reasons for allowing some degree of inconsistency in a set of beliefs, see Peter Klein, "The Virtues of Inconsistency," *The Monist*, Vol. 68, No. 1 (January, 1985).

34. For an explanation of the internalist-externalist distinction(s), see my "Internalism and Externalism in Epistemology," *Philosophical Topics*, 14, No. 1 (1986).

35. This is analogous to the "fideist" move in religion. Pessimistic about the chances of directly establishing the truth of the existence of God, one seeks to show that it is rational for one to believe in God, as a postulate of pure practical reason, as a requirement for fullness of life, or whatever.

36. Particularly "Concepts of Epistemic Justification" and "An Internalist Externalism."

37. At least this is the story with respect to beliefs. Our approach does countenance a sort of universalism with respect to practices. We need, and have, universally applicable principles for the evaluation of doxastic practices. But even here, as we saw, there are severe limits on what can be expected from the application of these principles. This is, at most, a very weak universalism.

38. Note that this point does not strictly rule out a deontological conception of justification in terms of obligations, duties, blameworthiness, etc. For the stress on reliability can be preserved in the view that the justification of a particular belief is a matter of that belief's being formed with due regard to one's obligation to see to it that one forms beliefs only by procedures that, so far as one can tell, are reliable.

39. Ancestors of this paper have been presented at the Institute of Philosophy in Moscow, Wayne State University, and the University of Utah. I am indebted to my discussants on those occasions for many useful reactions. I am especially grateful to Robert Audi and Jonathan Bennett for comments that greatly improved the paper.

2
Understanding Human Knowledge in General

Barry Stroud

The philosophical study of human knowledge seeks to understand what human knowledge is and how it comes to be. A long tradition of reflection on these questions suggests that we can never get the kind of satisfaction we seek. Either we reach the skeptical conclusion that we do not know the things we thought we knew, or we cannot see how the state we find ourselves in is a state of knowledge.

Most philosophers today still deny, or at the very least resist, the force of such reflections. In their efforts to construct a positive theory of knowledge they operate on the not-unreasonable assumption that since human perception, belief, and knowledge are natural phenomena like any other, there is no more reason to think they cannot be understood and explained than there is to think that digestion or photosynthesis cannot be understood and explained. Even if there is still much to be learned about human cognition, it can hardly be denied that we already know a great deal, at least in general, about how it works. Many see it now as just a matter of filling in the details, either from physiology or from something called "cognitive science." We might find that we understand much less than we think we do, but even so it would seem absurd simply to deny that there is such a thing as human knowledge at all, or that we can ever understand how it comes to be. Those traditional skeptical considerations, whatever they were, therefore tend to be ignored. They will be refuted in any case by a successful theory that explains how we do in fact know the things we do.

It would be as absurd to cast doubt on the prospects of scientific investigation of human knowledge and perception as it would be to declare limits to our understanding of human digestion. But I think that what we seek in epistemology — in the philosophical study of human knowledge — is not just anything we can find about how we know things. We try to understand human knowledge in general, and to do so in a certain special way. If the philosophical investigation of knowledge is something distinctive, or sets itself certain special or unique goals, one might question whether those goals can really be reached without thereby casting any doubt on investigations of human knowledge which lack those distinctive philosophical features. That is what I shall try to do. I want to raise and examine the possibility that, however much we came to learn about this or that aspect of human knowledge, thought, and perception, there might still be nothing that could satisfy us as a philosophical understanding of how human knowledge is possible.

When I say nothing could satisfy us I do not mean that it is a very difficult task and that we will never finish the job. It *is* very difficult, and we *will* never finish the job, but I assume that is true of most of our efforts to understand anything. Rather, the threat I see is that once we really understand what we aspire to in the philosophical study of knowledge, and we do not deviate from the aspiration to understand it in that way, we will be forever unable to get the kind of understanding that would satisfy us.

That is one reason I think skepticism is so important in epistemology. It is the view that we do not, or perhaps cannot, know anything, and it is important because it seems to be the inevitable consequence of trying to understand human knowledge in a certain way. Almost nobody thinks for a moment that skepticism could be correct. But that does not mean it is not important. If skepticism really is the inevitable outcome of trying to understand human knowledge in a certain way, and we think it simply could not be correct, that should make us look much more critically at that way of trying to understand human knowledge in the first place. But that is not what typically happens in philosophy. The goal itself is scarcely questioned, and for good reason. We feel human knowledge ought to be intelligible in that way. The epistemological project feels like the pursuit of a perfectly comprehensible intellectual goal. We know that skepticism is no good; it is an answer, but it is not satisfactory. But being constitutionally unable to arrive at an answer to a perfectly comprehensible question is not satisfactory either. We therefore continue to acquiesce in the traditional problem and do not acknowledge that there is no satisfactory solution. We proceed as if it must be possible to find an answer, so we deny the force, and even the interest, of skepticism.

What we seek in the philosophical theory of knowledge is an account that is completely general in several respects. We want to understand how any knowledge at all is possible — how anything we currently accept amounts to knowledge. Or, less ambitiously, we want to understand with complete generality how we come to know anything at all in a certain specified domain.

For example, in the traditional question of our knowledge of the material bodies around us we want to understand how we know anything at all about any such bodies. In the philosophical problem of other minds we want to understand how any person ever comes to know anything at all about what is going on in the mind of any other person, or even knows that there are any other minds at all. In the case of induction we want to understand how anyone can ever have any reason at all to believe anything beyond what he himself has so far observed to be true. I take it to be the job of a positive philosophical theory of knowledge to answer these and similarly general questions.

One kind of generality I have in mind is revealed by what we would all regard as no answer at all to the philosophical problem. The question of other minds is how anyone can know what someone else thinks or feels. But it would be ludicrous to reply that someone can know what another person thinks or feels by asking a good friend of that person's. That would be no answer at all, but not because it is not true. I *can* sometimes find out what someone else thinks by asking his best friend. But that would not contribute to the solution to the philosophical problem of other minds. We are not simply looking for a list of all the ways of knowing. If we were, that way of knowing would go on the list. But in fact we seek a more inclusive description of all our ways of knowing that would explain our knowledge in general.

What is wrong with that particular way of knowing the mind of another is not that it is only one way among others. The trouble is that it explains how we know some particular fact in the area we are interested in by appeal to knowledge of some other fact in that same domain. I know what Smith thinks by knowing that Jones told me what Smith thinks. But knowing that Jones told me something is itself a bit of knowledge about the mind of another. So that kind of answer could not serve as, nor could it be generalized into, a satisfactory answer to the question how we know anything at all about any other minds. Not because it does not mention a legitimate way of knowing something about the mind of another. It does. Coming to know what Smith thinks by asking Jones is a perfectly acceptable way of knowing, and it is a different way of getting that knowledge from having Smith tell me himself, or from reading Smith's mail. There is nothing wrong with it in itself as an explanation. It is only for the general philosophical task that it is felt to be inadequate.

The same holds for everyday knowledge of the objects around us. One way I can know that my neighbor is at home is by seeing her car in front of her house, where she parks it when and only when she is at home. That is a perfectly good explanation of how I know that fact about one of the things around me. It is a different way of knowing where my neighbor is from seeing her through the window or hearing her characteristic fumblings on the piano. But it could not satisfy us as an explanation of how I know anything at all about any objects around me. It explains how I know something about one object around me — my neighbor — by knowing something about another object around me — her car. It could not answer the philosophical question as to how I know anything about any objects around me at all.

The kind of generality at stake in these problems takes its characteristic philosophical form when we come to see, on reflection, that the information available to us for knowing things in a particular domain is systematically less than we might originally have thought. Perhaps the most familiar instance of this is the *First Meditation* of Descartes,[1] in which he asks about knowledge of the material world by means of the senses. It apparently turns out on reflection that the senses give us less than we might have thought; there is no strictly sensory information the possession of which necessarily amounts to knowledge of the material world. We could perceive exactly what we perceive now even if there were no material world at all. The problem then is to see how we ever come to get knowledge of the material world on that sensory basis.

In the case of other minds we find on reflection that the only evidence we can ever have or even imagine for the mental states of other people is their bodily behavior, including the sounds coming out of their mouths, or even the tears coming out of their eyes. But there is no strictly physical or behavioral information the possession of which necessarily amounts to knowledge of another person's mind or feelings. With induction the general distinction is perhaps even more obvious. The only reason we could ever have for believing anything about what we are not observing at the moment is something we have observed in the past or are observing right now. The problem then is how any knowledge of strictly past or even present fact amounts to knowledge of, or reasonable belief in, some unobserved or future fact.

These apparently simple, problem-generating moves come right at the beginning of epistemology. They are usually taken as so obvious and undeniable that the real problems of epistemology are thought to arise only after they have been made. In this paper I simply assume familiarity with them and with how easily they work. They are the very moves I think we eventually must examine more carefully if we are ever going to understand the real source of the dissatisfaction we are so easily driven to in philosophy. But for now I am concerned with the structure of the plight such reflections appear to leave us in.

If we start by considering a certain domain of facts or truths and ask how anyone could come to know anything at all in that domain, it will seem that any other knowledge that might be relevant could not be allowed to amount to already knowing something in the domain in question. Knowledge of anything at all in that domain is what we want to explain, and if we simply assume from the outset that the person has already got some of that knowledge we will not be explaining all of it. Any knowledge we do grant to the person will be of use to him only if he can somehow get from that knowledge to some knowledge in the domain in question. Some inference or transition would therefore appear to be needed — for example, some way of going from what he is aware of in perception to knowledge of the facts he claims to know. But any such inference will be a good one, and will lead the person to knowledge, only if it is based on something the person also knows or has some reason to believe. He cannot just be making a guess that he has got good evidence. He has to know or at least have reason to believe something that will help get him from his evidential base to some knowledge in the domain in question. That "something" that he needs to know cannot simply be part of his evidential base, since it has to get him beyond that base. But it cannot go so far beyond that base as to imply something already in the domain in question either, since the knowledge of anything at all in that domain is just what we are trying to explain. So it would seem that on either possibility we cannot explain with the proper generality how the kind of knowledge we want to understand is possible. If the person does know what he needs to know, he has already got some knowledge in the domain in question, and if he does not, he will not be able to get there from his evidential base alone.

This apparent dilemma is a familiar quandary in traditional epistemology. I think it arises from our completely general explanatory goal. We want to explain a certain kind of knowledge, and we feel we must explain it on the basis of another, prior kind of knowledge that does not imply or presuppose any of the knowledge we are trying to explain. Without that, we will not be explaining the knowledge in question in the proper, fully general way. This felt need is what so easily brings into the epistemological project some notion or other of what is usually called "epistemic priority" — one kind of knowledge being prior to another. I believe it has fatal consequences for our understanding of our knowledge. It is often said that traditional epistemology is generated by nothing more than a misguided "quest for certainty," or a fruitless search for absolutely secure "foundations" for knowledge, and that once we abandon such a will-o'-the-wisp we will no longer be threatened by skepticism, or even much interested in it.[2] But that diagnosis seems wrong to me — in fact, completely upside down. What some philosophers see as a poorly motivated demand for "foundations" of knowledge looks to me to be the natural consequence of seeking a certain intellectual goal, a certain kind of understanding of human knowledge in general.

In the philosophical problem of other minds, for example, we pick out observable physical movements or "behavior" and ask how on that basis alone, which is the only basis we have, we can ever know anything about the mind behind the "behavior." Those observable facts of "behavior" are held to be "epistemically prior" to any facts about the mind in the sense that it is possible to know all such facts about others' "behavior" without knowing anything about their minds. We insist on that condition for a properly general explanation of our knowledge of other minds. But in doing so we need not suppose that our beliefs about that "behavior" are themselves indubitable or incorrigible "foundations" of anything. Levels of relative epistemic priority are all we need to rely on in pressing the epistemological question in that way.

In the case of our knowledge of the material objects around us we single out epistemically prior "sensations" or "sense data" or "experiences" or whatever it might be, and then ask how on that basis alone, which is the only basis we have, we can know anything of the objects around us. We take it that knowledge of objects comes to us somehow by means of the senses, but if we thought of sensory knowledge as itself knowledge of material objects around us we would not get an appropriately general explanation of how any knowledge of any objects at all is possible by means of the senses. We would be explaining knowledge of some material objects only on the basis of knowledge of some others. "Data," "the given," "experiences," and so on, which traditional epistemologists have always trafficked in, therefore look to me much more like inevitable products of the epistemological enterprise than elusive "foundations," the unmotivated quest for which somehow throws us into epistemology in the first place.

But once we accept the idea of one kind of knowledge being prior to another as an essential ingredient in the kind of philosophical understanding we seek, it immediately becomes difficult even to imagine, let alone to find, anything that could satisfy us. How *could* we possibly know anything about the minds of other people on the basis only of truths about their "behavior" if those truths do not imply anything about any minds? If we really are restricted in perception to "experiences" or "sense data" or "stimulations" which give us information that is prior to any knowledge of objects, how *could* we ever know anything about what goes on beyond such prior "data"? It would seem to be possible only if we somehow knew of some connection between what we are restricted to in observation and what is true in the wider domain we are interested in. But then knowing even that there was such a connection would be knowing something about that wider domain after all, not just about what we are restricted to in observation. And then we would be left with no satisfactorily general explanation of our knowledge.

In short, it seems that if we really were in the position the traditional account in terms of epistemic priority describes us as being in, skepticism would be correct. We could not know the things we think we know. But if, in order to resist that conclusion, we no longer see ourselves in that traditional way, we will not have a satisfactorily general explanation of all our knowledge in a certain domain.

Theorists of knowledge who accept the traditional picture of our position in the world obviously do not acknowledge what I see as its skeptical or otherwise unsatisfactory consequences. Some philosophers see their task as that of exhibiting the general structure of our knowledge by making explicit what they think are the "assumptions" or "postulates" or "epistemic principles" that are needed to take us from our "data" or evidence in a particular area to some richer domain of knowledge we want to explain.[3] The fact that certain "postulates" or "principles" can be shown to be precisely what is needed for the knowledge in question is somehow taken to count in their favour. Without those "principles," it is argued, we wouldn't know what we think we know.

However illuminating such "rational reconstructions" of our knowledge might be, they cannot really satisfy us if we want to understand how we actually do know the things we think we know. If it had been shown that there is a certain "postulate" or "principle" which we have to have some reason to accept if we are to know anything about, say, the world around us, we would not thereby have come to understand how we do know anything about the world around us. We would have identified something we need, but its indispensability would not show that we do in fact have good reason to accept it. We would be left with the further question whether we know that that "principle" is true, and if so how. And all the rest of the knowledge we wanted to explain would then be hanging in the balance, since it would have been shown to depend on that "principle." Trying to answer the question of its justification would lead right back into the old dilemma. If the "principle" involved says or implies something richer than anything to be found in the prior evidential base — as it seems it must if it is going to be of any help — there will be nothing in that base alone that could give us reason to accept it. But if we assume from the outset that we do know or have some reason to accept that "principle," we will be assuming that we already know something that goes beyond our prior evidential base, and that knowledge itself will not have been explained. We would therefore have no completely general explanation of how we get beyond that base to any knowledge of the kind in question.

The threat of a regress in the support for any such "principles" leads naturally to the idea of two distinct sources or types of knowledge. If the "principles" or presuppositions of knowledge could be known independently, not on the basis of the prior evidence, but in some other way, it might seem that the regress could be avoided. This might be said to be what Kant learned from Hume:[4] if all our knowledge is derived from experience, we can never know anything. But Kant did not infer from that conditional proposition the categorical skeptical conclusion he thought Hume drew from it. For Kant the point was that if we do have knowledge from experience we must also have some knowledge that is independent of experience. Only in that way is experiential knowledge possible. We must know some things *a priori* if we know anything at all.

As a way of explaining how we know the things we do, this merely postpones or expands the problem. It avoids the skeptical regress in sensory knowledge of the world by insisting that the basic "principles" or presuppositions needed for such empirical knowledge do not themselves depend on empirical, sensory support. But that says only that those "principles" are *not* known by experience; it does not explain how they are known. Merely being presupposed by our empirical knowledge confers no independent support. It has to be explained how we know anything at all *a priori*, and how in particular we know those very things we need for empirical knowledge. And then the old dilemma presents itself again. If our *a priori* knowledge of those "principles" is derived from something prior to them which serves as their evidential base, it must be shown how the further "principles" needed to take us from that base to the "principles" in question could themselves be supported. If we assume from the outset that we do know some "principles" *a priori*, not all of our *a priori* knowledge in general will have been explained. It would seem that *a priori* knowledge in general could be explained only in terms of something that is not itself *a priori* knowledge. But empirical knowledge cannot explain *a priori* knowledge — and it would be no help here even if it could — so either we must simply accept the unexplained fact that we know things *a priori* or we must try to explain it without appealing to any other knowledge at all.

I do not want to go further into the question of *a priori* knowledge. Not because it is not difficult and important in its own right, but because many theorists of knowledge would now argue that it is irrelevant to the epistemological project of explaining our knowledge of the world around us. They find they can put their finger precisely on the place where the traditional philosophical enterprise turns inevitably towards skepticism. And they hold that that step is wrong, and that without it there is no obstacle to finding a satisfactory account of our epistemic position that avoids any commitment to skepticism. This claim for a new "enlightened" theory of knowledge that does not take that allegedly skeptical step is what I want to question.

I have already sketched the hopeless plight I think the old conception leaves us in. The trouble in that conception is now thought to enter at just the point at which the regress I have described apparently gets started. To get from his "evidence" to any of the knowledge in question the person was said to need some "principle" or assumption that would take him from that "evidence" to that conclusion. But he would also need some reason for accepting that "principle" — he would have to know something else that supports it. And then he would need some reason for accepting that "something else," and it could not be found either in his evidential base or in the "principles" he originally needed to take him beyond that base. It must be found in something else in turn — another "something else" — and so on *ad infinitum*. What is wrong in this, it is now thought, is not the idea that the person cannot find such reasons, or that he can only find them somehow mysteriously *a priori*. What is wrong is the requirement that he himself has to find such reasons, that he has to be able to support his "principles," at all. The new "enlightened" approach to knowledge insists that there is a clear sense in which he does not.

The objection can be put another way. What is wrong with the traditional epistemological project that leads so easily to skepticism, it is said, is that the whole thing assumes that anyone who knows something must know that he knows it. He must himself know that his reasons are good ones, or that his prior "evidence" is adequate to yield knowledge of the kind in question. And then, by that same assumption, he must know that he knows that, and so on. But that assumption, it is argued, is not correct. It is obviously possible for someone to know something without knowing that he knows it. The theory of knowledge asks simply whether and how people know things. If that can be explained, that is enough. The fact that people sometimes do not know that they know things should not make us deny that they really do know those things — especially if we have a satisfactory theory that explains that knowledge.

Now it certainly seems right to allow that someone can know something even when we recognize that he does not know that he knows it. Think of the simplest ordinary examples. Someone is asked if he knows who won the battle of Hastings, and when it took place, and he tentatively replies "William the Conqueror, 1066." He knew the answer. He had learned it in school, perhaps, and had never forgotten it, but at the time he was asked he did not know whether he had really retained that information. He was not sure about the state of his knowledge, but as for the winner and the date of the battle of Hastings, he knew that all along. He knew more than he thought he did. So whether somebody knows something is one thing; whether he knows that he knows it is something else. That seems to be a fact about our everyday assessments of people's knowledge.

The question is not whether that is a fact, but what significance it has for the prospects of the philosophical theory of knowledge. Obviously it turns on what a satisfactory philosophical account is supposed to do. The goal as I have presented it so far is to take ourselves and our ways of knowing on the one hand, and a certain domain of truths that we want to know about on the other, and to understand how we know any of those truths at all on the basis of prior knowledge that does not amount to already knowing something in the domain we are interested in. The question was what support we could find for the bridge that would be needed to get us from that prior basis to the knowledge in question. The present suggestion amounts in effect to saying that no independent or *a priori* support is needed on the part of the knower. All that is needed is that a certain proposition should be true; the person doesn't have to know that it is true in order to know the thing in question. If he has the appropriate prior knowledge or experience, and there is in fact a truth linking his having that knowledge or experience with his knowing something in the domain in question, then he does in fact know something in that domain, even if he is not aware of the favorable epistemic position he is in.

The truth in question will typically be one expressing the definition of knowledge, or of having reason to believe something. The search for such definitions is what many philosophers regard as the special job of the philosophical theory of knowledge. If knowing something could be defined solely in terms of knowledge or experience in some unproblematic, prior domain, then that definition could be fulfilled even if you didn't know that you knew anything in that domain. You yourself would not have to find a "bridge" from your evidential basis to the knowledge in question. As long as there actually was a "bridge" under your feet, whether you knew of it or not, there would be no threat of a skeptical regress.

In one form, this anti-skeptical strategy has been applied to the problem of induction. Hume had argued that if a long positive correlation observed to hold between two sorts of things in the past is going to give you some reason now to expect a thing of the second sort, given an observed instance of the first, you will also have to have some reason to think that what you have observed in the past gives you some reason to believe something about the future. P.F. Strawson replied that you need no such thing. Having observed a long positive correlation between two sorts of things under widely varied circumstances in the past is just what it is — what it means — to have reason to expect a thing of the second sort, given that a thing of the first sort has just appeared.[5] If that is a necessary truth about reasonable belief it will guarantee that you do in fact have a reasonable belief in the future as long as you have had the requisite experience of the past and present. You do not have to find some additional reason for thinking that what you have observed in the past gives you good reason to believe something about the future.

This has come to be called an "externalist" account of knowledge or reasonable belief. It would explain knowledge in terms of conditions that are available from an "external," third-person point of view, independent of what the knower's own attitude towards the fulfillment of those conditions might be. It is not all smooth sailing. To give us what we need, it has to come up with an account of knowledge or reasonable belief that is actually correct — that distinguishes knowledge from lack of knowledge in the right way. I think the account just given of inductive reasons does not meet that test. As it stands, it does not state a necessary truth about reasons to believe.[6] To come closer to being right, it would have to define the difference between a "law-like" generalization and a merely "accidental" correlation which does not give reason to believe it will continue. That task is by no means trivial, and it faces a "new riddle of induction" all over again.[7] But if we do draw a distinction between having good reasons and not having them it would seem that there must be some account that captures what we do. It is just a matter of finding what it is.

The same goes for definitions of knowledge. One type of view says that knowing that p is equivalent to something like having acquired and retained a true belief that p as a result of the operation of a properly functioning, reliable belief-forming mechanism.[8] That general scheme still leaves many things unexplained or undefined, and it is no trivial task to get it to come out right. But I am not concerned here with the details of "externalist" definitions of knowledge. My reservations about the philosophical theory of knowledge are not just that it is difficult. I have doubts about the satisfactoriness of what you would have even if you had an "externalist" account of knowledge which as far as you could tell matched up completely with those cases in which we think other people know things and those in which we think they do not.

Here we come up against another, and perhaps the most important, dimension of generality I think we seek in the theory of knowledge. We want an account that explains how human knowledge in general is possible, or how anyone can know anything at all in a certain specified domain. The difficulty arises now from the fact that we as human theorists are ourselves part of the subject-matter that we theorists of human knowledge want to understand in a certain way. If we merely study another group and draw conclusions only about them, no such difficulty presents itself. But then our conclusions will not be completely general. They will be known to apply only to those others, and we will be no closer to understanding how our own knowledge is possible. We want to be able to apply what we find out about knowledge to ourselves, and so to explain how our own knowledge is possible.

I have already suggested why I think we cannot get a satisfactory explanation along traditional Cartesian lines. The promise of the new "externalist" strategy is that it would avoid the regress that seems inevitable in that project. A person who knows something does not himself have to know that what he has got in his prior evidential base amounts to knowledge in the domain in question. As long as he in fact satisfies the conditions of knowing something in the domain we are interested in, there is nothing more he has to do in order to know things in that domain. No regress gets started.

The question now is: can we find such a theory satisfactory when we apply it to ourselves? To illustrate what I find difficult here I return to Descartes, as we so often must do in this subject. Not to his skeptical argument in the *First Meditation*, but to the answer he gives to it throughout the rest of the *Meditations*. He eventually comes to think that he does know many of the things that seemed to be thrown into doubt by his earlier reflections on dreaming and the evil demon. He does so by proving that God exists and is not a deceiver and that everything in us, including our capacity to perceive and think, comes from God. So whatever we clearly and distinctly perceive to be true is true. God would not have it any other way. By knowing what I know about God I can know that He is not a deceiver and therefore that I do know the things I think I know when I clearly and distinctly perceive them. If I am careful, and keep God and his goodness in mind, I can know many things, and the threat of skepticism is overcome.

Many objections have been made to this answer to Descartes's question about his knowledge. One is the "externalist" complaint that Descartes's whole challenge rests on the assumption that you don't know something unless you know that you know it. Not only do my clear and distinct perceptions need some guarantee, but on Descartes's view I have to know what that guarantee is. That is why he thinks the atheist or the person who denies God in his heart cannot really know those things that we who accept Descartes's proof of God's existence and goodness can know.[9] But according to "externalism" that requirement is wrong; you don't have to know that you know in order to know something.

Another and perhaps the most famous objection is that Descartes's proof of the guarantee of his knowledge is no good because it is circular. The knowledge he needs in order to reach the conclusion of God's existence and goodness is available to him only if God's existence and goodness have already been proved. What he calls his clear and distinct perception of God's existence will be knowledge of God's existence only if whatever he clearly and distinctly perceives is true. But that is guaranteed only by God, so he can't know that it is guaranteed unless he already knows that God exists.

Taking these two objections together, we can see that if the first is correct, the second is no objection at all. If Descartes is assuming that knowing requires knowing that you know, and if that assumption is wrong, then the charge of circularity has no force against his view. If "externalism" were correct, Descartes's inability to prove that God exists and guarantees the truth of our clear and distinct perceptions would be no obstacle to his knowing the truth of whatever he clearly and distinctly perceives. He would not have to know that he knows those things. As long as God did in fact exist and did in fact make sure that his clear and distinct perceptions were true, Descartes would have the knowledge he started out thinking he had, even if God's existence and nature remained eternally unknown to him. The soundness of his proof would not matter. All that would matter for the everyday knowledge Descartes is trying to account for is the truth of its conclusion — God's existence and goodness. If that conclusion is in fact true, his inability to know that it is true would be no argument against his account.

To develop this thought further we can try to imagine what an "enlightened" or "externalist," but still otherwise Cartesian, theory might look like. It would insist that the knowing subject does not have to know the truth of the theory that explains his knowledge in order to have the knowledge that the theory is trying to account for. Otherwise, the theory would retain the full Cartesian story of God and his goodness and his guarantee of the truth of our clear and distinct perceptions. What would be wrong with accepting such an "enlightened" theory? If we are willing to accept the kind of theory that says that knowing that p is having acquired the true belief that p by some reliable belief-forming mechanism, why would we not be equally or even more willing to accept a theory that says that knowing that p is having acquired the true belief that p by clearly and distinctly perceiving it — a method of belief formation that is reliable because God guarantees that whatever is clearly and distinctly perceived is true? It is actually more specific than a completely general form of "externalism" or "reliabilism." It explains *why* the belief-forming mechanism is reliable. What, then, would be wrong with accepting it?

I think most of us simply don't believe it. We think that God does not in fact exist and is not the guarantor of the reliability of our belief-forming mechanisms. So we think that what this theory says about human knowledge is not true. Now that is certainly a defect in a theory, but is it the only thing standing in the way of our accepting it and finding it satisfactory? It seems to me it is not, and perhaps by examining its other defects, beyond its actual truth-value, we can identify a source of dissatisfaction with other "externalist" theories as well.

We have to admit that if the imagined "externalist" Cartesian theory were true, we would know many of the things we think we know. So skepticism would not be correct. But in the philosophical investigation of knowledge we want more than the falsity of skepticism and more than the mere possession of the knowledge we ordinarily think we've got. We want to understand how we know the things we know, how skepticism turns out not to be true. And even if this "enlightened" Cartesian story were in fact true, if we didn't know that it was, or if we didn't have some reason to believe that it was, we would be no further along towards understanding our knowledge than we would be if the theory were false. So we need some reason to accept a theory of knowledge if we are going to rely on that theory to understand how our knowledge is possible. That is what I think no form of "externalism" can give a satisfactory account of.

Suppose someone had said to Descartes, as they in effect did, "Look, you have no reason to accept any of this story about God and his guarantee of the truth of your clear and distinct perceptions. Of course, if what you say were true you would have the knowledge you think you have, but your whole proof of it is circular. You could justify your explanation of knowledge only if you already knew that what you clearly and distinctly perceive is true." Could an "enlightened" "externalist" Descartes reply: "That's right. I suppose I have to admit that I can give no good reason to accept my explanation. But that doesn't really bother me any more, now that I am an "externalist." Circularity in my proofs is no objection to my theory if "externalism" is correct. I still do believe my theory, after all, and as long as that theory is in fact true — whether I can give any reason to accept it or not — skepticism will be false and I will in fact know the things that I clearly and carefully claim to know."

I take it that that response is inadequate. The "externalist" Descartes I have imagined would not have a satisfactory understanding of his knowledge. It is crucial to what I want to say about "externalism" that we recognize some inadequacy in his position. It is admittedly not easy to specify exactly what the deficiency or the unsatisfactoriness of accepting that position amounts to. I think this much can be said: if the imagined Descartes responded only in that way he would be at best in the position of saying, "If the story that I accept is true, I do know the things I think I know. But I admit that if it is false, and a certain other story is true instead, then I do not." If "externalism" is correct, what he would be saying here is true. His theory, if true, would explain his knowledge. The difficulty is that until he finds some reason to believe his theory rather than some other, he cannot be said to have explained how he knows the things he knows. That is not because he is assuming that a person cannot know something unless he knows that he knows it. He has explicitly abandoned that assumption. He admits that people know things whether they know the truth of his theory or not. The same of course holds for him. And he knows that implication. That is precisely what he is saying: if his theory is true he will know the things he thinks he knows. But he is, in addition, a theorist of knowledge. He wants to understand how he knows the things he thinks he knows. And he cannot satisfy himself on that score unless he can see himself as having some reason to accept the theory that he (and all the rest of us) can recognize would explain his knowledge if it were true. That is not because knowing implies knowing that you know. It is because having an explanation of something in the sense of understanding it is a matter of having good reason to accept something that would be an explanation if it were true.

The question now is whether an "externalist" scientific epistemologist who rejects Descartes's explanation and offers one of his own is in any better position when he comes to apply his theory to his own knowledge than the imagined "externalist" Descartes is in. He begins by asking about all knowledge in a specified domain. A philosophically satisfactory explanation of such knowledge must not explain some of the knowledge in the domain in question by appeal to knowledge of something else already in the domain. But the scientific student of human knowledge must know or have some reason to believe his theory of knowledge if he is going to understand how knowledge is possible. His theory about our belief-forming mechanisms and their reliability is a theory about the interactions between us and the world around us. It is arrived at by studying human beings, finding out how they get the beliefs they do, and investigating the sources of the reliability of those belief-forming mechanisms. Descartes claimed knowledge of God and his goodness, and of the relation between those supernatural facts and our earth-bound belief-forming mechanisms. A more naturalistic epistemologist's gaze does not reach so high. He claims knowledge of nothing more than the familiar natural world in which he thinks everything happens. But he will have an explanation of human knowledge, and so will understand how people know the things they do, only if he knows or has some reason to believe that his scientific story of the goings-on in that world is true.

If his goal was, among other things, to explain our scientific knowledge of the world around us, he will have an explanation of such knowledge only if he can see himself as possessing some knowledge in that domain. In studying other people, that presents no difficulty. It is precisely by knowing what he does about the world that he explains how others know what they do about the world. But if he had started out asking how anyone knows anything at all about the world, he would be no further along towards understanding how any of it is possible if he had not understood how he himself knows what he has to know about the world in order to have any explanation at all. He must understand himself as knowing or having reason to believe that his theory is true.

It might seem that he fulfills that requirement because his theory of knowledge is meant to identify precisely those conditions under which knowledge or good reason to believe something is present. If that theory is correct, and he himself fulfills those conditions in his own scientific investigations of human knowledge, he will in fact know that his theory of knowledge is true, or at least he will have good reason to believe it. He studies others and finds that they often satisfy the conditions his theory says are sufficient for knowing things about the world, and he believes that theory, and he believes that he too satisfies those same conditions in his investigations of those other people. He concludes that he does know how human beings know what they do, and he concludes that he therefore understands how he in particular knows the things he knows about the world. He is one of the human beings that his theory is true of. So the non-Cartesian, scientific "externalist" claims to be in a better position than the imagined "externalist" Descartes because he claims to know by a reliable study of the natural world that his explanation of human knowledge is correct and Descartes's is wrong. In accepting his own explanation he claims to fulfill the conditions his theory asserts to be sufficient for knowing things.

I think this theorist would still be in no better position than the position the imagined "externalist" Descartes is in. If his theory is true, he will in fact know that his explanation is correct. In that sense he could be said to possess an explanation of how human beings know the things they know. In that same sense the imagined "externalist" Descartes would possess an explanation of his knowledge. He accepts something which, if true, would explain his knowledge. But none of this would be any help or consolation to them as epistemologists. The position of the imagined "externalist" Descartes is deficient for the theory of knowledge because he needs some reason to believe that the theory he has devised is true in order to be said to understand how people know the things they think they know. The scientific "externalist" claims he does have reason to believe his explanation of knowledge and so to be in a better position than the imagined "externalist" Descartes. But the way in which he fulfills that condition, even if he does, is only in an "externalist" way, and therefore in the same way that the imagined Descartes fulfills the conditions of knowledge, if he does. *If* the scientific "externalist's" theory is correct about the conditions under which knowledge or reasonable belief is present, and if he does fulfill those conditions in coming to believe his own explanation of knowledge, then he is in fact right in thinking that he has good reason to think that his explanation is correct. But that is to be in the same position with respect to whether he has good reason to think his explanation is correct as the imagined "externalist" Descartes was in at the first level with respect to whether he knows the things he thinks he knows.

It was admitted that if that imagined Descartes's theory were true he would know the things he thinks he knows, but he could not be said to see or to understand himself as possessing such knowledge because he had no reason to think that his theory was true. The scientific "externalist" claims to have good reason to believe that his theory is true. It must be granted that if, in arriving at his theory, he did fulfill the conditions his theory says are sufficient for knowing things about the world, then if that theory is correct, he does in fact know that it is. But still, I want to say, he himself has no reason to think that he does have good reason to think that his theory is correct. He is at best in the position of someone who has good reason to believe his theory if that theory is in fact true, but has no such reason to believe it if some other theory is true instead. He can see what he *would* have good reason to believe if the theory he believes were true, but he cannot see or understand himself as knowing or having good reason to believe what his theory says.

I am aware that describing what I see as the deficiency in this way is not really satisfactory or conclusive. It encourages the "externalist" to re-apply his theory of knowing or having good reason to believe at the next level up, and to claim that he can indeed understand himself to have good reason to believe his theory because he has good reason to believe that he does have good reason to believe his theory. That further belief about his reasons is arrived at in turn by fulfilling what his theory says are the conditions for reasonably believing something. But then he is still in the same position two levels up that we found the imagined "externalist" Descartes to be in at the first level. If the imagined Descartes's claim to self-understanding was inadequate there, any similar claim will be equally inadequate at any higher level of knowing that one knows or having reason to believe that one has reason to believe. That is why our reaction to the original response of the imagined "externalist" Descartes is crucial. Recognition of its inadequacy is essential to recognizing the inadequacy of "externalism" that I have in mind. It is difficult to say precisely what is inadequate about that kind of response, especially in terms that would be acceptable to an "externalist." Perhaps it is best to say that the theorist has to see himself as having good reason to believe his theory in some sense of "having good reason" that cannot be fully captured by an "externalist" account.

So even if it is true that you can know something without knowing that you know it, the philosophical theorist of knowledge cannot simply insist on the point and expect to find acceptance of an "externalist" account of knowledge fully satisfactory. If he could, he would be in the position of someone who says: "I don't know whether I understand human knowledge or not. If what I believe about it is true and my beliefs about it are produced in what my theory says is the right way, I do know how human knowledge comes to be, so in that sense I do understand. But if my beliefs are not true, or not arrived at in that way, I do not. I wonder which it is. I wonder whether I understand human knowledge or not." That is not a satisfactory position to arrive at in one's study of human knowledge — or of anything else.

It might be said that there can be such a thing as unwitting understanding, or understanding you don't know you've got, just as there can be unwitting knowledge, or knowledge you don't know you've got. Such "unwitting understanding," if there is such a thing, is the most that the "externalist" philosophical theorist about human knowledge could be said to have of his own knowledge. But even if there is such a thing, it is not something it makes sense to aspire to, or something to remain content with having reached, if you happen to have reached it. We want witting, not unwitting, understanding. That requires knowing or having some reason to accept the scientific story you believe about how people know the things they know. And in the case of knowledge of the world around us, that would involve already knowing or having some reason to believe something in the domain in question. Not all the knowledge in that domain would thereby be explained.

I do not mean that there is something wrong with our explaining how people know certain things about the world by assuming that they or we know certain other things about it. We do it all the time. It is only within the general epistemological enterprise that that otherwise familiar procedure cannot give us what we want. And when I say that "externalism" cannot give us what we want I do not mean that it possesses some internal defect which prevents it from being true. The difficulty I am pointing to is an unsatisfactoriness involved in *accepting* an "externalist" theory and claiming to understand human knowledge in general in that way. And even that is too broad. It is not that there is any difficulty in understanding other people's knowledge in those terms. It is only with self-understanding that the unsatisfactoriness or loss of complete generality makes itself felt. "Externalism," if it got the conditions of knowledge right, would work fine for other people's knowledge. As a third-person, observational study of human beings and other animals, it would avoid the obstacles to human understanding apparently involved in the first-person Cartesian project. But the question is whether we can take up such an "external" observer's position with respect to ourselves and our knowledge and still gain a satisfactorily general explanation of how we know the things we know. That is where I think the inevitable dissatisfaction comes in.

The demand for completely general understanding of knowledge in a certain domain requires that we see ourselves at the outset as not knowing anything in that domain and then coming to have such knowledge on the basis of some independent and in that sense prior knowledge or experience. And that leads us to seek a standpoint from which we can view ourselves without taking for granted any of that knowledge that we want to understand. But if we could manage to detach ourselves in that way from acceptance of any truths in the domain we are interested in, it seems that the only thing we could discover from that point of view is that we can never know anything in that domain. We could find no way to explain how that prior knowledge alone could yield any richer knowledge lying beyond it. That is the plight the traditional view captures. That is the truth in skepticism. If we think of our knowledge as arranged in completely general levels of epistemic priority in that way, we find that we cannot know what we think we know. Skepticism is the only answer.

But then that seems absurd. We realize that people do know many things in the domains we are interested in. We can even explain how they know such things, whether they know that they do or not. That is what the third-person point of view captures. That is the truth in "externalism." But when we try to explain how we know those things we find we can understand it only by assuming that we have got some knowledge in the domain in question. And that is not philosophically satisfying. We have lost the prospect of explaining and therefore understanding all of our knowledge with complete generality.

For these and other reasons I think we need to go back and look more carefully into the very sources of the epistemological quest. We need to see how the almost effortlessly natural ways of thinking embodied in that traditional enterprise nevertheless distort or misrepresent our position, if they do. But we should not think that if and when we come to see how the epistemological enterprise is not fully valid, or perhaps not even fully coherent, we will then possess a satisfactory explanation of how human knowledge in general is possible. We will have seen, at best, that we cannot have any such thing. And that too, I believe, will leave us dissatisfied.[10]

NOTES

1. R. Descartes, *Meditations on First Philosophy* in *The Philosophical Writings of Descartes*, vol. I, tr. J. Cottingham, R. Stoothoff, D. Murdoch, (Cambridge, 1985).

2. This charge has been laid against traditional epistemology at least since Dewey's *The Quest for Certainty* and is by now, I suppose, more or less philosophical orthodoxy. For more recent expressions of it see, for example, Michael Williams, *Groundless Belief* (Oxford, 1977), and Richard Rorty, *Philosophy and the Mirror of Nature* (Princeton, 1979).

3. Perhaps the best example of this, with a list of metaphysical and epistemological "postulates" deemed to be necessary, is B. Russell, *Human Knowledge: Its Scope and Limits* (London, 1948). For a more recent version of the same project concentrating only on "epistemic principles" see the epistemological writings of R. Chisholm, e.g., *Theory of Knowledge* (Englewood Cliffs, N.J., 1977) or *The Foundations of Knowing* (Minneapolis, 1980).

4. See, e.g., I. Kant, *Critique of Pure Reason*, tr. N. Kemp Smith (New York, 1965), B 19-20.

5. P.F. Strawson, *Introduction to Logical Theory* (London, 1952), pp. 256-257.

6. I have made the point in more detail in my *Hume* (London, 1977), pp. 64-66.

7. See N. Goodman, "The New Riddle of Induction," in *Fact, Fiction, and Forecast* (Cambridge, Mass., 1955).

8. What the mechanism is, how its reliability is to be defined, and what other conditions are necessary vary from one "externalist" theory to another. See, e.g., F. Dretske, *Knowledge and the Flow of Information* (Cambridge, Mass., 1981), or A. Goldman, *Epistemology and Cognition* (Cambridge, Mass., 1986).

9. R. Descartes, "Third Set of Objections with the Author's Replies" and "Author's Replies to the Sixth Set of Objections," in *The Philosophical Writings of Descartes*, vol. I, pp. 137, 289, (Cambridge, 1985).

10. I would like to thank Janet Broughton, Thompson Clarke, Fred Dretske, Alvin Goldman, Samuel Guttenplan, and Christopher Peacocke for helpful comments on earlier versions of this paper.

3
The Skeptic's Appeal

Ernest Sosa

Skepticism, preeminent in the history of our subject, has since suffered decades of neglect, and only in recent years has reclaimed attention and even applause.

We shall take up some recent influential discussions as well as some older arguments, neglected of late. The paper will close with a positive proposal on how to deal (negatively) with the skeptic's appeal, along with some objections and replies.

1. SKEPTICAL ARGUMENTS, SKEPTICAL RESPONSES

Consider the following two principles:

PDC (The Principle of Deductive Closure):
If (one knows that p1) & ... & (one knows that pn); and one deduces that q from one's beliefs (that p1), ..., (that pn); and believes that q on that basis; then one knows that q — all of course at the same time t.

PMC (The Principle of Meta-Coherence):
For any arbitrary proposition, that-p, one is never justified in being quite sure that both it is the case that p and at the same time one has no knowledge at all of that fact.

These principles are placed up front so that their preanalytic intuitive plausibility may be assessed before their consequences or entanglements are highlighted below. We shall return to each of them later, in connection with the following two arguments, which will serve to focus our discussion of skepticism.

SA (The Simple Argument):
(S1) Assumption: One knows that f (that there is at the moment a fire before one)
(S2) Assumption: One deduces that one is not merely dreaming that f from one's belief that f, and on that basis believes that one is not merely dreaming that f
(S3) From S1 and S2: One knows that one is not merely dreaming that f
(S4) Conditionalization: If S1 then S3
(S5) Assumption: One does not know that one is not merely dreaming that f
(S6) From S4 and S5: One does not know that f

CA (The Complex Argument):
(C1) Assumption: One knows that if one knows that f, then one must not be dreaming that f
(C2) Assumption: If C1, then if one is to know that f, one must know that one is not dreaming that f
(C3) From C1, C2: If one is to know that f, one must know that one is not dreaming that f
(C4) Assumption: One does not know that one is not dreaming that f
(C5) From C3, C4: One does not know that f

(The "complexity" of CA derives from its reliance on premise C2, which requires supplementary, and complicating, defense.)

Two patterns of response to our arguments are discernible in the literature: the radical and the moderate. The radical response accepts S5 and is hence forced to deny PDC. The moderate response endorses only C4 and is hence at least initially enabled to sidestep the controversy over PDC.[1]

It is a problem for the complex argument, however, that it must rely on assumption C2, the assumption that if we know a certain circumstance to be incompatible with our knowing something, then if we are to know that thing we must knowingly preclude that circumstance. Thus if (a) one knows that if one knows that there is a fire before one, then one is not dreaming that, then (b) one knows there is a fire before one only if one knows one is not dreaming that; or, in symbols: $K[K(f) \rightarrow \text{not-}d] \rightarrow [K(f) \rightarrow K(\text{not-}d)]$ — i.e., (C1 $\rightarrow$ C3), i.e., C2. J.L. Austin attempts to discredit C2, but his arguments have been rejected plausibly as resting on confusion between what we are allowed to say in ordinary conversation and for practical purposes, on one hand, and on the other what is really true.

The fact remains that C2 is an assumption of argument CA which, though not implausible, yet seems less than axiomatic. There is however a related argument which dispenses with that assumption. Call it the *modified complex argument*:

MA (The Modified Complex Argument):
(M1) Assumption: One knows that if one knows that f, then one must not be dreaming that f
(M2) Assumption: One deduces that one is not dreaming that f from one's beliefs that one knows that f and that if one knows that f, then one must not be dreaming that f
(M3) From M1, M2: If one knows that one knows that f, then one knows that one is not dreaming that f
(M4) Assumption: One does not know that one is not dreaming that f
(M5) From M3, M4: One does not know that one knows that f

M4 and PDC, therefore, along with M1 and M2, may all be retained compatibly with K(f) but then *not* with KK(f). Accordingly, when one reflects on one's assurance that one knows that f and considers whether one knows that one knows that f, if one reasons properly one must deny that one has any such knowledge of one's knowledge that f. But in that case one is committed to being quite sure that it is a fact that one knows that f while yet at the same time one has no knowledge of that fact. And this clashes with PMC.

Both the radical and the moderate responses are hence sooner or later led to face PDC. The former rejects PDC outright, and may be seen to collide with PMC as well. For it grants that, if one is ever to explain *how* one knows that f (that there is a fire before one), one must affirm that not-d' (that one is not merely dreaming that f). Yet while affirming that not-d' one would of course retain one's conviction that not-K(not-d'). And this collides with PMC.

As for the moderate response, it again faces the dilemma of colliding either with PDC or with PMC. If with the moderate response one is to retain that one knows there is a fire before one, i.e., K(f), and does *not* know one is not dreaming that, i.e., not-K(not-d), along with PDC, then in any case where one deduces that one is not dreaming that not-d from K(f) and (K(f) -> not-d) — a case that is easy enough to produce — one is left no choice but to reject KK(f), since otherwise K(not-d) would follow by PDC. Thus in such a case one is stuck with [K(f) & not-KK(f)] — colliding with PMC.

So we seem after all to be left with the question that our responses have been hoping to avoid: namely, if one does know that not-d and one does know that not-d', how does one manage to know such things? *What is more:* even if one is persuaded that one does not know any such things, the explanation of why it is that one does not know them and the explanation of how one does know whatever it is that one does know may yet require that one believe with robust conviction that not-d and that not-d', which would leave us with the question of how one can become justified in believing any such things. Much of traditional epistemology would hence remain in place, and much of the skeptic's attack would remain unmet, for these may be cast in terms of justification, let knowledge fall where it 'may.'[2]

2. DOES JUSTIFICATION ENTAIL KNOWLEDGE?

It has been argued, however, that there is an intimate relation between knowledge and justification beyond the familiar requirement of justification for knowledge. The further relation goes indeed in the *opposite* direction and requires rather knowledge for justification. Traditional questions of justification for belief (and for actions and attitudes generally) hence cannot after all "let knowledge fall where it may." We pause to consider this argument.

There are three premises:

(1)   If someone S is (at all) reasonable in something X, then there is something which is S's reason for X or there are some things which are S's reasons for X.

(2)   If there is something which is S's reason for something X, then there is some propositional value of 'p' such that S's reason is that p and if there are some things which are S's reasons for X, then there are some propositional values of 'p' and 'q' and so on such that S's reasons are *that p* and *that q* and so on.

(3)   If S's reason (for something X) is *that p*, then S *knows* that p; and if S's reasons (for X) are *that p* and *that q* and so on, then S *knows* that p and S *knows* that q and so on.

The conclusion to be drawn from these three premises is:

(4)   If someone is (at all) *reasonable* in something X, then there is a propositional value of 'p' such that S *knows* that p or else there are some propositional values of 'p' and 'q' and so on such that S *knows* that p and S *knows* that q and so on.[3]

This is the Argument for the Dependence of Reasons on Knowledge (DRK). It follows from DRK that if someone S is at all reasonable in believing that such and such, then there must be something which is at least one of his reasons (and perhaps his only reason) for believing that such and such. But if there is something which is at least one of S's reasons, then there is a propositional value of 'p,'*that p*, which is at least one of S's reasons. And if *that p* is at least one of S's reasons, then S *knows* that p. Thus if someone S is at all reasonable in believing anything, then there must be a propositional value of 'p' such that S *knows* that p. Hence if no one really *knows* anything, then no one is at all reasonable in believing anything. Q.E.D.

Here is a short story.

> Abigail looks out the window and seems to see and hear rain and to learn that (to stay dry) she must carry an umbrella. Basil wakes up, has an intuition that it rains, and superstitiously believes that it rains (never having had such an intuitive feeling before and in the absence of any supporting evidence whatever). On her way out Abigail picks up her umbrella, to avoid getting drenched. On his way out Basil picks up his umbrella, to shoot some ducks with it.

Basil is as unreasonable as Abigail is reasonable; this despite the fact that the rain Abigail thought she saw and heard was just, unbeknownst to her, a mere hoax, and despite the fact that, unbeknownst to her, opening her umbrella would reveal only bare wires and tattered shreds. What then are Abigail's reasons for (reasonably) believing that to stay dry she must carry an umbrella and for (reasonably) carrying her umbrella? It would not be plainly true to say that one of Abigail's reasons for believing that she must carry the umbrella is that it rains. For it does *not* rain. Nor would it be flatly true to say that Abigail's reason for taking the umbrella is that it will protect her from the rain. For it will not do so.

As I see it, the best answers to DRK begin by stressing that reasonableness does (often) require reason*ing*. But reasoning can rest on false premises (as does Abigail's reasoning) and yet be good reasoning. It may thus be argued that good reasoning does not necessarily require actual reasons. One may reason well in the absence of actual reasons (as Abigail does: "It rains, and so on. So I must carry an umbrella") inasmuch as actual reasons cannot be false. (Abigail's reason for carrying the umbrella cannot be that it rains, for it does not rain.) Reasoning requires only adduced or intended reasons. If one reasons (well) one must adduce considerations that one (well) takes to be reasons (at least *in foro interno*). Thus if we replace 'S's reason' wherever it occurs in 1 (or 2) by 'consideration (correctly) adduced by S as a reason,' the resulting propositions are quite acceptable, and the undesirable consequences are no longer forthcoming. In summary, then, this answer simply rejects premise 1 as it stands in favor of a more acceptable substitute, one whose conjunction with premises 2 and 3 will no longer yield either the undesirable consequence or conclusion 4.

A second answer also begins by stressing that reasonableness often requires reason*ing* and that reasoning can rest on false premises, and it goes on to reject 2 as it stands. Since it does not rain, Abigail's reason for carrying the umbrella cannot be that it rains, but that does not mean she has no reason for carrying the umbrella. In fact among her reasons for carrying the umbrella is *what she takes to be the fact* that it rains. Thus if we replace 'that p' and 'that q' wherever they occur in 2 by 'what he takes to be the fact that p' and 'what he takes to be the fact that q,' the resulting proposition is quite acceptable. In summary, then, this answer simply rejects premise 2 as it stands in favor of a more acceptable substitute, one whose conjunction with premises 1 and 3 will no longer yield either the undesirable consequence or conclusion 4.

We have found two likely ways of rejecting DRK. Each rejects one of the essential premises in favor of a substitute that preserves what is plausible and acceptable in the rejected premise.

There are of course many other ways to argue for skepticism about justification, but here I should like to reconsider only one much debated years ago, but neglected of late, following which I shall conclude with a line of argument towards a more general refutation of skepticism.

3. SPILL-OVER ARGUMENTS

The conclusion that *no observation report can constitute conclusive knowledge* has often been drawn from the assumption that our observation reports always yield implications beyond those we can have verified, implications that can never be contained within our observation plus memory. Take this as the first of our Spill-Over Arguments, SOA1. Once known as the Verification Argument, it may be put more formally as follows:

Consider an arbitrary present-tense observation report O.

(A) There is a (possibly long) conjunction P of contingent predictions implied by O, such that if P fails to come true that will provide absolutely conclusive grounds against O.

(B) (i) There are no present absolutely conclusive grounds for P and, in virtue of this, (ii) there is no present absolutely conclusive evidence that there will not later be absolutely conclusive evidence against C.

(C) If there is no present absolutely conclusive evidence that there will not later be absolutely conclusive evidence against O, then no one now verifies absolutely (for certain) that O is true.

Conclusion: No one does now verify absolutely (for certain) that O is true.

Norman Malcolm objects to premise B(i) by challenging anyone to prove it, to find a true premise or conjunction of premises from which it may be seen to follow. His own search discloses several possibilities, from among which the following seems the likeliest 'candidate':

β   No contingent prediction P implied by O is necessarily entailed by any present grounds for P.

But we are told that though β is true it does *not* really entail B(i) after all.[5] Nevertheless, it might be argued as follows that in fact it does:

Let 'P' stand for a contingent prediction implied by an arbitrary present-tense observation report O.

(1)   If grounds in favor of a statement are absolutely conclusive, then they could not be strengthened.

    Assumption

(2)   If grounds in favor of a statement do not necessarily entail that statement, then they could always be strengthened (through judicious addition).

    Assumption

(3)   If grounds in favor of a statement do not necessarily entail that statement, then they are not absolutely conclusive.

    1, 2

(4)   No present grounds for P necessarily entail P.

    Assumption

(5)   There are no present absolutely conclusive grounds for P.

    3, 4

Thus 5 is necessarily entailed by the conjunction of 1, 2, and 4. But 5 is tantamount to B(i), and 4 is tantamount to β. If each of 1 and 2 is necessarily true, then β does after all entail B(i).

There appears no promising way to counter this argument except by questioning the truth or at least the necessity of premise 2. Concerning this premise, however, I can find no plausible example of a contingent singular statement which, first, is made certain (to the extent that it is certain) by grounds that do not entail it, and which, second, could not be made more certain by adding judiciously to those grounds. Thus leave aside such risky reports as those about natural kinds (with their attendant implications about hidden powers and properties), and let us test our hypothesis directly against the sort of case that appears hardest for it to handle, the case of simple observation reports. If an observer has no reason whatever, all things considered, for judging the conditions to be in any way abnormal, if in those conditions something looks red to him, and if the observer knows himself not to be color blind, then he has excellent grounds for thinking that the thing is red. However, his grounds could surely be strengthened, this in at least three ways: first, by reference to his own physiological and mental state (perceptual, intellectual, and emotional); second, by reference to the surrounding conditions prevailing at the time; and, finally, by adding concurrent testimony by witnesses known to be generally reliable on the matters under consideration. Thus *if* he consciously tests himself and finds himself to be mentally stable and alert; *if* he finds further reason to believe that his eyes have not been affected surgically or otherwise; *if* he thoroughly investigates for special lighting and finds none; *if* he determines that the thing is an apple; *if* he gathers supporting testimony; and *if* the thing continues to look red to him just as before; *then* surely that the thing is red is at least somewhat more certain (to him) than it was before. But even the new grounds *could* be strengthened. One systematic way of doing so is to find properties that we reasonably believe to be lawfully correlated with redness and to be present in the thing. There seems no *a priori* limit to the number of such properties.

Although the foregoing objections to SOA1 can apparently be answered in the ways described, there appears no way of meeting the following additional objection. The objection is aimed at premise A, which may be seen not to hold true (as claimed) for any randomly selected observation report O. The argument relies on a conclusion reached earlier, to the effect that grounds G provide absolutely conclusive grounds against O only if G conjointly entail not-O. Thus it follows from premise A that not-P must entail not-O. Hence, by contraposition, O must entail P. This means that if A is true for any arbitrary observation report O, then any arbitrary observation report O must entail some statement P about the future. But there are at least many observation reports that entail nothing about the future. For instance, the statement (O) that there is now something white before me is an observation report, a paradigm of the type of statement that the SOA is about. But statement O entails nothing about the future (except something trivially or formally about the future, such as that a day from now it will have been true that a day earlier there had been something white before me, but this is irrelevant to the SOA).

We may finally consider a further Spill-Over Argument: SOA2. This version argues for the conclusion that no observation statement S about one's immediate surroundings can be certain *at all* (rather than just absolutely certain). The argument is that any such statement S must be based on grounds, and for S to be certain the grounds upon which it is based must be conclusive. Now grounds are *conclusive* when they enable us to *conclude* inquiry, and to reach a *conclusion*. We can never conclude inquiry on an observation statement O; however, we can never close the case (or our minds), since in every such instance there are always relevant questions still outstanding. Thus if the observation statement is that I see something red on the facing surface when I seem to see an apple in what seem to be normal conditions of perception, there always remain such questions as: Would my hand go right through it if I next tried to pick it up? Would I feel and hear the characteristic crunch if I next tried to bite it? Would I taste the characteristic acid sweetness? And in every such case there is always the more general question: Will I next find myself going through the experiences characteristic of (my) waking up? Surely we would be in a better position to answer such questions *after* the relevant tests had been made. Should we not therefore postpone judgment on the question whether I do see something red on the facing surface? If indeed we should postpone judgment, then of course present evidence is *not conclusive*, and hence it is *not now certain* that I do see something red on the facing surface. Despite the fact that questions about the *future* are raised when we ask whether we can be certain about our *present* surroundings, however, and despite the fact that we will no doubt be in a better position to answer the questions about the future *in* the future — nevertheless, it is at least uncertain that we should therefore postpone judgment about the present. For (i) although we will be in a better position to answer the questions about the future *in* the future, and (ii) although answers to these questions about the future are very much relevant to questions about the present, and (iii) although we will therefore *in that respect* be in a better position in the future to determine whether I now do see something red (or am merely the victim of an illusion, a hallucination, or a dream), it does *not* follow that (iv) we will *all things considered* be in a better position in the future. For although we may gain something by waiting we will also certainly lose something, namely, the present sensory experience relevant to the question whether I *now* see something red. Later we will have to rely on memory where now we rely on sensory experience. It seems clear, therefore, that we may well be in a position where no *overall* epistemic gain is to be derived by postponing judgment. Hence the idea that there is always such a gain to be derived with respect to any contingent statement about our physical surroundings cannot serve as a general argument for the inconclusiveness of present grounds for present-tense observation reports and thus for the general uncertainty of such reports.

Our discussion also suggests a way of returning to Malcolm's claim that β above, though true, does not entail B(i). We considered an argument against that claim on the basis of two assumptions, one of them the assumption that the following is a necessary truth: that if grounds in favor of a statement are absolutely conclusive, then they could not be strengthened (meaning in effect that they neither could be nor could have been strengthened). But is this assumption so much as true — much less necessarily true? We now have reasons for doubt, which tends to restore Malcolm's challenge to our SOA1: our argument in terms of A, B, and C above, leading to the conclusion that no one now does make absolutely certain that O is true. What is more, our most recent reflections also raise serious doubt about assumption C in our formulation of the argument: namely, the assumption that if there is no present absolutely conclusive evidence that there will not later be absolutely conclusive evidence against O, then no one now verifies absolutely (for certain) that O is true. For example, might we not now be in the best possible sort of situation for judging whether O is the case, without necessarily being in the best possible situation for judging whether or not there will later be evidence against O that will later (from the perspective of that later time and one's situation at that time) prove conclusive against O?

What then may we conclude about Spill-Over Arguments? Two objections against the first of them, SOA1, were both shown to be ill-taken. However, since its first premise requires that every observation report entail a contingent prediction, and since many observation reports entail no contingent prediction, that argument is anyhow unsound. A further variety of SOA was then suggested — the SOA2 — with the stronger conclusion that no observation report can be certain *at all* (rather that just *absolutely* certain). This boils down approximately to the idea that since there are always relevant questions outstanding on observation reports, we can never close the case, i.e., present evidence is never conclusive. In reply to this it was urged that although indeed there is a good sense in which there are always relevant questions left outstanding on observation reports, there is also important present evidence to be lost by waiting, and that — at least sometimes — we may well be in a position for judging that can only be weakened by time, with no compensating improvement to be gained; a position, moreover, where we do have excellent present grounds for belief. In such circumstances our grounds may reasonably be regarded as conclusive — as good enough to permit concluding inquiry — and the belief may be regarded as among the *most* certain available to us about the external world, and in that sense as certain. Finally, these latest reflections were shown to reinstate Malcolm's challenge to an assumption of our SOA1, and to weaken a further assumption on which that argument depends.

4. NATURALISM

There is a response to the skeptic more radical than any we have considered thus far, a response so radical that it might with justice be viewed as not only antiskeptical but more aptly antiphilosophical. Indeed, in a way it is a deliberate *non*-response. By its lights skeptical arguments are best *neglected*. This so-called "naturalism"⁶ appeals to a distinction between two sorts of beliefs: first, those which are based on a particular reason or experience; second, those which have rather the character of "scaffolding, framework, background, substratum, etc." The second set of beliefs are not the products of any reasoning, no matter how implicit or subconscious; they are rather the banks along which the river of reason may flow. And the argument concerning this second group of beliefs amounts to the following:

1. The general beliefs that there are bodies, that there are other minds, that there has been a determinate past — none of these is one that we choose or decide to have for a reason, none is based on inference or argument or reasoning. Further, we cannot help accepting them and retaining them.
2. Therefore, skeptical arguments against such beliefs are *idle*.
3. Therefore, such skeptical arguments are *negligible*, and indeed they are "to be neglected."

Against such "beliefs" (commitments, claims, presuppositions, convictions, prejudices, or "elements") skeptical arguments aim to show that they are no knowledge nor even justified. Now the "idleness" of skeptical arguments presumably amounts to their inability, singly or in combination, to budge any such beliefs. And from this it is supposed to follow that skeptical arguments are best ignored.

Several questions need to be faced about this argument. First of all, it seems artificial to focus exclusively on general, philosophical beliefs as those unyielding to the skeptic. Given the right circumstances, plenty of ordinary beliefs will hold just as firm against all comers, or at least against all *argumentative* comers; and, lest we libel some skeptics, are there not circumstances in which the general, "philosophical" beliefs do totter or fall?

Secondly, it is not quite clear what the idleness of skeptical arguments amounts to. Is it that the skeptic will never persuade one that one's belief in body, or in others, or in the past is no knowledge, or is not even justified; or is it rather that the skeptic's arguments will not in any case move anyone to give up any such belief as our belief in body, etc.? In either case more is needed in support of the proposed premise before us. For instance, what is involved in this general belief in the existence of body which is supposed prevalent among us? Is it a belief in the existence of things spatiotemporal and independent of thought? And if so is it really so clear that it cannot be given up? What do we say of Berkeley and his idealist colleagues? As for the existence of other minds, what to say of the "disappearance theorists" in our midst? But let us put these doubts aside.

Let us suppose that in some sense there are general "beliefs" — in body, in others, and in the past, etc. — which the skeptic cannot make us doubt: not in the sense of leading us to suspend them; nor yet in the sense of leading us to deny them the title of knowledge, or even that of justified or warranted belief. Still the master argument of the epistemic naturalist is less than obviously sound. Even if the skeptic, less consequential than Sysiphus, is unable to budge our framework convictions; even if skeptical arguments fail to dislodge our belief that we are justified in such convictions: What follows even so? Is the skeptic therefore worthy of nothing better than neglect?

In fact the skeptic might here trip the naturalist with his own momentum. What if a skeptical argument once well understood cannot be budged by framework convictions? Would it follow that framework convictions are "idle" and "negligible"?

Is it not possible, after all, that even though there are reasons against skepticism, at least reasons with *prima facie* force, even so we cannot give it up, simply because it seems so certain and well founded? What is most surprising is that we might at the same time find it *also* impossible to give up our many everyday beliefs, framework beliefs included, even despite the obvious conflict between these many beliefs and our philosophical belief in skepticism.

We need therefore some way to avoid both the pendulum of skepticism and the pit of naturalism. The search goes on for a better response to the skeptic. The remainder of this paper argues that the skeptic is unable to live coherently.

5. THE SKEPTIC'S VITAL INCOHERENCE

Let's begin with the most radical of skepticisms, *total skepticism*. What is required for one to be a total skeptic? It is not enough simply to accept neither the affirmative nor the negative with regard to every question, simply always in that sense to "suspend judgment." For a blow on the head and total amnesia do not necessarily make one a skeptic. Nor is one made a skeptic by pushing a button that removes all belief, nor by carrying out an arbitrary decision to suspend all belief. Apparently one must suspend judgment in a certain way, on a certain basis, with certain causal roots. What form, basis, or roots are required? More specifically: What form, basis, or roots can one have for universal suspension of judgment on every question, in order for this to turn one not only into a total skeptic, but also one with some possibility, however remote, of being reasonable in one's skepticism? Since such total suspension of judgment is not intrinsically and obviously reasonable *per se* or in itself, in order to be reasonable it must hence be based on ulterior reasons or at least on some ulterior reason. But in order to base an attitude on some ulterior reason in such a way that what is thus based may thereby be reasonable, one needs to believe reasonably whatever it is that constitutes one's ulterior reason. Since, deprived as he is of all belief, the total skeptic cannot have any such reasonable belief, he is cut off from any hope of being reasonable in his attitude of universal suspension of judgment.

Even though the total skeptic hence lacks any reasonable basis for his skepticism, it is replied, he may still retain a certain justification for his attitude, one that derives from the justification he has for adopting it at the moment of adoption, even if he does lose that particular basis with the adoption of total skepticism. He is rather like the justified suicide, and in effect the total skeptic commits intellectual suicide.

Let us hence look more closely at the exact situation of the prospective total skeptic at the precise moment of his decision. In order to reasonably decide and carry out his intellectual suicide, the skeptic at that moment has need of some rational basis. For suspending judgment with respect to every question, something that presents itself to the skeptic at that moment for his consideration, is not a reasonable attitude *per se*, obviously and in itself. In order to adopt it reasonably one needs some consideration in its favor. But in order to become thus justified one cannot draw such a consideration by arbitrary magic out of some hat; one needs instead some consideration accepted with justification considered reasonable. At a minimum one needs to accept that consideration with justification that *is* reasonable, whether one considers it so or not. Accordingly, for one's total suspension of judgment to be reasonable, one needs what seems quite out of reach; which explains why one now contemplates such total suspension. It cannot be the mere repeated frustration of one's search for reasonable belief that justifies the total suspension. One must at least *remember* some or many cases of such frustration, or one must be aware in some other way of such repeated frustration, or one must at the very least believe reasonably that one has been thus repeatedly frustrated. Once again it seems clear one needs reasonable belief for reasonable total suspension of judgment. In a certain sense, therefore, total skepticism is self-refuting. For it is the lost hope for reasonable belief that prompts total skepticism. But the reasonable adoption of total skepticism logically requires reasonable belief after all (even if we conceive of total skepticism *not* as itself an attitude of belief but only as a sort of withholding). So we set aside total skepticism as intolerably incoherent.

Super-radical skepticism is more moderate and requires accepting only what is really apparent, what is present to the mind *per se*, with no need of extrinsic support. But super-radical skepticism (that one must accept only the apparent *per se*) does not satisfy its own requirement, and hence declares itself unacceptable and is again incoherent with itself.

That brings us at last to the most influential skepticism in modern philosophy, the *radical* skepticism based on a rationalist conception of the nature and conditions of true knowledge. We are told that true knowledge must be accepted either because it presents itself as intrinsically obvious *per se*, with no need of any supporting reasoning whatever, or else because it is established by logical deduction grounded in the intrinsically obvious *per se*. What of this more moderate skepticism?

We are often told that radical skepticism is irrefutable. But whoever believes that is already a skeptic, at least in principle, and of course to start with that assumption rules out any such refutation. But here I assume, controversially, that a refutation can be question-begging when the question demands begging: thus anyone who denies the principle of noncontradiction is refuted by the affirmation of what he denies. In any case, let us now take a fresh look on our own.

In considering radical skepticism it is important to bear in mind a principle we might name Pyrrhonic:

> P   If a belief is neither more nor less reasonable than the *opposite* belief (its negation), then what is most reasonable on the matter is to suspend judgment and to adopt neither the original belief nor the opposite.

To throw some light on this principle there is no better example than one already used by the skeptics of antiquity: the belief that the total number of stars is even. For us that belief is neither more nor less reasonable than the opposite belief that the total number is odd. According to the Pyrrhonic principle, what is most reasonable on that matter is to suspend judgment. For many ancient skeptics the very same form of reasoning applies far more broadly. Their skepticism is very radical.

Another principle, also important here, is that of "vital coherence":

> VC   If one believes that all things considered acting a certain way or being a certain way is not reasonable (is irrational, incorrect, wrong, bad, *et cetera*) but one yet wittingly acts in that way or is that way, one falls thereby into incoherence in one's life, into vital incoherence.

For example, if one believes that being impulsive is unwise, yet knowingly remains so, one falls into vital incoherence. That is a case in which the incoherence involves a psychological state — being impulsive — but there can also be such incoherence with regard to a physical state: say, bearing so many pounds of excess weight. If I believe that being overweight is unhealthy and yet remain obese, I fall thereby into vital incoherence. Finally, it is also possible to fall into such incoherence with respect to a particular action of one's own at a given moment: say, eating some peanuts before one.

Any human being who accepts radical skepticism must fall into vital incoherence. For one must retain a multitude of beliefs all of which are by one's own skepticism unreasonable (incorrect, bad, or irrational). Of that I feel confident at least in my own case. What response is now open to the skeptic? We can imagine at least six objections by the skeptic:

First Objection: "It is a *petitio* against the skeptic to suppose that he (and people in general) retain their normal beliefs even after adopting skepticism. How can we possibly know any such thing?"

Reply: But no pronouncement about other minds is needed if one sticks to the first person. Proceeding thus, I at least must declare myself confident that I could not abandon the bulk of my ordinary beliefs. And here I mean the vital ones held crucial for a minimum of success in an ordinary day. Hence by adopting radical skepticism I would fall into vital incoherence. And that seems all I need for a reason, a *prima facie* reason against radical skepticism. If I wish to avoid the charge of *petitio* by the skeptic, I cannot suppose that the same is true of you, or so I am willing to grant for the sake of argument, but I can yet invite anyone who understands me to consider their situation as I have done mine, to see if they do not get the very same result. (Moreover, if I have already adopted skepticism, or if I find it very plausible, then I find myself in a certain incoherence, from which I must try to escape.)

Second Objection: "Once in ignorance so deep, no cognitive attitude can really improve on any other. One is reduced to groping in near total darkness. What reason can there possibly be in such circumstances to proceed one way in preference to any other? In default of such reason one cannot be blamed for sticking to common sense: total inaction would be neither more nor less reasonable than an ordinary life."

Reply: The skeptic is right to argue that his doctrine reduces all forms of ordinary action to the same level: there is no more reason for jumping than for not doing so when a truck looms, . . . nor is there any less. Even so, it is incautious of the skeptic to object as he does, for he forgets precisely the principle that so well served his predecessors of antiquity: the Pyrrhonic principle, according to which it is *impossible* that all intellectual options with respect to a certain question or hypothesis really be on a par. Whenever it is all the same to affirm as to deny, it is always best to suspend judgment. And the skeptic's objection does not touch this point, no matter how plausible he may be on forms of action that are not forms of believing or suspending judgment. Even setting all of that aside, moreover, there remains the vital incoherence that would attend my own skepticism: for I surely would retain not only certain forms of physical action but also certain beliefs and intellectual procedures.

Third Objection: "Ought implies can; and a multitude of our ordinary beliefs brook no alternative. If we see a large truck loom as we cross the road, that *forces* not only our appropriate motion but also our corresponding beliefs."

Reply: But let us be honest: *Would* we suspend judgment? *Would* we do so if only we could? For if we persist in the attitude that we would *not* do so even if we could, that leaves a remainder of culpable incoherence (which must yet be explained). Besides, there is much that we could do but do not even consider. For example, we could stop reading many books and periodicals. If a radical skeptic is convinced that: (i) almost the totality of the beliefs acquired by reading are irrational and unjustified; (ii) non-literary reading has no gain to balance off its irrational results; and (iii) he could easily abandon non-literary reading; then that skeptic incurs culpable incoherence if he does not so much as try to give up such reading. For he persists knowingly and deliberately in what he considers both incorrect and under his control.

Fourth Objection: "Despite all the theoretical reasoning in favor of skepticism, there are important *practical* reasons for retaining the great bulk of our beliefs, which is why we are reasonable to retain them."

Reply: But to be reasonable in retaining a belief requires either that we grasp the intrinsic value of that belief, which in general cannot be grasped since it does not exist, or else that we grasp some pertinent connection (generally causal) between the belief and some good(s) accessible at least in part by means of the belief. However, both of these ways are regularly closed to the radical skeptic.

Fifth Objection: "The clash between skepticism and ordinary beliefs gives a *prima facie* reason against skepticism but it also gives a *prima facie* reason against ordinary beliefs. In that case why should the reasoned philosophical principle yield to the vulgar beliefs socially or biologically derived?"

Reply: In the first place we have once again the impossibility of abandoning our many beliefs with biological roots: for example, our shifting perceptual beliefs as we negotiate an ordinary day. In the second place, there is the numeric difference. The philosophical belief is one, and the ordinary beliefs are a great host. Besides, since there is no known set of eligible alternatives for our ordinary beliefs, if we can formulate a plausible enough way to avoid philosophical skepticism, we may need look no further to escape our dilemma. How then might we conceive of the nature and conditions of knowledge so as to avoid the radical skepticism prompted by the rationalist conception of knowledge?

Sixth Objection: "By parity of reasoning the argument from vital incoherence could be used to support the silliest wishful thinking, which reduces to absurdity any such form of argument. Thus a weak-willed smoker could argue from vital incoherence for rejecting the belief that smoking is 'unhealthy.'"[7]

Reply: But the hypothesis that smoking is unhealthy presumably does not just lie unattached in the smoker's corpus. Much else would have to go with it, much else of enough value that retaining it may well outweigh the disvalue of the vital incoherence in the smoker's life. (This would vary from case to case and would depend on how much evidence one has and how sophisticated is one's epistemology and scientific methodology.) Of course the sophisticated skeptic is not wholly unlike the sophisticated smoker. The skeptic too has reasons for skepticism. The vital incoherence that is one's inevitable lot as a human skeptic gives only a *prima facie* reason *against* retaining one's skepticism. Is it outweighed by the price of giving it up? That would depend on how much is tied together with what has to go. Fortunately, skepticism has usually enjoyed little by way of close support except for a couple of intuitions said to be obvious or axiomatic, and a short bit of deductive reasoning. Therefore, if we are able to cast doubt on the supposed axiom that only deductive proof can yield knowledge; and if we can develop an alternative, more liberal account of knowledge, one with its own degree of intrinsic plausibility and acceptable coherence with whatever else we regard as plausibly true; to that extent will we have enhanced the combination of costs and benefits attaching to some route of escape from the vital incoherence of skepticism.

NOTES

1. Further discussion of these views along with references may be found in my "Beyond Skepticism, to the Best of Our Knowledge,"*Mind* 97 (1988), part A.

2. For further support see *ibid*.

3. Cf. Peter Unger's "Two Types of Skepticism," *Philosophical Studies* 25 (1974) 79-96; 79-80; also the introduction and chapter five of his book *Ignorance* (Oxford: Oxford University Press, 1975).

4. Norman Malcolm, "The Verification Argument," in *Empirical Knowledge*, ed. R.M. Chisholm and R.J. Swartz (Englewood Cliffs, N.J.: Prentice-Hall, Inc., 1973), 155-202.

5. *Ibid.*, p. 182.

6. Again, for references and further discussion, see "Beyond Skepticism, to the Best of Our Knowledge."

7. I owe this objection to Arthur Walker.

4
Précis and Update of
Epistemology and Cognition

Alvin I. Goldman

1. NATURALISTIC EPISTEMOLOGY AND EPISTEMICS

Since W. V. Quine's paper "Epistemology Naturalized" (1969) was published, the idea of linking epistemology with psychology has had some currency. But Quine's proposal is very radical. It requires "dislodging" epistemology from its old status, of "surrendering" the epistemological burden to psychology (cf., Quine, 1969, pp. 87, 75). Quine appears to preach what Hilary Kornblith (1985) calls a "replacement thesis": traditional epistemology is to be abandoned and replaced by psychology. One element that would be abandoned — though not an element Quine himself stresses — is the evaluative strain in epistemology. Traditionally, epistemology has been a normative or critical enterprise; but it cannot remain so if it is an enterprise wholly within natural science, since natural science itself is strictly positive.

My own attempt to give a naturalistic twist to epistemology began with "A Causal Theory of Knowing" (Goldman, 1967), which also paid no attention to evaluative issues. But in *Epistemology and Cognition* (1986) I urge a squarely evaluative conception of epistemology, consonant with the dominant tradition. At the same time I advocate a close linkage between epistemology and empirical psychology, or cognitive science in general. But how can these themes be joined? If epistemology is primarily evaluative, how can there be a role for the empirical sciences? What contributions can they make to a normative discipline?

The first part of *Epistemology and Cognition* (henceforth, E & C) lays theoretical foundations for a conception of epistemology that is simultaneously evaluative and yet emphatic in the need for inputs from the sciences of the mind. The second part illustrates the proposed linkage by surveying a selected range of work from cognitive science, work that bears on certain normative-epistemic questions. It thereby puts flesh on the multi-disciplinary conception of the field that I like to call "epistemics" (cf., Goldman, *primary individual* epistemics. Epistemics as a whole would have a larger scope, encompassing secondary as well as primary individual epistemology, and social epistemology in addition.

2. EPISTEMIC EVALUATION

There are a variety of terms of intellectual evaluation, many of interest to epistemology. The ones most commonly used in the discipline are 'justified' and 'rational.' Another central term of intellectual appraisal, which oddly has received only scant attention in the field, is 'intelligent.' Epistemology should be concerned, on my view, with (at least) this range of intellectual assessments. It should try to elucidate the standards associated with these terms and try to indicate whether and how those standards can be met.

In speaking of 'standards,' I mean *factual* or *substantive* standards. The working assumption is that the evaluative status of an action, trait, institution or any other object of evaluation supervenes on some sort of factual properties or relations. The evaluation merited by an athletic performance, for example, hinges on such physical variables as distance jumped, or elapsed time to reach the finishing line, or on a comparison of such scores with those of other performers. Similarly, if a belief is to qualify as justified, it must have some factual property or properties for which it merits this appraisal. An initial task is to specify the pertinent properties.

Much of my attention is devoted to 'justified.' This can plausibly be viewed as a deontic term of appraisal. Roughly, to say that a belief is justified is to say that it is *permitted* by a right system of rules of epistemic justification. Of course, this just introduces another normative notion — 'right system of rules' — and does not provide factual standards. But if we can specify the criteria of rightness for these rules in non-normative terms, and ultimately specify the content of the rules themselves, then we would have spelled out in factual terms how beliefs can "earn" the status of being justified. The framework of rules is attractive not only for formulating my own eventual account of justifiedness, but also for examining various alternative approaches.

The notion of an epistemic rule is ambiguous. It might be understood as a rule that cognizers can apply in guiding their doxastic conduct. Alternatively, it might be understood as a tool of theoretical appraisal, appropriate for judging a belief's justificational status, whether or not it can serve a "regulative" function. That there are two such distinct uses, or roles, for moral principles is argued by Holly M. Smith (1988). She refers to these as the "first person practical" use and the "theoretical" use, respectively. In E & C, justificational rules are understood as tools of theoretical appraisal only, not as regulative principles. This contrasts with the conception of epistemic norms of, for example, John Pollock (1986).

3. THE FRAMEWORK PRINCIPLE

The theory of justification proposed in E & C articulates a three-tiered structure. At the first level is a *framework principle*, intended to be largely (though not completely) neutral among competing epistemological theories. The main content of the framework principle was already expressed in the preceding paragraph: a justified belief is one that is permitted by a right system of J-rules (justificational rules). But a further proviso is also incorporated, viz., that the belief's permissiveness *not* be "undermined" by the state of the believer. Varieties of undermining of S's belief in q would include S's believing that he is not permitted to believe q (although he is so permitted), and S's being permitted (or obligated) to believe that he is not permitted to believe q.

Although this framework principle is neutral insofar as it leaves unspecified what makes for rightness of rules, there are some epistemological theories that introduce what amounts to a stronger framework principle. They impose a "second level" condition, requiring not merely that the belief be permitted by right rules, but that the believer be justified in believing that his belief is so permitted. Roughly this sort of requirement is implied by Laurence Bonjour's principle of "doxastic ascent" (Bonjour, 1985). But this principle is too strong as a requirement for our *analysandum*, viz., a belief's *being* justified. It seems more appropriate for an iterated *analysandum*, namely, "S is justified in believing that his belief B is justified." To propose the stronger principle in an account of first-level justifiedness therefore seems to constitute a case of what William Alston (1980) has called a "level-confusion" in epistemology. My own non-undermining proviso imposes a weaker, merely negative, condition and is not open to the same objection.

4. RIGHTNESS OF J-RULES

Granted that a justified belief is one permitted (without undermining) by a right system of J-rules, the next natural question is: What makes a system of J-rules right? This leads to the second level of theory: the criterion of J-rule rightness. A criterion of rightness is sought that is couched in factual or substantive terms.

Many kinds of criteria for J-rule rightness are possible. Some criteria might be social in nature, for example, a criterion that makes rightness a function of the methods accepted by one's community or culture. I argue against any such social criterion. Mere acceptance by a community is not sufficient for rightness, for a system to be *really* right as opposed to being thought to be right. (At this juncture E & C contains a discussion of relativism versus absolutism and objectivism versus subjectivism in epistemology; but I skirt these topics here.) Alternative criteria might be purely formal, appealing to truths of logic or probability theory. For example, right rules might be those entailed by truths of logic.

At this point some rough indication must be given of the nature of J-rules. As a preliminary characterization, J-rules are construed as *cognitive-state transition* rules. Such rules approve of certain types of transitions from prior to subsequent cognitive states, for example, moving from perceptual appearances or prior beliefs to immediately succeeding beliefs or subjective probabilities. Thus, a belief is justified if and only if it results (without undermining) from a sequence of steps, each step of which is permitted by a right rule system. As this formulation makes clear, the conception of justification is a *historical* conception. The justificational status of a belief is a function of its ancestry.

5. LOGIC AND J-RULES

Given this tentative characterization of J-rules, the strategy is explored of trying to derive right J-rules from logic. An obvious problem with this strategy is that J-rules concern beliefs or other doxastic states, but the truths of formal logic are, as such, simply silent about doxastic phenomena. Formal logic concerns semantic and syntactic properties of formulae or formal systems, but says nothing whatever about belief states. Moreover, J-rules are rules of permission (or perhaps of obligation); they are normative in nature. But logic is not normative in this way. There is no obvious way of deducing the permissibility of making this or that cognitive state transition from semantic or syntactic properties of sentences or sets of sentences.

Nonetheless, it might seem as if correct rules of cognitive state transition ought to be based, in some sense, on logic. For example, if proposition P logically implies Q, and you believe P, isn't it permissible to add to your belief corpus a belief in Q? Won't such an addition always make the belief in Q justified, at least if the belief in P was justified? No, for two reasons. First, there is Gilbert Harman's (1973) point that sometimes it may be more appropriate to delete P than to add Q. When you notice that P implies Q — where Q is, let's say, "I don't have a head" — perhaps you should recognize that you have been wrong all along to believe P. Instead of adding a belief in Q, you should hasten to abandon P. Second, a belief in Q is not justified simply because Q is logically implied by P, belief in which was antecedently justified. A belief's justificational status depends on exactly how one arrives at it (or sustains it). If you just chance to believe Q, or believe it as a result of some illicit process (e.g., wishful thinking), then that belief is not justified simply because there happens to be a justified belief in your head with a content that entails Q. Justificational status depends on *causal* provenance. More specifically, I argue, it is the specific mental processes, or operations, which get deployed in belief formation (or sustenance), that are critical to justificational status.

One conclusion is that the cognitive-state transition format is not quite adequate for a satisfactory criterion of rightness. No criterion of rightness is satisfactory unless it places constraints on the cognitive *processes* by which beliefs are produced. Thus, instead of licensing state "transitions," which are neutral concerning causal production, an acceptance criterion must license (or mandate) belief-forming processes (more precisely, process types). Since pure logic does not specify mental processes at all, this is another reason why logic alone cannot generate adequate justificational rules.

6. J-RULES AND COGNITIVE PROCESSES

The foregoing arguments set the stage for my "connection thesis," i.e., the thesis that there should be an intimate connection between epistemology and cognitive science. The stage is set because it is cognitive processes that are to be the permitted objects of right J-rule systems. Which cognitive processes are available, and which are to be approved, are matters that can only be settled with the help of cognitive science. Only cognitive science can tell us which processes belong to the human repertoire; and cognitive science is needed to help ascertain which processes in this repertoire possess the epistemically relevant properties.

Of course, we have not needed help from psychology or cognitive science to support any of the theses presented thus far (including the connection thesis itself). Thus, psychology does not enter the picture at either the first or the second level of justification theory. That is, it does not play a role in finding a framework principle or in identifying a suitable criterion of rightness. But given the proposed constraint on a rightness criterion, psychology is needed to determine what specific J-rule systems will satisfy an adequate criterion. So psychology will be needed at the third level of justification-theory, the level that tries to specify one or more right rule systems. However, this runs ahead of the story; for I have not yet presented a full criterion of rightness, merely one constraint on an acceptable criterion. What is the complete criterion?

7. EVIDENTIALISM

In seeking such a criterion, we will find it useful to examine analogies in the sphere of ethical theory. Ethics distinguishes consequentialist and deontological types of theories, and epistemology can utilize this distinction. An example of a deontological theory in epistemology is what I call "evidence proportionalism," or what others (e.g., Feldman and Conee, 1985) call "evidentialism." Evidentialism says that a J-rule system is right just in case it makes degrees of belief proportional to the weight of one's evidence. This is analogous to the deontological theory of punishment, which says that punishment should be proportioned to the seriousness of a crime, no matter what the consequences. One reason I find this sort of theory unacceptable has already been given: the absence of any causal-process requirement. Applying this point to the present case, consider a detective with a degree-of-belief .80 in the hypothesis (= H) that the butler committed the crime. As it happens, this degree of belief is correctly proportioned to the detective's evidence, since a correct confirmation theory — assuming the existence of such a creature — implies that his total evidence confirms H to degree .80. Our foolish detective, however, has no real understanding of why the evidence gives such support to H. Nobody has explained this relationship to him, and he is so dim-witted that he could not follow the tortuous argument in any case. He has arrived at his degree-of-belief by "eyeballing" the butler and the other suspects and "feeling" that .80 is an appropriate degree of conviction. Surely this degree of belief isn't justified, contrary to the precept of evidentialism.

Another dissatisfaction with evidentialism is that it is forced to adopt a fundamentally bifurcated account of justification. A distinction must be drawn between evidence beliefs and other beliefs. Proportioning credence to the weight of evidence is the alleged mark of justification for "other" beliefs; but what about the evidence beliefs themselves? Presumably, calling them "evidence" beliefs entails that they are justified. But what substantive properties confer this epistemic status on them? A totally different account will have to be offered. (Merely being highly confirmed by *some* propositions won't do the job because every proposition highly confirms itself.) Such a bifurcated theory is inevitably unsatisfactory, however. Why, one would like to know, are the two components of the theory both relevant to justificational status? What do they have in common? Other things equal, a single, unified account should be sought. That is what I ultimately offer.

Turning from deontological to consequentialist types of theories, it may be suggested that what makes a psychological process (type) justificationally suitable is that its deployment tends to produce good consequences.

More precisely, what makes a system of rules right is that conformity with that system has, or would have, good consequences. What sorts of consequences, though, are good in the relevant respect, good as far as justification goes?

8. VERIFIC CONSEQUENTIALISM

I canvass and reject proposals involving (A) coherence consequences, (B) explanatory consequences, and (C) pragmatic or biological consequences. Instead I endorse an approach that highlights *verific* consequences, i.e., having beliefs with certain truth properties. Even verific consequentialism, however, admits of several varieties. One variant would say that a rule system is right just in case conformity with it would maximize the number of true beliefs. Another variant would say that a rule system is right just in case conformity with it would realize a high *truth ratio*. In other words, a rule system is right if its instantiation would generate a class of beliefs with a high proportion of truths. This is the variant of the verific consequences approach to which I subscribe. The upshot, then, is a kind of process reliabilism, a theory close to one I advanced earlier in Goldman (1979).

There are still ambiguities in the theory as presented thus far. In particular, what does it say about the justificational status of beliefs in imaginary cases? Such cases may involve possible worlds in which rule systems would have different truth ratios than they do in the actual world. How is justification fixed in those possible worlds? One approach is to say that a belief in world W is justified if it is formed in conformity with a rule system that is right in W; and that a system is right in W just in case it has a high truth ratio in W. This approach allows rightness to vary from world to world. Another possibility is to "rigidify" rightness, requiring that a given rule system R is either right in all worlds or not right in all worlds. E & C adopts the latter approach. It does not propose, however, that R's rightness is fixed by its truth ratio in the actual world; rather, it is fixed by its truth ratio in "doxastically normal" worlds, i.e., by worlds that have the general characteristics we *believe* the actual world to have.

One upshot of this approach is to accommodate intuitions about demon victim cases, which would otherwise pose a *prima facie* problem for reliabilism. In a demon victim case, most people feel that the victim's perceptual beliefs are justified despite the fact that, by hypothesis, his perceptual belief-forming processes are unreliable in that world. This would be a difficulty if the rightness of a rule system were fixed by its truth ratio in the world of the example. However, the difficulty is avoided if rightness is fixed by doxastically normal worlds. Presumably, a rule system permitting (among other things) ordinary perceptual belief-forming processes would be reliable in worlds having the general characteristics we believe the actual world to have (though not in demon worlds). So the demon victim's beliefs are formed in accordance with a right rule system, and hence is justified.

9. STRONG AND WEAK JUSTIFICATION

There are objections, however, to the normal worlds approach. (For example, it is not wholly clear how doxastically normal worlds are to be fixed.) With these objections in mind, plus additional considerations, a new version of a reliabilist theory of justification has been formulated. This appears in "Strong and Weak Justification" (Goldman, 1988). The leading idea here is that there are really two distinct conceptions of justified belief: (1) a belief formed by *adequate* or *proper* belief-forming procedures, and (2) a *blameless* or *non-culpable* belief. A cognizer in an intellectually benighted community may use belief-forming procedures that are objectively unsound and improper. On the first conception of justifiedness, his beliefs are unjustified. However, since he has no access to ways of telling, or reasons for suspecting, that his procedures are unsound and improper, we may regard his beliefs as blameless and non-culpable: we wouldn't expect him to be doing better epistemically. Hence, these beliefs are justified according to the second conception of justifiedness. Call the first conception that of "strong" justification, and the second that of "weak" justification. Applying this distinction to the demon victim case, we may say that the victim's perceptual beliefs are not strongly justified, since they are formed by unsound and inadequate procedures (for his world). But they are weakly justified: since he has no way of telling that his perceptual procedures are unsound and inadequate, he is epistemically blameless in using them.

Can the intuitive contrast between strong and weak justification be captured within a broadly reliabilist framework? I propose that it can. Proper, adequate, or sound procedures are reliable procedures — more precisely, procedures that are reliable in the world of the example, or the (modal) neighborhood of that world. Thus, a belief is strongly justified if it is formed (without undermining) by reliable procedures (or in conformity with a reliable rule system). A belief is weakly justified if the procedures by which it is formed are unreliable, but (A) the cognizer does not believe that they are unreliable, (B) he neither possesses nor has available to him a reliable way of telling that they are unreliable, and (C) there is no procedure he believes to be reliable which, if used, would lead him to believe that the procedures are unreliable. (For further details, see Goldman, 1988.)

10. KNOWLEDGE

The reliability theory of justification (especially "strong" justification) is intimately connected with the theory of knowledge offered in E & C. Very briefly, to count as an item of knowledge, a (strongly) justified belief must also (i) be true, and (ii) be such that it would not be false in any relevant counterfactual situation. For example, consider a visually formed belief that a certain object in the field is a barn. To count as knowledge, this belief must be true, and there must be no relevant alternative situation — e.g., there being a papier-mache facsimile of a barn — in which the same belief would be formed but in which it would be false (cf. Goldman, 1976). The latter sort of condition is the chief component in the theories of knowledge of Dretske (1981) and Nozick (1981). But those theories omit the *generic* reliability condition that I impose, an omission which renders them (I argue) too weak. This emerges, for example, in examples of beliefs in necessities, which are allowed to qualify too easily as instances of knowledge.

11. PROCESSES VERSUS METHODS

An important distinction drawn in E & C is the distinction between *processes* and *methods* of belief formation. Processes are basic psychological operations, either innate parts of our cognitive architecture or merely the results of maturation as opposed to learning. Methods, on the other hand, are acquired principles or techniques for guiding assent, acquired either by explicit tutelage, self-invention, or induction and habit formation. Methods can either be highly domain specific — e.g., rules of how to solve a narrow class of problems in a particular branch of mathematics — or relatively domain independent — e.g., the logical technique of reductio. When we use methods in belief formation, they are explicitly represented in the head (though not necessarily consciously). Processes, by contrast, are not explicitly represented. They are the operations with which we think, not the rules, recipes, or precepts to which we may appeal in thinking.

The account of justification in E & C (and in "Strong and Weak Justification") delineates two levels of justification: the level of processes and the level of methods. A fully justified belief is justified at both levels. The process/method distinction, however, is perhaps less important for its place in the theory of justification than for its place in the general conception of epistemics. The division of "individual" epistemics into two branches, primary and secondary, relies on the process/method distinction. Primary epistemics would consist in the epistemic evaluation of basic cognitive processes, roughly speaking, of human cognitive architecture. Secondary epistemics would consist in the evaluation of methods. While primary epistemics would be closely allied with the sciences of human mentation, secondary epistemics would have no such essential affiliation.

12. INTELLIGENCE AND PROBLEM-SOLVING

This discussion has focused heavily on justification. But 'justified' is not the only significant term of epistemic evaluation, as noted earlier. Another such term is 'intelligent.' Although E & C offers no full-blown account of intelligence, it suggests that a central strand in the notion of intelligence is that of problem-solving ability. (This is a commonplace, of course, in artificial intelligence.) By problem-solving capacity, I mean a skill at getting (and believing) *true* answers to questions one wants to answer. There are at least two types of epistemic evaluation linked to problem-solving capacity: *power* and *speed*. Power is the ability to solve a large proportion of problems one wants to solve (answer questions one wants to answer). Speed is the ability to solve problems quickly. Thus, the notion of true belief again plays an important conceptual role in specifying standards, or criteria, of epistemic evaluation. These standards are not equivalent to reliability. Reliability consists of a low error rate, which could be achieved (partly) through doxastic caution. Mere cautiousness, however, does not yield problem-solving power, nor problem-solving speed. Indeed, it is compatible with getting very few answers to the questions one wants to answer, or getting them very slowly. So problem-solving power and speed are distinct epistemic desiderata. Primary epistemics should be interested in assessing our cognitive operations not only for reliability, but for power and speed as well.

13. TRUTH AND CONTENT

The epistemological theses of E & C continually appeal to the notions of truth and belief, both controversial notions in philosophy. The last two chapters of Part One take up these notions, in order to forestall certain objections that might be lodged against the structure of the philosophical program. First, some writers have contended that truth itself is at bottom an epistemic notion, to be explicated in terms of rational credibility (perhaps in some idealized situation). If this were correct, it would defeat our claim of providing factual, non-epistemic standards for such epistemic notions as justification, intelligence, and so on. Chapter 7 therefore defends a realist conception of truth, according to which it is not reducible to epistemic notions. Chapter 8 addresses the topic of belief and belief content, responding very briefly to various attempts to undermine these notions, or challenge the role that the book assigns to empirical investigation of the truth-properties of belief-forming processes. For example, if high truth ratio can be guaranteed for people's beliefs *a priori*, simply in virtue of a charity principle of content assignment, that would seem to undermine the relevance of empirical assessments of reliability. Such a thesis is therefore examined and rejected.

14. EMPIRICAL EPISTEMIC PERFORMANCE

Having provided a theoretical rationale for incorporating cognitive science into the enterprise of epistemology, Part Two of E & C attempts to illustrate the manner in which the enterprise should proceed. In other words, it offers some selected specimens of primary epistemics. The idea is, first, to draw on research in cognition to identify fundamental belief-forming and problem-solving processes of the human mind-brain. Second, these processes, or concatenations of processes, are evaluated in terms of reliability, power, speed, and so on. Some readers have imagined that this second half of the book is intended as a *survey* of cognitive science. That, I should emphasize, was never its intention. Part Two merely consists of selected examples, which struck me as usefully illustrative of how primary epistemics should proceed and what sorts of judgments it might issue.

In the remainder of this discussion, I shall give four examples of the indicated procedures. The first three examples are drawn from E & C, although substantial supplementary material is included as well. The fourth is an entirely new example.

15. DEDUCTIVE REASONING

What basic resources do people have for deciding the validity or invalidity of arguments? How do they go about trying to execute such tasks? What does this reveal about their "logicality" or "illogicality," about the reliability or power of their logical endowments?

In one study of propositional reasoning, Lance Rips (1983) constructed a model that imputes to the reasoner only sound inference procedures, each procedure being associated with a familiar sort of natural deduction rule. The assumption of the model is that human reasoners, confronted with the task of assessing the validity of a given argument, try to construct a mental proof of the conclusion from the premises. The model does not assume that, at each stage of a proof attempt, a relevant inference procedure is accessed by the reasoner. Nor does the model feature all sound propositional inference procedures. (In particular, it omits *modus tollens*, which is not consistently recognized as valid by naive subjects.) As a result, subjects do not always succeed in constructing proofs for valid arguments. Having failed to construct a proof, they are forced to guess about the argument's validity, and their guesses are often wrong. Nonetheless, if Rips' model is correct — and it does very well in matching the performance of actual subjects — then all the cases in which proofs were constructed are cases where the subjects used entirely reliable processes in forming their beliefs of validity.

This makes it look as if people's reasoning powers — at least a certain subset of these powers — are very good. And I think this may well be a tenable conclusion. *Certain* deductive reasoning processes, or concatenations of such processes, may indeed have high reliability. This is compatible with the fact that subjects have substantial error rates in their judgments of validity and invalidity. In Rips' study, the valid arguments were wrongly judged invalid 49% of the time, and the invalid arguments were wrongly judged valid 23% of the time. The point is that most if not all of these mistakes may have arisen when subjects were forced to guess (not having managed to construct a proof). Guessing is obviously a different way of forming a belief about validity than the process-sequence that consists of constructing a proof and then inferring that the argument is valid. The latter process-sequence is completely reliable, while the former (failing to construct a proof and guessing) is of course quite unreliable. From the proportion of errors, one can infer that *no* processes used by subjects are very reliable. But one cannot infer that *not all* process (or concatenation of processes) used by the subjects is reliable.

A second point worth emphasizing (and one not clearly made in E & C) concerns the fact that subjects were presented with a "forced choice." They had to judge each argument as either valid or invalid, even if this meant making a guess. Now if a person answers "invalid" merely as a guess, this answer does not record a genuine belief. Hence, we cannot infer from false *answers* that the subjects had false *beliefs*. This means that the reported error rate is not necessarily a belief-error rate. Indeed, we cannot draw any confident conclusion about the truth ratio of the subjects' beliefs. No pessimistic conclusion is warranted about unreliable *belief*-forming processes merely from the error rate in the answers.

The same point is worth making in connection with Wason's well-known "selection task." Subjects were given a group of four cards with markings on both sides. The top faces of the cards showed E, K, 4, and 7. The subjects were asked to identify exactly those cards that have to be turned over to verify whether they conform to the rule: "If a card has a vowel on one side, then it has an even number on the other side." The correct answer is: E and 7. But only 4% of the subjects in the original experiment gave this answer! Ostensibly, this shows very poor logical powers.

But, again, we should caution against excessively hasty conclusions, at least as far as reliability is concerned. It may be that most of the subjects in the experiment are quite uncertain about the answer, and wind up guessing. They may not actually *believe* the incorrect answer that they give. To be sure, they must not believe the correct answer either, since they would presumably give it if they did. So the experiment certainly shows that not many of them have the *power* to solve the problem correctly. But it does not conclusively show erroneous belief.

A second reason for caution in drawing pessimistic conclusions from this case is this. While most subjects certainly gave the wrong answer to the target question, many of them had the right answers to some of the subquestions "contained" in the target question. Subjects had to decide for each card whether it was *one* of the cards that needed to be turned over. Most of the subjects correctly selected E as one such card and correctly selected K as a card that did not have to be turned over. The incorrect choices mostly concerned the 7 and the 4. Viewed in this fashion, we can say that even the subjects who gave the wrong answer to the target question did not display total logical ineptitude.

Sorting out the exact respects of (belief) unreliability is important. Some theorists have been tempted to draw extremely pessimistic conclusions about people's logical powers from experiments like the selection task. But only if we bear in mind that some questions are being answered correctly, and that some incorrect answers may not be genuinely believed, will we have a balanced assessment of logical abilities and disabilities. Certain kinds of logical relationships seem to be easily and accurately grasped by people, but others seem unnatural or hard to recognize. While this certainly shows that people are not natively perfect logicians — who would have thought otherwise? — it does not so obviously warrant conclusions of a global sort about human irrationality. So, at least, I contend.

16. BELIEF PERSEVERANCE

Studies by Lee Ross and colleagues (e.g., Ross, Lepper, and Hubbard, 1975) reveal that subjects, under certain conditions, persist in believing things even after their original grounds for belief have been undercut. Subjects are given deliberately misleading evidence about their own or someone else's skills at a certain task, e.g., discriminating authentic from inauthentic suicide notes. Later they are told of the deception; in effect, they are advised that their old evidence was worthless. Nonetheless, they commonly (though by no means invariably) persist in believing propositions that were derived from that evidence, seemingly in violation of canons of rationality.

Although E & C does not formulate any theory of rationality, its theory of justification makes it clear how a perseverant belief could be deemed unjustified. Making beliefs responsive to one's total evidence is likely to be reliability enhancing. If one ignores changes in total evidence — which can occur through evidence discrediting — this will lower reliability. Since this is what (some of) the subjects seem to be doing — viz., ignoring changes in their evidence — they must not be conforming with a right system of J-rules.

But the matter is more complicated than this. Nisbett and Ross (1980) explain the perseverance phenomenon partly by reference to mental search activities which provide additional supporting evidence beyond the original, discredited evidence. For example, suppose Jane receives feedback in the experiment that she is uncannily successful at the suicide note discrimination task. She then generates additional "evidence" that seems consistent with her apparent social sensitivity, e.g., her good performance in an abnormal psychology course, her ability to make new friends easily, and so on. Once such explanations are generated and found convincing, they remain to support her high assessment of her ability even after the original evidence is discredited.

Now is such gathering of additional "evidence" epistemically permissible, more specifically, justificationally permissible? This is a complex matter, but let us assume that it is. Then even when the original evidence is discredited, the retention of the target belief may be permissible according to a right system of process-permitting rules, because there may be enough *other* evidence to license retention of the target belief. However, shouldn't the cognizer be expected to remember that the supplementary evidence was itself inferentially linked to the original (now discredited) evidence? If she fails to do so, isn't the persisting belief unjustified?

Here matters get quite tricky. Can *failure* to recall something render other beliefs unjustified? Should it be built into a right J-rule system that a belief in p is permitted only if one first retrieves *everything* from long-term memory that is relevant to it, and then correctly assesses its impact? If such a strong requirement is built into a right J-rule system, it is doubtful that anyone will have any justified beliefs. Moreover, it is unclear that this is required to ensure that a J-rule system has a high enough truth ratio. Perhaps it should be required, more conservatively, that the cognizer *search* long-term memory (LTM) for anything relevant. This requirement can be satisfied even if LTM fails to deliver the goods, so to speak. Even the requirement of search, however, may be unreasonably strong. Should it be required that for every belief p that you believed a moment earlier, you should not continue to believe it unless you search LTM for any changes in your old evidence that might undercut p? Or should it be required that for every newly rejected belief q, you should search LTM for connections with other beliefs that might have originated through q? It isn't clear that these requirements are strictly required for high reliability, though the second has some plausibility. But conformity with these requirements might so occupy the mind as to interfere with other operations that enhance reliability. And such activity might also impede the mind's *power* to answer new questions on its agenda. Thus, when we take seriously the sorts of mental operations required for memory retrieval, and once we take cognitive limits into account, it becomes a very delicate matter to delineate the exact contours of a right J-rule system.

17. ACCEPTANCE AND CONNECTIONIST NETWORKS

While the main epistemological application of cognitive science discussed in E & C is evaluative in purpose, there are also descriptive issues that would benefit from empirical research. The notion of belief, in particular, needs to be addressed. When considering the fine-structure of the mind, the concept of belief is bound to seem less than fully satisfactory, possibly in need of major refinement. The question of belief *content* is one area of controversy, but that question is set aside here. Focusing exclusively on the question of what sorts of *states* beliefs are supposed to be, we find that there is need for a richer and more supple taxonomy than our ordinary language provides. E & C proposes that we must distinguish active from stored beliefs, acknowledge both modality-specific and modality-neutral beliefs, and find some psychologically satisfactory rendering of both the binary notion of belief, i.e., acceptance, and the graded notion of belief, i.e., degrees of confidence. I argue that the Bayesian approach to subjective probability is dubious from a psychological standpoint. Among other things, it provides no natural niche for binary belief, which seems to have great intuitive appeal.

One possible realization of the acceptance notion within a cognitivist framework, I propose, can be found in connectionist winner-take-all (WTA) networks (Feldman and Ballard, 1982). Simplifying somewhat, let such networks consist of *units*, crudely analogous to neurons, which for present purposes are understood as representing propositions (or, rather, mental attitudes toward propositions). This "localist" representational assumption may not be essential, but it is useful for expository purposes. Units are connected to each other by excitatory and inhibitory links. The potential of a unit U is updated by considering the potentials of the units to which it is linked. If it has an excitatory link to some U' which has positive output, this will tend to increase the potential of U; if the link is inhibitory, then U' will tend to depress the potential of U. The output of a unit is some function of its own potential and inputs. In epistemological terms, we can think of the inhibitory links as representing incompatibility relations between propositions, and the excitatory links as representing evidential ones. Networks can be run with cycles of updating the potentials of all units until they settle into a stable state in which all units have acquired resting potentials.

The critical property of a WTA network is that only the unit with the highest potential (among a set of contenders) will have output above zero after some settling time. This is what might correspond, at the micro-level, to the macro-phenomenon of acceptance. A proposition is accepted only when all its rivals are rejected, while uncertainty consists in the absence of a clear-cut winner.

The epistemological fruitfulness of connectionist ideas similar to those found in WTA networks is amplified and enhanced by Paul Thagard's computer program ECHO. (Cf. Thagard, 1988a; my summary is drawn from Thagard, 1988b.) ECHO is particularly directed at modeling belief systems in terms of explanatory coherence. ECHO's units represent propositions, its excitatory links represent relations of explanatory coherence, and its inhibitory links represent relations of contradictoriness (properly qualified). The main respect in which ECHO differs from the WTA networks is that there is no explicit requirement that only one of a set of competitors finish with activation greater than 0. There is a pressure for this to happen, and it does happen if one unit gets a lot more activation than its competitors. But in closer cases two competing propositions can both end up with positive activation (potential). This is intended to model scientific reasoning, where, if two contradictory hypotheses have roughly equal amounts of evidence, some plausibility may be attributed to both. In ECHO, two units that both have lots of excitation can settle with activation greater than zero, although they inhibit each other.

An evaluative question about these connectionist networks is whether they are capable of producing beliefs with a high truth ratio. This will depend on whether there are sources of belief strength, i.e., potential or activation, which stem from "the facts." Now, in ECHO, units representing pieces of evidence are distinguished from units representing hypotheses. The former are linked to a special evidence unit whose activation is always kept at 1, so there is a steady flow of activation. Thus evidence is given a certain priority over hypotheses, even though units representing evidence can be de-activated if the evidence coheres only with bad hypotheses. If we assume that evidence-based activation is highly correlated with truth, then the prospect for a high truth ratio among all belief elements in the network may well be favorable.

In E & C it is conjectured that coalitions of units may be important, and this is related to the epistemologist's notion of coherence. Thagard's network develops this theme in detail. In ECHO's simulations of scientific cases, complexes of hypotheses get evaluated together because they cooperate in explanations, forming coalitions against competing complexes even though the contradictory (i.e., inhibitory) relations between units directly relate only pairs of propositions. If two hypotheses explain a piece of evidence, then the units representing the hypotheses are linked to each other as well as to the unit representing the evidence, so the hypothesis units will tend to rise and fall together. Two units that are each linked to a third unit will similarly affect each other indirectly. Thus, a global notion of the coherence of a set of propositions emerges from pairwise relations of coherence derived from shared participation in explanations.

18. MOTIVATED INFERENCE

In this final section, I shall introduce a topic that certainly belongs on the agenda of primary epistemics, although it was not treated in E & C, and relatively little psychology of the requisite sort has been done to date. A standard example in the literature of an unreliable process is "wishful thinking." But what exactly is this process? How exactly do desires or wishes affect thought? It is unlikely that there is a *unique* manner in which desires influence belief, and some of the ways in which desires influence belief need not be unreliable. For example, a desire can influence belief simply by posing a question to be answered, which guides the choice of problem-solving activities that ultimately produce a belief. There is no reason to suppose that this kind of influence of desire on belief increases error. Primary epistemics therefore must be more specific: Which kinds of desire-infected processes are biased against truth?

One proposal on this score, made by Paul Thagard and Ziva Kunda (in press), concerns motivated memory search. (Actually they make a couple of proposals, but I shall confine my attention to one.) Suppose that Sandra wants to believe that she is extroverted, for this will enhance her self-conception. Thagard and Kunda analyze the possible upshot of this desire using the PI system developed in Holland, Holyoak, Nisbett, and Thagard (1986), in which goals and subgoals can direct the search of memory for specific categories of fact. For example, given this desire, the system may set as a goal the activation of information about Sandra's being sociable, which in turn leads the system to ask if Sandra goes to lots of parties. Retrieving positive information to this effect will then make possible the inference that Sandra is sociable and thus is extroverted. If the desired conclusion is reached, the search stops, so the system does not go on to find conflicting information that might imply that the self is introverted. Similarly, a person can be motivated to believe that all A's are B's, in which case she will want to retrieve as many A's that are B's as possible. Motivated retrieval here consists of giving the "problem-solving" unit the goal of finding things that are A's and B's and storing this information with the concepts A and B, for use as evidence in favor of the generalization.

Although Thagard and Kunda don't put it this way, what seems crucial is that the system searches memory for information that will support a particular proposition p, not information that will support either p or its denial. In other words, it does not look indifferently for any information relevant to p's truth-value, whatever that may be, but only for information that supports p's truth. This is what is elsewhere called a "confirmation bias." Thus, on my current reconstruction, one way in which desires can influence beliefs is by creation of a confirmation bias, which obviously has the potential to operate against reliable belief formation. This contrasts with the case in which search is guided by a desire for an answer — any answer — to a targeted question. Where directed search is not prejudiced toward a particular answer, reliability is presumably not threatened.

Many other domains of cognitive research are sampled for epistemic applications in chapters of E & C that I have not reviewed here — such domains as perception, imagery, constraints on representation, probability judgment, and procedural learning. All these explorations are initial steps in a projected collaboration between psychology and philosophy that would comprise primary epistemics.

REFERENCES

Alston, William (1980). "Level-Confusions in Epistemology," in Peter French, Theodore Uehling, Jr., and Howard Wettstein, eds., *Midwest Studies in Philosophy*, V, Minneapolis: University of Minnesota Press.

Bonjour, Laurence (1985). *The Structure of Empirical Knowledge,* Cambridge, Mass.: Harvard University Press.

Dretske, Fred (1981). *Knowledge and the Flow of Information,* Cambridge, Mass.: MIT Press.

Feldman, Fred and Earl Conee (1985). "Evidentialism," *Philosophical Studies*, 48: 15-34.

Feldman, Jerome, and Dana Ballard (1982). "Connectionist Models and Their Properties," *Cognitive Science*, 6: 205-254.

Goldman, Alvin I. (1967). "A Causal Theory of Knowing," *The Journal of Philosophy*, 64: 355-372.

_____ (1976). "Discrimination and Perceptual Knowledge," *The Journal of Philosophy*, 73: 771-791.

_____ (1978). "Epistemics: The Regulative Theory of Cognition," *The Journal of Philosophy,* 75: 509-523.

_____ (1979). "What Is Justified Belief? " in George Pappas, ed., *Justification and Knowledge,* Dordrecht: D. Reidel.

_____ (1986). *Epistemology and Cognition*, Cambridge, Mass.: Harvard University Press.

_____ (1988). "Strong and Weak Justification," in James Tomberlin, ed., *Philosophical Perspectives*, II, Atascadero, Calif.: Ridgeview Publishing Co.

Harman, Gilbert (1973). *Thought*, Princeton: Princeton University Press.

Holland, J., K. Holyoak, R. Nisbett, and P. Thagard (1986). *Induction*, Cambridge, Mass.: MIT Press.

Kornblith, Hilary (1985). "Introduction" to *Naturalizing Epistemology*, Cambridge, Mass.: MIT Press.

Nisbett, Richard, and Lee Ross (1980). *Human Inference*, Englewood Cliffs, N. J.: Prentice-Hall.

Nozick, Robert (1981). *Philosophical Explanations*, Cambridge, Mass.: Harvard University Press.

Pollock, John (1986). *Contemporary Theories of Knowledge,* Totowa, N. J.: Rowman & Littlefield.

Quine, W. V. (1969). "Epistemology Naturalized," in *Ontological Relativity and Other Essays*, New York: Columbia University Press.

Rips, Lance (1983). "Cognitive Processes in Reasoning," *Psychological Review,* 90: 38-71.

Ross, L., M. R. Lepper, and M. Hubbard (1975). "Perseverance in Self Perception and Social Perception: Biased Attributional Processes in the Debriefing Paradigm," *Journal of Personality and Social Psychology,* 32: 880-892.

Smith, Holly M. (1988). "Making Moral Decisions, *Nous,* 22: 89-108.

Thagard, Paul (1988a)."Explanatory Coherence," Princeton University Cognitive Science Laboratory Technical Report, Princeton, N. J.

————— (1988b). "Connectionism and Epistemology: Goldman on Winner-Take-All Networks," *Philosophia.*

Thagard, Paul and Ziva Kunda (in press). "Hot Cognition: Mechanisms for Motivated Inference," in Earl Hunt, ed., *Proceedings of the Ninth Annual Conference of the Cognitive Science Society,* Hillsdale, N. J.: Erlbaum.

5
The Need to Know

Fred Dretske

Getting things right is not just a useful skill. It is a biological imperative. Behavior has to be coordinated with the external conditions on which its success depends. An animal doesn't want to be running *all* the time; only *when* there is something chasing it. Courtship and mating activities are nice, but only *with* a partner. No point in biting, chewing and swallowing unless there is something *in* the mouth. The only way to bring about this kind of coordination is to have the causal processes culminating in motor output triggered by accurate and timely representations of the conditions *with which* output must be synchronized. If behavior b has offspring-producing, danger-avoiding, or need-fulfilling outcomes *when* c obtains, but is otherwise ineffective, perhaps even a wasteful expenditure of energy, one needs, as an internal cause of b, something that indicates, and in this sense represents, the existence of c. Animals lacking these representational skills, those who don't get things right often *enough*, are eliminated. Their behavior (or failure to behave) occurs at the wrong time, in the wrong place, and with the wrong results. They are soon replaced by more discriminating competitors.

According to a certain crude picture of knowledge, then, it seems to follow that animals *have* to know, if not everything, then a lot of things, in order to survive. Those that don't know get eaten. Hence, those that don't get eaten know. The superior representational skills of the survivors, whatever heritable capacities enable them to behave in appropriate and timely ways, become more prevalent in succeeding generations. That is why *we*, the descendants of successful competitors, are blessed with the capacity to know, if not everything, then a lot of things.

Three things — well *at least* three things — prevent one from executing this slam dunk against skepticism.[1]

1. There is, first, the questionable identification of belief with internal representation. Even if we need reliable representational mechanisms in

order to survive and flourish, why suppose that *belief* is, or is a product of, a mechanism of this kind?

2. Secondly, even on a crude picture of knowledge, the above argument shows, not that animals have to *know* anything, but that they must, more often enough, be *right* about the things on which the success of their behavior depends. There is, presumably, a competive advantage (and, hence, contribution to overall fitness) in having true and accurate internal representations. But what additional advantage is conferred by having these true and accurate representations generated by *reliable* mechanisms? Do reliable mechanisms somehow make the behavior produced by true representations *more* successful? If not, where is the selectional pressure for reliability and, hence, knowledge?

3. Even if we set this question aside by assuming that there is selection for reliable belief-generating mechanisms (*and* that knowledge *is* some form of reliably produced true belief), why should one suppose that selection has actually *reached* the degree of reliability required for knowledge? Selection can favor something without ever accumulating much of it. So why suppose that at *this* (or indeed *any*) stage of the evolutionary process, our beliefs are reliable *enough* to add up to knowledge?

I think each of these questions has a satisfactory answer. The answers, taken together, serve to articulate, and thereby help to define, a Reliability Theory of Knowledge. Since I have long advocated such a theory,[2] I take this occasion to exhibit a few of its more attractive assets. Aside from its resources for countering skepticism, I am particularly interested in the way this theory of knowledge helps one gain a better understanding of why we *need* knowledge, of what knowledge, insofar as it is understood to be something more than true belief, is *good for*. Any theory of knowledge that leaves it a mystery why we need or want knowledge, why we prefer it to mere true belief, is a theory that leaves *knowledge* a mystery.

BELIEF AND REPRESENTATION

Animals need internal indicators of the conditions, generally *external* conditions, *in which* their behavior occurs and *on which* its success depends. But so do plants. There must be something *in* the plant, something that not only stimulates growth, the formation of flowers and buds, the germination of seeds, and the removal of leaves, but also *signals, indicates*, and thereby *represents* the kind of external conditions — having mainly to do with temperature and the availability of water — with which such activities must be coordinated for optimum effect. The plant must have some way of "recognizing" spring, some way of distinguishing it from merely temporary periods of warm weather, so that it can begin the process of growth, flowering, and germination. The ability to exploit environmental cues for this purpose is of the greatest survival importance to the plant.

So plants, too, need accurate and reliable representational mechanisms. They, too, depend on internal representations for their welfare and the success of their reproductive efforts. Unless these representations are, by and large, correct, neither the individual nor the species will survive. Or, if the species manages to survive, it will be because its members got smarter, because there developed, quickly enough, *better* ways of coordinating behavior with the availability of those resources on which growth and reproduction depend.

Plants and very simple animals — bacteria, protozoa, sea slugs, for example — may not exhibit much in the way of behavior, but as long as their survival and reproduction depend to some degree on what they do, they need some way of internally registering the conditions on which the success of this behavior depends. And, other things being equal, the better, the more accurate, these internal representations, the greater will be the competitive advantage they confer on their possessor.

The same might be said for the *parts* of organisms. Many animals depend on the operation of automatic regulatory systems to maintain uniform body temperature, blood pH, and concentrations of sugar in the body. A system can't maintain q at the proper level unless it has some way of *telling* what the value of q is, and telling *is*, or at least requires, successful representation.

So, if our opening argument against skepticism shows what I think it shows, it shows the *same* thing for bugs, plants, and bodily organs. Everything that does anything, where the success of what is done depends on the conditions *in which* it is done, needs a way of representing the conditions in which things are being done. And the more accurate the representation, the greater are the chances of success. The greater the chances of success, the greater will be the selectional pressures for the mechanisms, *reliable* mechanisms, on which continued success depends.

It is true, of course, that knowledge is not just *any* form of representation. If we follow the traditional path on this matter, knowledge requires belief, and belief is a very special kind of internal representation. Plants, bugs, and bodily organs presumably do not possess *this* way of representing external affairs. Plants may register the arrival of spring and behave accordingly, but they do not, at least not in the relevant sense, *know* that spring has arrived. Plants don't have *beliefs*.

This is true, but irrelevant. As long as belief is *a form* of internal representation, however exclusive this form of representation may be, the evolutionary pressure for reliability in the mechanisms for producing and fixing belief will remain the same. Our opening argument was a very general argument, an argument applying to internal representations of whatever kind. As long as belief is of this kind, the argument applies.

Still, some may be uncomfortable with the treatment of belief as a kind of internal representation. If nothing else, it gives belief some rather strange bedfellows. Perhaps, it will be thought, belief is *not* a mode of representation at all. Or, if it is, perhaps because the notion of representation is being used *very* broadly, belief has special qualities that put it outside the scope of our opening argument.

While I am prepared to admit the legitimacy of such worries, I propose (invoking the standard space-time excuse) to bypass them by assuming, without argument, that belief *is* a form, albeit a very special and interesting form, of internal representation. I will assume, therefore, without (further) argument that if there are selectional pressures, not only for true representations, but for reliability in their production, then these pressures apply equally well to beliefs and the mechanisms for generating belief. Other things being equal, true beliefs, like accurate representations in general, contribute more to an animal's overall fitness than do false beliefs. If, then, it can be shown that in addition to *accurate* (i.e., *true*) representations, natural selection also favors *reliable* mechanisms for their production, then natural selection will favor increased reliability in the mechanisms for producing true beliefs.

SELECTION, TRUTH, AND RELIABILITY

What confers an advantage in the struggle for survival is not *knowing* more than your competitors but being *right* more often than they. It may be hard to see how, in the long run, one could maintain an edge on being right without knowing more, but the fact remains that one needn't know to be right — even in the long run. My fortune is made if I am right about oil stocks doubling in the next week. I needn't *know* they will double. And what goes for me goes for the rabbit in his quest to avoid the coyote. What gets the rabbit through the day is his running, hiding, or executing other evasive maneuvers *when* a hungry coyote is nearby. To do this the rabbit needn't *know* the coyote is nearby. Lucky rabbits, those who happen to be right, those who merely run *when* a coyote is nearby, will survive as well. Assuming they *stay* lucky, they, the ignorant rabbits, will have their genes as well represented in the succeeding generation as those of their keen-sighted and quick-witted neighbors.

So even on a spartan view of knowledge, one that equates knowledge with reliably produced true belief, it isn't knowledge itself that is important, but what is implied by the possession of knowledge, the fact that one has got things *right*, that fact that one has got the *truth*, the fact that one has *correctly* represented conditions in one's surroundings. *That*, and not some fact about *why* you enjoy that advantage, is what gives you the competitive edge. Since this is so, it would seem that, from an evolutionary point of view, the property of interest is *truth*, not reliability. It is getting things right, not knowledge, that is selected *for*.[3]

Most of the beliefs, not to mention other representational products, important to survival and reproduction are what we can (for obvious reasons) call *indexical* beliefs, beliefs about what is happening *here* and *now*. The rabbit has to know that *those* are coyotes! They are coming *this* way! Right *now*! Perhaps, in order to use this indexical information to its best advantage, the rabbit also has to know *that* coyotes are to be avoided, that they are dangerous, a generalized piece of knowledge that is not itself indexical.[4] Be that as it may, the indexical representations, constantly being up-dated by new information, about prey, predators, obstacles, and opportunities, are absolutely essential. Without them, general knowledge is quite useless. What good is it for an animal to know that coyotes are dangerous, or to be genetically programmed to run from coyotes, if it can't tell whether *that* is a coyote or a centipede?

These facts, I hope, are obvious enough. An indexical representation is really just another name for a *perceptual* representation, and it is *perception*, the capacity to see, hear, smell, or otherwise tell what is going on *here* and *now* (in a way that classifies what is going on here and now under appropriate categories) that is of primary importance to an animal's success in negotiating its way through an environment. But these facts, obvious though they are, change the way we must evaluate the objection to our opening argument.

It is, to be sure, the truth (at some behavior-relevant level of specificity) of a representation, and not the fact (if it is a fact) that it was produced by a reliable mechanism, that is important to the survival and well-being of its possessor. Nonetheless, the fact that many of the representations on which an organism's well-being and survival depend are what I am calling indexical representations, representations about *current* conditions, shows that, at least for these representations, the *only* way to select truth is by selecting for reliability. Indexical representations, whether true or false, are not, as such, heritable. Whatever is passed along in the genes, it is *not* the belief that *that* is a coyote and he is coming *this* way. Rabbits may be able to pass along to their descendants a healthy fear of coyotes, an instinct to avoid coyotes, a tendency to run from coyotes, a disposition to hide from coyotes, but they can't pass their knowledge that *now* is the time to run or hide because *that* is a coyote.

Though one can imagine true beliefs being generated by unreliable processes, one cannot imagine either the beliefs themselves or the mechanisms that generate them being selected *for*. For the beliefs, being indexical, aren't heritable and the mechanisms, though heritable, do not, because unreliable, increase fitness. What is both heritable and contributes to overall fitness (by generating accurate indexical representations) is the sensory and cognitive *hardware* used to generate true representations: an acute sense of smell, sharp eyesight, good memory, and the intelligence to use information in ways that promote personal welfare. This being so, selection *of* true indexical representations, the ones that confer benefits, must necessarily be done via selection *for* reliable mechanisms for their production.

If we could select, directly as it were, for truth, we wouldn't have to worry about knowledge or reliable mechanisms. But the only way to select for rabbits who will run or hide *when* a coyote is approaching, rabbits who will have (often enough anyway) *true* coyote representations, is by selecting for rabbits who possess heritable mechanisms for reliably representing, when the occasion arises, coyotes and their whereabouts. The only way to select rabbits with true beliefs is to select for rabbits who, when the time for believing comes, will *know*.

It is a bit like being asked to equip someone with true beliefs about newspaper headlines for the next ten years. There is nothing you can do if the petitioner wants the beliefs *now*. There are no crystal balls, no way of telling what will be newsworthy years in the future. But if it turns out that the request comes from someone who wants the beliefs only *when* the headlines appear, you can be of some help. Assuming he can read, what this person probably needs is something to help him *see* the headlines — perhaps a good pair of reading glasses. That gift, when properly deployed, will generate the desired beliefs when the time is right. But this gift isn't a gift of true belief — at least not *just* a gift of true belief. It is the gift of knowledge. And necessarily so. There is no way to give the person what is wanted, true beliefs about future events, without giving *more* than what is wanted. Truth, at least the kind of truth now in question, is like that. It is something you can't buy. The only thing for sale is a *means*, a reliable process, for producing true belief, a means which, when deployed, thereby produces, not merely true belief, but *knowledge*.

WHAT GOOD IS KNOWLEDGE?

Stock answers to a question about why knowledge is good and ignorance is bad, why it is, say, worth *paying* for an education, is that knowledge is knowledge of the truth and the truth, as we all know, is a useful thing. It is even supposed to set one free. But why, one is tempted to ask, is it so much better to *know* the truth than merely to *believe* the truth? Is one less free if one merely believes the truth? Is there something one is missing in life if one merely believes what others know?

Often, of course, a person who doesn't know, but nonetheless has a true belief, exhibits a hesitation, a lack of confidence, characteristic of people who don't know. Such people are less prepared to *act*, less prepared to *use* the truths in their possession. Compared to people who know, then, they are, though possessed of the same truths, at something of a disadvantage. This, though, is a disadvantage that can easily be remedied without conferring knowledge. Let the believer be *as certain* as those who know. We can imagine, if we like, that the mere believer *thinks* (mistakenly, of course) that he knows — thus, being certain of what he (mistakenly) thinks he knows. Such a person is not only in possession of all the truths that his better informed neighbors are, he is *as well* disposed to *use* these truths in the conduct of his daily affairs. Is there, then, something *this* person is missing in life by being ignorant of (at least not knowing) what everyone else knows? What good is knowledge for *this person*?

These rhetorical questions are intended to dramatize the point already made: truth, or confidently held truth, is what you want, the marketable commodity as it were, but the relevant truths aren't for sale. In order to ensure yourself a proper supply when the time for action arrives, you have to be blessed with (or somehow arrange to purchase) their means of production, some *reliable* way of generating them. One needs, in other words, keen eyesight, good hearing, a sharp intelligence and whatever else helps one to believe p when, and only when, p.

Critics of externalism, those who think knowledge requires something *other than*, or at least *more than*, reliably produced true belief, something (usually) in the way of a justification for the belief that one's reliably produced beliefs *are* being reliably produced, have, it seems to me, an obligation to say what benefits this justification is supposed to confer. Though reliability itself contributes nothing directly to the benefits of true belief (true beliefs, indexical or otherwise, assuming one is prepared to *act* on them, are just as useful as reliably produced true beliefs), the Reliability Theorist can at least demonstrate the necessity, hence the *value*, of reliability in the acquisition process. The reading glasses become as important as the headlines when you can't read the headlines without the glasses. If, then, knowledge is something more than this, something more than true beliefs produced by reliable mechanisms, what good is this something extra? Who needs it and why? If an animal inherits a perfectly reliable belief-generating mechanism, and it also inherits a disposition, everything being equal, to *act* on the basis of the beliefs so generated,[5] what additional benefits are conferred by a justification that the beliefs *are* being produced in some reliable way? If there are no additional benefits, what good is this justification? Why should we insist that no one can have *knowledge* without it? How does it contribute to the *value* of knowledge?

This is not to say that justification is not a good thing. Of course it is. But it has an *instrumental* utility, a utility in promoting the reliability of the beliefs for which it is available. If it didn't do that, it would be hard to see what value it would have. People who have no evidence, no reasons, no justification for the things they believe end up, more often than not, believing false things. And even when it does not promote reliability — because, we may suppose, the belief is generated by mechanisms that are already reliable (or whose reliability cannot be enhanced by subjective considerations) — it may acquire a utility in the way it affects a person's preparedness to *act* on the belief. Even if my informant is perfectly reliable, I won't trust him, and won't therefore benefit from his communications, if I am given no reason to think he is reliable. So justification is important *to me*. But if it doesn't affect a person's willingness to believe, and by this I mean a person's willingness to *act* on what he believes, nor the reliability of the beliefs on which he acts, as I think it is clear it doesn't in the case of most *perceptual* beliefs (paradigmatic cases of knowledge), of what possible value could a justification be? This, I submit, is why we all find justification to be largely irrelevant to what we can *see* (hence *know*) to be the case.

DEGREE OF RELIABILITY

I have spoken glibly about natural selection favoring reliable mechanisms for the generation and fixation of belief. This is glib because x can favor y, and it can favor y for a very long time, without ever accumulating much y. Selecting for high jumpers doesn't mean that we will eventually get people leaping tall buildings at a single bound. There are natural limits beyond which it becomes harder and harder to go, beyond which it becomes less and less useful to go. Even if one can continue to make improvements, the magnitude of the improvements becomes smaller and smaller. And there are trade-offs. The resources required to make marginal improvements in a given capacity, not to mention the compromises in performance or potential of other capacities, may not be worth the effort. There are no further benefits to be enjoyed — often quite the reverse — by continued improvement. So no further improvement occurs.

So the question arises: Even supposing that selection favors reliability in our representational mechanisms, *how* reliable are these mechanisms? And are they reliable *enough* to qualify the beliefs so generated, the true ones, as knowledge? How reliable must a process be to qualify its product as knowledge?

How reliable a representational system is depends on *what* we take it to be representing.[6] If we take a pressure gauge and calibrate its face in feet above sea level, call it an altimeter, and install it in the cockpit of an aircraft, it will, of course, be less reliable (as in indicator of altitude) than if we merely took it to be a pressure gauge. There are more ways for such an instrument to go wrong about altitude than about air pressure. The more ambitious we get about what r represents, the less reliable r becomes in doing its job. And, correspondingly, the less demanding we are in what we ask r to represent, the more reliable it becomes in representing it. We can, in fact, achieve any level of reliability in a representational device if we are prepared to be modest enough about what it represents. Newspapers, we are told, often misrepresent the views of public figures; if it is the views of public figures that they are representing, they are far from reliable. Their reliability improves if we take them to be representing, not what public figures think, but *their own* best judgment of what these public figures think. And they become nearly infallible purveyors of information (admittedly about matters of less interest) if we take them to be representing, not the views of public figures, not their own judgment about newsworthy events, but what they, for whatever reasons, would like their readers to believe about such matters.

To describe *what* an animal believes about the world around it is, I am assuming, to describe the way it represents its surroundings. And just as we can "make" an instrument more reliable by describing its representational efforts in more modest terms, we can "make" an animal know more by making it believe less. The trick is the same. By making it say less we make it easier for it to say what is true. Moths initiate evasive maneuvers when a bat approaches. There is something in the moth, an internal representation of its surroundings, that tells it *when* to do this. Is this internal representation a representation of a bat, of the movements and whereabouts of its arch-enemy? Or is it merely a representation of the properties of the acoustical input? If the former, we can fool the moth with a high-frequency sound generator. We can make it "think" a bat is coming when there are no bats around. If, on the other hand, the moth is representing the acoustical input, our deceptive efforts with the sound generator are futile. The moth still takes a nose dive when we turn it on, but the moth no longer misrepresents anything. The acoustical input has exactly the character the moth represents it as having. The moth is making no mistake. The reason it isn't is because it isn't *taking* anything to be other than it is. Since there is no bat, the moth doesn't "know" there is a bat closing in. But neither does it *"believe"* there is a bat closing in. The moth lives in a world of acoustic vibrations. And on this modest portrayal of the moth's representational efforts, the moth enjoys virtual infallibility.

It will doubtless be said that although it may be up to us to say what instruments represent (they are, after all, *our* instruments, to do with as we please), it is *not* up to us to tinker with an animal's representational efforts in the same way. We can't inflate a moth's cognitive achievements, its record of doxastic successes (true beliefs), by arbitrarily scaling back on *what* (if anything) it believes. There is a fact of the matter, if not with moths and frogs, then with human beings. From a third-person point of view it may be hard to say whether Clyde is simply unreliable in his judgments about reality or perfectly reliable in his judgments about appearances, but from Clyde's point of view, from the inside as it were, his thought, what he believes, is either something about the way things are or something about the way things appear. What Clyde's internal representations are representations *of*— whether, for instance, they represent objects as red or merely as looking red — is a matter to be determined, not by *us*, but by what is going on in Clyde's head. He either believes it is red and he is wrong or he believes it looks red and he is right. In the latter case, with regard to a belief about how things *look*, he evinces a degree of reliability that may be enough for knowledge. In the former case, with regard to the way things *are*, he may be much less reliable. Perhaps not reliable *enough* to know. So Clyde either knows or he doesn't know. It depends on what he believes. But whether he knows or not is not up to us. It isn't up to us because what he believes is not up to us. It is up to Clyde.

But things aren't this simple. If Clyde's beliefs are internal representations, then Clyde's beliefs are certainly in *his* head. So in that sense a question about what Clyde believes, a question about what his current representations are representation *of*, is a question about what representations are currently in Clyde's head. But a representation can be in Clyde's head without the facts that determine *what* it represents being in Clyde's head. The snapshots of my children are in the dresser drawer, but what makes them snapshots of my children, what makes them representations of these two people (rather than, say, my niece and nephew), is *not* in the drawer. You can't find out whether these two pieces of paper misrepresent anything by looking in the drawer. The reason you can't is because the facts that make them pictures of my children are not facts that reside in the drawer. What makes these pieces of paper (in the drawer) pictures of my children are (roughly) facts about the causal source of the patterns that appear on them. These are facts that can be determined only by looking to the history of the paper and the causal relations of the paper to things outside the drawer. Who was standing in front of the camera when the film was exposed from which these pictures were developed?

If we think of Clyde's beliefs on this model, then although whether Clyde believes that p (rather than q) is a matter of what is going on in his head, what makes what is going on in his head a belief that p (rather than a belief that q) is something that is not going on in his head. It is, just as with the photos in the drawer, a matter of the history of these representations and the causal relations between them and the things they are representations of.

If Clyde can talk, he will certainly *say* one thing and not another. He will, let us suppose, either say, "It *is* red" or he will say "It *looks* red." But what will this show? Will it show that these words, given their conventional meaning, give accurate expression to the way he is representing *it*? If we can teach Clyde to say "It's a muskrat" when he thinks its a gopher, why can't we make him *say* "It's red" when all he *thinks* is that it looks red? If we could make moths talk, and moths had beliefs, we could no doubt teach them to say "A bat is coming" whenever they had a certain belief about the properties of the acoustic input. And the interesting fact is that, give or take a few slips (but certainly no more slips than we customarily make in applying our concepts), what the moth said (assuming that what it said when it used the word "bat" was that there was a bat coming) would be generally true. There generally *would* be a bat closing in when the moth said, "A bat is coming." We might even use this as evidence that the moth was talking about the bat. Would this show that the moth had bat-beliefs, beliefs which were sometimes wrong (when generated by our high-frequency generator)? Or would we simply have given the moth a misleading (to us) way of expressing its perfectly reliable beliefs about the properties of the acoustic input?

These rhetorical questions are meant to have a point. They are meant to suggest a certain connection between two problems, a connection that, if it can be properly exploited, is capable of taking the sting out of both. The first problem, a problem in epistemology, is one of saying *how* reliable a belief-generating mechanism must be to confer on the beliefs so generated the status of knowledge. Natural selection may favor reliability, but can we (against the skeptic) count on it to promote, to *have* promoted, the degree of reliability required to know? The second problem is a problem in the philosophy of mind, a problem about saying what determines the content or meaning of those internal states we describe as beliefs. Assuming that beliefs are internal representations, what makes the representations in our heads representations of p rather than representations of q? Since, as we have just seen, the reliability of a representation-producing mechanism, including belief-fixation processes, is dependent on the content of the representation so produced, on *what* they represent, there is deep connection between these two problems. We cannot determine *how* reliable a representation-generating mechanism is until we have the means of determining *what* the representations it produces are representations *of*, until we have a means of saying what makes the stuff in the head say, mean, or represent one thing rather than another. If we put these two problems together, we can, as it were, pass the buck. Perhaps, that is, the degree of reliability (between a representation and the conditions it represents) required to make the representation *say* (whether truly or falsely) that these conditions exist is exactly the degree of reliability required to make what it says, *when it says it truly*, a *knowledge* that these conditions exist. We needn't say *how* reliable anything must be if we are willing to put the same price on meaning that we put on knowledge. That, in the last analysis, is the hope of a Reliability Theory of Knowledge. Such a theory of knowledge, of what it takes to *know* that p, is, I think, inextricably linked to a reliability theory of representation, meaning, and intentionality, of what it takes for something to *mean* that p.

NOTES

1. I ignore the familiar, but irrelevant, skeptical objection that such arguments beg the question against the skeptic by assuming that we know, or have reason to believe, that there *is* selection for more reliable representational processes. No one is arguing that we know we know, that we *know* evolution works in this way. To put it most cautiously, the argument is that things *might* work this way and, *if* they do, we know. Furthermore, since the skeptic doesn't know, and gives us no reason to think, things do *not* work this way, the skeptic gives us no reason to think we don't know. *That*, I assume, is an effective counter against one classical form of skepticism.

2. The first effort was in *Seeing and Knowing*, Chicago, University of Chicago Press, 1969, Chapter III. Though I lack space to develop the point in this paper, I think it important to distinguish between different versions of the reliability theory of knowledge. Those, for instance, that require the *beliefs* (rather than the *grounds* on which these beliefs are based) to be reliable are, I think, too crude to work. I also think it important to distinguish reliability theories *of knowledge* on the one hand (which I think can be made plausible) and reliability theories *of justification* (which I think are quite implausible).

3. To say that knowledge is not selected for is not to say that it is not selected. If all ripe apples are red, and I am selecting *for* ripe apples, I will, perforce, select red apples. But I am not selecting *for* red apples. See Elliott Sober's discussion of this distinction in *The Nature of Selection*, Cambridge, Mass.: MIT (Bradford) Press, 1984. I return to this point in a moment to reject the idea that it is truth, and not reliability, that is selected for.

4. Perhaps all it needs to know is *what to do* when it sees a coyote, a kind of knowing *how* that we can imagine to be innate, embodied in the way the control system is wired, and, thus, genetically transmittable.

5. I take it that nature has equipped us with something like this disposition — the tendency to believe, indeed a difficulty in *not* believing, and thus a preparedness to *act on*, the "evidence" of our own senses. There would be little point in equipping an organism with reliable belief-generating mechanisms (which I take the senses to be) unless there was, as part of the package, an "actionable" quality to the beliefs so generated.

6. I have an earlier discussion of this point in "The Epistemology of Belief," *Synthese*, 55.1 (April 1983).

6
Convention, Confirmation, and Credibility

Henry E. Kyburg, Jr.

1. CONVENTION

Conventionalism, particularly in the treatment of scientific theories, has a long history, though a rather unclear meaning. There may be important historical roots going arbitrarily far back, but the first widely familiar modern conventionalist was Mach,[1] who argued that Newton's second law, $f = ma$, was nothing but a disguised definition of "force," on the ground that we have no other way to measure force than by directly or indirectly measuring acceleration. If we measure a force in terms of the strain on a spring, for example, we are indirectly measuring force in terms of the stress on the spring, and we know the stress in terms of experiments in which the spring accelerates known masses (for example). How far beyond Newton's second law conventionalism extended for Mach is not clear, and not really to the point of our inquiry. It suffices for us that he took a statement that was clearly regarded as an empirical generalization, and argued that it should better be construed as a convention concerning one of the *terms* of discipline involved.

A view of convention as somewhat more pervasive within a single discipline is that of Poincaré. Poincaré took all of the axioms of geometry to be implicit definitions of "space" and thus conventional. He argued that whether you regard space to be Euclidean, or Riemanian, or Lobachevskian, or some combination thereof, was not determined by "facts" about space, but was a matter of convention.[2] He also made a famous prediction that was falsified in the event (though this does not prevent his argument from having been a good one in its time): "Euclidean geometry is, and will remain, the most convenient. . . ."[3] He argued this on the ground — of interest to us in the latter part of this essay — that the increased complexity of geometries of variable curvature would never pay for itself in increased simplicity in the physical theory itself. In any event, for Poincaré it was not just the odd physical or mathematical law that was conventional in character, but all the assertions of a certain discipline often construed as empirical in character.

It was not merely geometry to which Poincaré ascribed a conventional element. Mach remarks, "Poincaré . . . is right in calling the fundamental propositions of mechanics conventions which might very well have proven otherwise."[4]

It was Pierre Duhem, a physicist, who made the strongest claim regarding the conventionality of what most people think of as empirical theory near the turn of the century.[5] He distinguished between *empirical* laws and *theoretical* laws, and argued that while empirical laws (by which he meant such laws as the law of thermal expansion) could be confirmed or disconfirmed by experiment, any really interesting law could not, since testing it involved a whole bundle of theoretical physical laws that could in principle perfectly well be called into question.

It is not germane to our purpose to examine in detail the ideas of Mach, Poincaré, and Duhem. That they had the idea that it could be philosophically respectable to regard scientific theory, the crowning glory of human knowledge, the pinnacle of human inquiry, as in some sense conventional is important and sufficient for the time being.

Their modern successor, Quine, is not altogether a successor, since his claim is not that certain statements of physics or mathematics should be regarded as conventional, but rather that the very distinction between what is conventional — definitional, analytic — and what is not, what is synthetic, what has empirical content — is an illegitimate and unenlightening distinction. In what follows later we shall argue that this distinction is indeed useful and enlightening, but only in a rather stronger conventionalist framework.

In order to discuss the elements of convention in scientific theory, we should have a clear notion of what a convention is. As a first approximation, let us take the characterization offered by David Lewis in his book, *Convention*.[6] (Surely the author of a book should have a clear idea as to the meaning of its title!) Lewis writes,

> It is redundant to speak of an *arbitrary* convention. Any convention is arbitrary because there is an alternative regularity that could have been our convention instead. (p. 70)

Let us take this notion of conventionality as a starting point, and see how far convention permeates our scientific knowledge. To give us a visual handle on what we are doing, suppose that the vision of Quine and Ullian[7] is roughly correct: our knowledge of the world is like a web. At the periphery of the web are statements that are direct reports of experience — occasion sentences. In the center of the web are statements representing the truths of logic and mathematics. In between are the statements representing the theories, laws, and generalizations of empirical science.

Quine, at least in *Mathematical Logic*,[8] regarded first order logic as conventionally true. The principle of charity invoked in *Word and Object*[9] is also used to defend conventional two-valued, extensional, first order logic as the basic framework for human thought, or at least for human conversation. Even those who would like to see some other form of logic taken as basic rarely argue that ordinary first order logic is false; they argue that some other logic might be "simpler," or less "unnatural" for certain purposes. The tradition that regards logic as being "without content" or analytic is an old one, and respectable. Let us not argue with it, since it surely "could have been otherwise" by making a judiciously different choice of logical primitives and axioms.

To keep our attention on the important part of our scientific knowledge, let us eliminate from our Quinean/Ullianian image of scientific knowledge these strongly conventional elements. From the center of our web, that is, let us eliminate the propositions of logic and mathematics.

Now a well-known result of Craig[10] shows that if you distinguish, as all these people seem to, between *observational* and *theoretical* terms, you can find a constructive procedure by which you can re-axiomatize your scientific theories in such a way that the theoretical terms are completely redundant and unnecessary. More explicitly, the theorem shows the following: if you can distinguish recursively between "theoretical" and "observational" terms, then your theory can be expressed recursively exclusively in observational terms. The theoretical terms are only of heuristic value in deducing consequences from your axioms.

Note, though, that this is *not* to say that theoretical terms "serve only a heuristic function." It may perfectly well still be the case that these theoretical terms and the axioms that govern them are central to explanation. It may also perfectly well be the case that these theoretical terms denote objects and properties and relations that actually exist — that is, that the theories with their abstract terms are *semantically* correct. This is quite consistent with the replaceability of theoretical terms.

Given this replaceability, however, we are quite free to eliminate theoretical terms and the axioms that govern them and that relate them to observational terms as "merely conventional"; they not only "could" be replaced, but we have a recipe for replacing them. We are left with a corpus of scientific knowledge that is written in a language containing only "observation" terms, and yet is just as useful for predicting as the corpus we think of as warranted by the collective institution of science.

But worse! As I have shown elsewhere,[11] you can replace a given theory, employing a given theoretical vocabulary, and embodying given theoretical axioms and given "coordinating definitions," with a new theory, employing whatever theoretical, non-observational terms you like, embodying whatever axioms strike you as plausible for those theoretical terms, in such a way that the new theory has *exactly* the same observational consequences as the old one.

If this is so, then everything inside the periphery of the web could be regarded as "conventional" — that is, it can equally well be replaced by something else. But the periphery itself is not immune to charges of conventionality. Any realistic view of observation must allow for *errors* of observation. Thus what happens to us does not uniquely determine what sentences at the periphery of our web of knowledge we should accept.

Note that this is *not* merely a matter of the fact that what sound you make when you see a crow is arbitrary. That would be what Grunbaum calls "TSC" — trivial semantic conventionalism.[12] What is importantly conventional is the fact that the *boundaries* of the categories into which we take our observations to fall are subject to arbitrary modification. It is open whether we should regard this observation rather than that one as being erroneous.

All this suggests that the standard, "might equally well have been otherwise," is a poor touchstone for conventionality. And in fact no conventionalist has suggested that other alternatives might *really* equally have been chosen. What the conventionalist suggests is rather, as is clear from what Poincaré says about geometry, that it is factors of simplicity, convenience, even familiarity, that dictate the choice of one alternative over another. There are always *reasons* for preferring one convention over another.

Since our concern here is epistemology, let us come right out and characterize an *arbitrary* linguistic convention (from the epistemological point of view) as a convention whose reason for adoption is *non-epistemic.* (By "non-epistemic" one means to include such considerations as simplicity, familiarity, computational efficiency, and the like.)

Henceforth, then, we want to consider only non-arbitrary conventions. If any!

2. FORMAL FRAMEWORK

We will consider formalized theories.[13] We will construe a theory in what is possibly a somewhat old-fashioned way as consisting of four parts:

(a) A recursive specification of the set of terms and predicates of the theory. We include logical and mathematical terms and predicates, as well as "observational" and "theoretical" empirical terms and predicates. We do not suppose that there is a procedure for telling which is which.

(b) A recursive characterization of the sentences and formulas of the theory. Logic and mathematics are to be included.

(c) A recursive characterization of the axioms of the theory. These are to include both sufficient axioms for whatever logic and mathematics you want, and "meaning postulates," and axioms "pertaining" to the empirical subject matter with which the theory is concerned. We do not require a procedure for distinguishing these classes of axioms.

(d) Rules of inference. Of course we *can* get by with just *modus ponens*, but we would like to be able to accommodate those who prefer to think of "material rules of inference" rather than axioms.[14]

We suppose that among the theorems of this formal theory we have all the theorems of first order logic, and as much set theory and mathematics as we need. Controversy about these items can be generated, but they are not typically what epistemologists worry about. We suppose that any "meaning postulates" or "logical" or "analytic" relations among terms of the theory (if there are any) are captured by our axioms and rules of inference.

We thus suppose that we have a standard deductive logic built into our theory, that we can characterize in a standard proof-theoretic way. In a similar vein, we suppose that we also have an inductive logic available. One can hardly call it "standard," of course, since the very idea of there being an inductive logic is controversial. Furthermore, our inductive logic is parasitic on our notion of probability, the general idea of the inductive logic being that you can believe stuff that is probable enough. All this will be unpacked as part of the generic formal framework within which we shall attempt to account for the epistemic status of scientific theories.

Let us look at probability first. Probability is defined for all of our theories in the same way. It is a syntactical notion, like that of proof, that we can spell out explicitly in the metalanguage.[15] We list here some of its properties.

(a) Probability is defined for a given language or theory.

(b) Probability is relativized to a corpus **K** of statements, representing the body of *evidence* relative to which the probability of a sentence is to be evaluated. **K** need not in general be deductively closed, but it will contain, at least potentially, all the theorems of the theory. In addition, **K** may contain *observation* statements, and statements warranted by *inductive inference*.

(c) Probability is an objective relation, a syntactically definable function from sentences and sets of sentences of a given

language to subintervals of [0, 1]. It is objective in the same
sense that provability is objective.

(d) Probability is also objective in another, indirect, sense. All
probabilities are based on the statistical syllogism, in which the
statistical premise represents *known* (in **K**) frequencies or
propensities. (In general, these statistical statements will be
empirical, but they *can* be set-theoretical truths such as: almost
all subsets of a given set contain approximately the same
relative frequency of objects with a given property as the given
set exhibits.)

(e) Probability is interval valued. The form of a probability statement (a metalinguistic statement, be it noted) is:

$$\textbf{Prob}_T(\textbf{S}, \textbf{K}) = [p, q]$$

(f) Probability can equally well be defined for the metalanguage;
thus we can talk about the probability that a certain *statement*,
for example, has a certain metalinguistic property, such as that
of being in error.

The general idea behind the epistemological view being presented here
is that when something is probable enough, you can simply believe it — that
is, *accept* it. Given an epistemic notion of probability, one is immediately
led to ask: "Probable enough, *relative to what*?" One answer, the one we will
endorse, is that the probability in question is to be computed relative to the
total evidence you have. Thus we will say:

(1) A sentence **S** will belong to your corpus of practical certainties
K' if and only if there is a p and a q such that $\textbf{Prob}_T(\textbf{S}, \textbf{K}) =$
$[p, q]$, and p exceeds whatever we have taken as a level of
"practical certainty," where **K** is the corpus of *evidence*.

Of course we may now inquire into the source of the statements in the
evidential corpus **K**.

One possibility would be to suppose that they were phenomenological
reports, incorrigible deliverances of the senses. But this is not of much help
to us; if we are talking about "evidence" in any ordinary sense, we must
include as evidence the results of measurement ("the table is 3.6 ± .05
meters long"), the content-laden results of observation ("there are thirty-
eight black crows in the cage"), and even — we shall see how shortly — the
results of technically sophisticated observation ("microscopic examination
shows the presence of gram-negative bacteria").

So we can raise the same old question again. One answer, this time, *is*
to say that an evidential statement gets into the evidential corpus **K** by being
probable enough relative to a corpus **K*** of incorrigibilia. The contents of

K* *might* be taken to be the propositional content of phenomenological events, expressed in the language of the theory **T**.

There are difficulties with this view, and we shall ultimately abandon it, but let us look at the picture it yields of the structure of our knowledge. We have, at base, a set of incorrigible statements, **K***. The set of evidential statements, **K**, consists of those statements S whose probability relative to **K*** is greater than p : S $\in$ **K** if and only if ($\exists$ p, q)(**Prob**$_T$(S, **K***) = [p, q] & $\vdash p > p$).

The set of practical certainties, **K'**, is correspondingly defined as the set of statements S whose probability relative to **K** is greater than p', where **p** is greater than **p'** : S $\in$ **K'** if and only if ($\exists$ p, q)(**Prob**$_T$(S, **K**) = [p, q] & $\vdash p > p$). It is the set of practical certainties that we use for making practical judgments. It is relative to the practical corpus that we compute the probabilities that we multiply by utilities to get the expectations we need for decision theory.

C. I. Lewis said that nothing can be probable unless something is certain.[16] In a very special sense, we will find that to be true; but a stronger claim is embodied in the structure suggested: Something can be judged probable only in relation to evidence that is of yet greater dependability. This is embodied in our requirement that **p** > **p'**.

The next stage in the development of our theory is to consider *meta*corpora. This is inspired by our natural interest in error. We must be able to attribute error to the sentences embodying our observations. In the metalanguage we will have predicates such as "veridical," "erroneous" that we can use to separate the sheep among our observations from the goats. The set of incorrigibilia here is quite straightforward: it is the set of sentences inscribed (say) by responsible scientists in their notebooks. No responsible scientist would ever withdraw (erase) such an inscription. But no one would ever take it as *evidence* without a consideration of the possibility of its being in error.

So let us emulate the object-language structure in the metalanguage. **MK*** will correspond to **K***: but now there is no problem of interpreting it. It consists of just those sentences (of the metalanguage of **T**) that are written down in our notebook, or in the notebooks of our community of scientists.

These sentences *mention* sentences of the object language. **MK**, the metacorpus of evidential certainties, will consist of those metalinguistic statements whose probability, relative to **MK***, is at least p . We'll explain this in detail in just a moment. Finally, **MK'** corresponds to the set of practical certainties: it is the set of metalinguistic statements whose probability, relative to **MK**, is at least p' .

We have so far mentioned no metalinguistic predicates other than the classical ones of 'is true' and 'is false.' More important than those are the predicates corresponding to 'is inscribed in **X**'s laboratory notebook,' where **X** may denote either an individual or a *group* of individuals. (Chemists, for example.) We may introduce such predicates, expressing relations between sentences of our theory **T**, individuals, and times, as:

(a) $O(X, S, t)$, to mean that the individual, or group, **X** wrote in his (their) notebook the sentence **S**, at some time before the time t; **O** will be a primitive relation of the metalanguage of **T**.

We may use this primitive to define such interesting subsets of the set of sentences of **T** as:

(b) $VO(X, S) = \{S | (\exists t)(O(X, S, t)\ \&\ S)\}$.

This is the set of veridical observations of **X**. Correspondingly, we have, for **X**'s errors,

(c) $EO(X, S) = \{S | (\exists t)(O(X, S, t)\ \&\ {\sim}S)\}$.

Clearly, we may define the sentences of a given form, the sentences involving a given predicate, etc., and we may divide those sets of sentences into the veridical and the erroneous. In the next section we will consider how to make use of this machinery.

3. REPRESENTING BODIES OF KNOWLEDGE

You recall that **K*** contained incorrigible statements of the object language. Are there any? It is hard to believe that there are. What observation statement about the world is proof against correction? Surely any statement that purports to be about the world can be explained away, if only by the strained device of appealing to illusion or hallucination. Incorrigibility can be bought only at the price of vacuity.

Within the framework under discussion, however, we can eliminate **K*** with no loss. This is how it comes about. In place of incorrigible *object language* sentences in **K***, let us look at the metalinguistic sentences in **MK***. There is no problem in regarding *these* sentences as incorrigible, since they merely report **X**'s judgments about the world. *That* **X** made such and such a judgment about the world does of course represent a fact about the world: **X** is in the world. But it is a fact of psychology (or sociology, or cognitive science), and not, in **MK**, an empirical claim. If we restrict our theories to physics, biology, and the like, it should not be difficult to keep object and metalanguage clear. We may have difficulty doing this if **X** is an individual introspecting, or if **X** is a collection of sociologists observing the behavior of sociologists. Even in these cases, the benefits may well outweigh the difficulty.

We are now in a position to make a simplification of our framework. The corpus **K*** will be empty if we suppose that we can make errors in any kind of object language statement judgment. The corpus **MK'** seems to serve no very interesting purpose. So we take **MK*** to contain our observation *reports*; **MK** to contain metalinguistic statements that are highly probable (p) relative to **MK***; *and* object-language statements that are highly probable (p) relative to statistical information in **MK** itself. We are thus left with three sets of statements:

(1) **MK***, containing observation *reports*. These reports may or may not be veridical, but we take the report itself to be incorrigible. It also contains logical and mathematical statements.

(2) **MK**: the set of *evidential* certainties. A statement is in **MK** if and only if (a) its probability, relative to **MK*** exceeds **p**, or (b) it is a statement in the object language, and its probability relative to the part of **MK** that does *not* include the object language is greater than **p**.

(3) **MK'**: the set of *practical* certainties. A sentence is in **MK'** if and only if its probability, relative to **MK**, exceeds **p'**.

Let us suppose we have had a lot of experiences that we might record as the observation of an alligator and of its blueness, of a non-alligator and its blueness, of an alligator and its non-blueness, and of a non-alligator and its non-blueness. Suppose that among these judgments, practically all the alligator judgments are accompanied by blue judgments.

Consider two theories, T_1 and T_2. T_1 contains an axiom to the effect that all alligators are blue: $(x)(Ax \rightarrow Bx)$; T_2 does not. **MK***, on both theories, will contain a lot of statements of the form "O(X, "Aa_1," t)," "O(X, "Ba_1," t)," and so on. It will also generally contain some "negative" statements "O(X, "~Ba_i," t)." **MK***, since it is populated by incorrigibilia, will also contain statistical information — e.g., to the effect that 98% of the observation reports that have the form "Aa_i" are accompanied by observation reports having the form "Ba_i."

Now let us see what happens according to the theory we employ. If we employ theory T_2, we have no reason to think that any of the observation reports are in error, while if we employ theory T_1, we do. But someone might say that we have no reason, on either theory, to think that our observations are not in error! We need some principled way to deal with the possibility (or certainty, in the case of T_1) of observational error.

Various answers are possible, but one answer I have given elsewhere[17] is particularly simple. Adopt two principles:

Minimization Principle: Minimize the attribution of error to your observation reports.

Distribution Principle: Subject to that condition, distribute the error you *must* attribute to your observational reports in as even a way as possible.

It is hard to see why anyone would want to impugn the first principle. It is true that a lot of our alligator observations might turn out to be wrong. Maybe they all are, since alligators are material objects and maybe there are no material objects. But this seems a silly thing to worry about, though it may not be a silly project to analyze what it *is* to be a material object. On the other hand, the principle seems a natural one: it is our knowledge about the world that provides us, in ordinary life, with a touchstone for reality. We may judge an object in a tree to be a black cat, but when it flies away, we know that our judgment was in error.

The second principle is less natural. In particular, it would seem that negative judgments ("~Aa_3") are less prone to error than positive ones. But this in fact follows from plausible assumptions concerning our judgments. We first minimize error: to do this, it seems plausible to suppose that far fewer negative judgments will need to be labelled false than positive judgments. Thus when we choose the distribution that is most even, it may well still be the case that the relative frequency of false positive judgments must be presumed to be much higher than the relative frequency of false negative judgments.

From the application of these two principles, we do not, of course, discover *which* observation reports are misleading. (If we did, we would cleverly excise them so that the rest could be taken at face value!) What we get are the "observed" relative frequencies of error for the various sorts of observation report. This sample data is in **MK***, which we may suppose to be deductively closed in virtue of the fact that the items in it are incorrigible.

In theory T_2, we don't have to suppose there are any errors of observation.

In theory T_1, we must suppose that a certain number of alligator judgments and a certain number of non-blue judgments are in error.

Now turn to **MK**. We have sample information in **MK*** about the relative frequencies of various sorts of errors. We can use this as the basis for a straightforward statistical inference concerning the long-run or general frequencies of errors of these various sorts. (We assume here that there are no problems concerning statistical inference, and that the result is the acceptance, in the evidential corpus **MK** of level **p**, of a statistical hypothesis such as: "In general, alligator judgments turn out to have to be rejected with a relative frequency between .04 and .08.")

In theory T_2, since we not only have no evidence of any errors in our sample of judgments, but know that we *can* have no such evidence, we accept in the evidential corpus the metalinguistic generalization "Between 0% and 0% of alligator judgments turn out to have to be rejected."

In theory T_1, we do have some evidence of error, and so we might accept the metalinguistic statistical statement "Between 4% and 8% of the alligator judgments have to be rejected."

We also have in **MK** all the observation *reports* from **MK***. This accounts for the interesting metalinguistic contents of **MK**. We also have in the evidential corpus some probable statements of the object language. In particular, if "Aa_i" is a random member of the set of (syntactically characterized) observation reports, and the proportion of such statements that belong to **VO** (the veridical ones) is known in **MK** to exceed **p**, then the probability that "Aa_i" belongs to **VO** is more than **p**. If this is so, then since "Aa_i iff "Aa_i" $\in$ **VO**" is in **MK**, "Aa_i" itself will be in **MK**.

Of course, "Aa_i" is not in general a random member of the general set of observation reports, but rather a random member of the subset that have the form "Ax." Whether this makes any difference or not depends on whether we are using T_1 or T_2. There is nothing in T_2 to entail any errors of observation, so that if we have an observation report, we can accept it at face value and include the corresponding statement in **MK**. In the case of T_1, if the relative frequency with which observation statements must be rejected is high, the fact that "Aa_i" is an observation report may *not* suffice to justify its inclusion among the evidential statements. In particular, this is so for those statements "Aa_i" that are paired with statements "$\sim Ba_i$" in **MK***. We are bound to lose some statements, on this ground.

On the other hand, since it is a theorem that if **S** entails **S'** then the probability of **S'** exceeds that of **S**, and in T_1, "Aa_i" entails "Ba_i," and "$\sim Ba_i$" entails "$\sim Aa_i$," the contents of **MK** should accordingly be expanded. In T_2 there are no interesting entailments. ("Aa_i" entails "Aa_i v Ba_j," but who cares?)

In theory T_1, containing the generalization, we lose some observation statements in **MK** due to error; but we gain some observation statements from entailment.

In theory T_2, lacking the generalization, we retain all of our observations. Since the chance of error is 0, the probability of a conjunction of observation statements is the same as the probability of each of them, and we may also have in **MK** a statement to the effect that in a sample of n alligators, 96% have been found to be blue.

It is, however, the corpus of practical certainties **K'** that we require in order to plan our lives and make our decisions. The part of the corpus of practical certainties that interests us is the part that contains sentences in the object language. These sentences fall into a variety of categories. First, there are the observational sentences that are inherited (indirectly) from **MK***. In general, T_2 will provide more of these than T_1. Second, there are statistical statements that are rendered practically certain by the data in **MK**. Thus the statistical statement "About 95% of alligators are blue" may be rendered so probable by the evidence in **MK** that it becomes included in **K'**. Then relative to the corpus **K'** the probability of "Ba_j" (assuming randomness) may be $0.95 \pm .03$. Finally, singular statements such as "Ba_j" can be rendered probable enough, relative to **MK**, to be included in **K'**, even when they are not probable enough to be included in **MK** itself. The most important case of this sort is when there are entailments in a theory that lead from observation statements to their implications.

In the theory T_2 we may have, in the set of practical certainties **K'**, all of the observation statements (e.g., "Aa_8") that correspond to observation reports in **MK***, e.g., "$O(X, "Aa_8," t)$." (Of course, we also have everything entailed by these statements, e.g., "$Ba_6 v \sim Ba_6$.") Since we have sample data represented in **MK**, there will be statistical hypotheses that are probable enough to be included in **K'**. For example, we may be practically certain that almost all alligators are blue. Relative to such a corpus we should predict that an alligator of unspecified color will be blue, though that statement will not appear in **K'**.[18]

In the theory T_1 the corpus of practical certainties **K'** may not contain all the observation statements corresponding to the observation reports in **MK*** (in fact, if our observations are, according to our theory, highly prone to error, we could end up with no observation statements at all in **MK**). But we have the additional observation statements entailed, according to the theory, by those we do retain. In addition, as in theory T_2, we have statistical statements rendered practically certain by the evidence in **MK**.

4. CHOOSING BETWEEN THEORIES

By considering what happens to our three-part bodies of knowledge when hypothetical incomplete observation reports are added to the meta-corpus **MK***, we can formulate criteria for the preferability of one theory over another in terms of the *predictive observational content* of the corpus of practical certainties **K'**. The predictive observational content of a corpus of practical certainties **K'** consists of observation sentences in **K'** that do *not* correspond to observation reports in the corresponding **MK***, together with sentences whose probability relative to **K'** exceeds the level of **K'**:[19]

(4) **POC (MK*, p, p')** = {S| S ∈ **K'** & ~S ∈ **MK*** v
Prob$_T$(S, K') > **p'**}.

In the example we have just been considering, we could add such statements as "$O(X,$ "Ax_1," $t)$," "$O(X,$ "$\sim Ax_2$," $t)$," and "$O(X,$ "$\sim Bx_3$," $t)$" to our corpus $MK*$, where $x_1, x_2, x_3, \ldots$ are distinct terms new to the language. Which of the two theories is preferable depends on our past experience. If our past experience has involved a lot of non-blue alligators, then we may obtain no predictive observational consequences under either theory, though we could still get some statistical advice from T_2. If our past experience has involved a few non-blue alligators, then T_2 may provide more in the way of predictive power, since it requires less attribution of error to our observations. If our past experience has involved very few non-blue alligators, T_1, in which "Ax_i" entails "Bx_i" and "$\sim Bx_i$" entails "$\sim Ax_i$," may well provide more predictive observational content.

What happens depends on what partial observations we add to $MK*$. We want to add enough, of various kinds, so that we can see what is happening; but we don't want what we are hypothetically adding to affect the error frequencies. (Since the new terms are all distinct, they will dilute the error frequencies of the original corpus, if we count them as ordinary observation reports.) Since we have a formal object to play with, we can accomplish all this. Let us add partial observations to $MK*$ in the same proportion as our past observations of the corresponding sorts; let us call the result "aug-$MK*$"; let us not use this information to update the statistical components of MK and K'; and let us then compare the POC of aug-$MK*$ on the two theories.

We still have the parameters p and p' to take account of. For present purposes, let us just take them to be fixed by context.[20]

In "Theories as Mere Conventions,"[21] I have argued that this standard of preference for one theory over another (I perhaps perversely called them "languages" there, to emphasize the *a priori* character of the theoretical axioms and generalizations) accounts for much of what Kuhn and Feyerabend have drawn our attention to. I claimed that we could account relatively neatly not only for the replacement of one theory by another, but also for the expansion of a theory by the addition of new generalizations, the (rare) contraction of a theory by the "refutation" of generalizations, and even for the replacement of "observational" terms as theories change. I will not repeat those arguments here, but merely claim that the epistemological framework adumbrated above supports a plausible empiricist view of scientific inference.

5. MORE EPISTEMOLOGY

There are some specifically epistemological questions that are important to consider in this framework. Perhaps the most pressing is the question of observation. I have been freely referring to "observation sentences," though I have also said that this framework did not require a sharp observational/theoretical distinction. Once we have admitted errors of observation, and eliminated **K***, we no longer need to worry about finding sentences of the object language that can be known with certainty on the basis of observation. We can take our observations at face value, in the form of observation reports.

The general idea is that observation reports represent judgments based directly on experience. By "directly" I mean non-inferentially, and by "experience" I mean what happens to me in response to what I do. By merely looking, I can judge that a certain object is an alligator, for example. By hefting a certain piece of iron, I can judge that it weighs about three pounds. Lots of learning can be involved. It is this possibility that I was depending on earlier when I referred to a sentence about gram-negative bacteria as "observational." In fact, we are at last in a position to remove observation from the hands and eyes of the physiologically normal amateur, and to allow the experienced expert — the histologist — full scope. What is more important, however, is that the theory of error to which we are led in **MK** provides control.

But in comparing theories, at least at an elementary level, we do have to count observation sentences. We cannot avoid the question: What sentences? Clearly we want to count only sentences that are going to be dependable guides to experience.

Dependability in prediction may be construed in the same way as dependability in observation. An observation report represents a dependable observation just in case it is unlikely that future observations will impugn the contents of that report. More explicitly: a *kind* of observation report is a dependable kind just in case the *general* frequency of error among reports of that kind is sufficiently low (less than $1 - \mathbf{p}$, where $\mathbf{p}$ is the evidential level). We obtain this frequency from considering the sample proportion of such reports we are forced to construe as false in an initial segment of our experience as an indication of the long-run relative frequency with which such reports will have to be construed as false. It is our theory — that is, our *general* knowledge about the world — combined with the minimization principle and the distribution principle, that tells us what we must take the relative frequency of error of various kinds of observation judgments to be.

When an observation judgment is made, there is only one thing that can go wrong: it may be the case that not-S obtains. Or, in epistemic rather than semantic terms, it may be the case that further experience may induce us to regard that kind of judgment as generally unreliable.

When an observation prediction is made, there is still only one thing that can go wrong: it may be that not-S obtains. Or, in epistemic rather than semantic terms, it may be the case that further experience may induce us to regard that kind of judgment as generally unreliable.

There is a difference, of course, between *verifying* a prediction and simply recording an observation. In order to verify the prediction, I must often put myself in the way of a certain kind of experience: I must open my eyes and look, or focus my attention, or *try* to see whether or not S obtains, or look into an instrument. But this difference is not related to a difference in the reliability of the observation. If I try to see S, and fail, that results in an observation report that enters into the data for determining the reliability of non-S observation, as well as the reliability of any other observation sentences that went into the prediction.

The point is that reliability is a matter internal to what I am calling a theory, and that observationality is a property that is a matter of degree and is related to the internal measure of reliability.

There is much to be said about special cases. For example, if we have a physical theory, and the physical theory predicts that (say) a certain temperature should be 55°C, and we measure the temperature with a reliable instrument (a reliable instrument is one that gives rise to reliable readings — that is, to reliable observation reports), and find 75° C, we may well reject the physical theory, or replace it with a more modest theory that does not lead to the prediction in question.

The argument goes as follows: we have a larger and more pervasive theory, of which the law in question is only a small part, which entails that if we get one *genuine* anomalous result, we can generate any number of them. So it is within the large theory itself that the deep negative import of finding a temperature of 75°C makes itself felt. This is simply the negative form of a procedure that in a positive form allows us to get a lot of information from very few experiments. (For example, from a single careful experiment, we can get a very narrow distribution for the melting point of a new chemical compound; why? Because our general theory requires that all samples of a pure chemical compound melt at the same temperature under standard conditions.)

How about the confirmation and disconfirmation of theories? If we identify a theory with the conjunction of the non-logical, non-mathematical axioms of the theory, then we have no difficulty in assigning a degree of probability to the theory relative to a body of knowledge. There are two cases. The theory is providing the background for the bodies of knowledge. Then the probability of each of its sentences (axioms and theorems) is 1.0. Alternatively, some other theory is providing the background. The probability of each of its sentences (axioms and theorems) is 0.0. The probabilities are perfectly well defined, but perfectly useless.

When we talk about the probability of a theory, I think we are not talking of the probability that the theory is true, in the sense in which when we talk of the probability of heads on the next toss, we are talking of the probability that the proposition that the coin lands heads on the next toss is true. I think we have in mind something quite different: for example, the probability that we will accept the theory in question ten years from now. This is a quite different question — a question in the sociology of scientific change, if you will — and one to which sensible answers might well be provided by a study of the history and sociology of science. That is, it is a question that is internal to another branch of science, and not a philosophical question at all.

6. CONCLUSION

What is the upshot of all this? That there are good arguments for conventionalism in science, but that if they are pursued too far they leave us with empty bodies of knowledge. We must have grounds for preferring one convention to another, and furthermore, they must be epistemic grounds. Such grounds cannot be provided directly by observation. As many conventionalists have pointed out, observation is always subject to error.

So suppose we take theory in a broad and general sense as providing a framework for our body of knowledge. We take our body of knowledge to consist of three sets of sentences: a set of sentences in the metalanguage of the theory, **MK***, containing observation reports. From this set of sentences, together with the background theory, we can derive the statistics of observational error that are required by that background theory. Given these statistics, we can determine the probability of statements of the object language, relative to the metalinguistic and theoretical background.

The statistics of error and the statements of the object language that are highly probable form the evidential corpus **MK**. Statements in the object language that are so probable relative to the corpus **MK** as to be regarded as practically certain form another corpus: **K**, the corpus of practical certainties. **K** contains both statistical knowledge and predictive observational knowledge.

The contents of all of these corpora are determined by the background theory and by the contents of **MK***, and by the selection of two parameters to distinguish evidential certainty and practical certainty.

Finally, the criterion by which we determine that one theory is to be preferred to another is the frankly pragmatic one of the number (or content) of the predictive observational statements in the practical corpus.

The notion of error, and hence of observationality, is relativized to a theory, but is determined, for a given theory, by our experience — by what happens to us. Thus, even though theories are regarded as "conventional" or *a priori*, even though the notion of error that determines the content of the practical certainties of a theory is internal to the language of the theory, we can still have an objective measure of the degree to which one theory rather than another satisfies our desire to anticipate the future.

This picture leaves certain puzzles to be resolved, but seems to offer a picture of scientific knowledge that is plausibly rooted in the empiricist tradition. It may well be that the general framework of metalinguistic report at one extreme, and object language prediction at the other, tied together by an analysis of error that involves both languages, has something to offer other areas in epistemology as well.

NOTES

Research bearing on the topic of this paper has been supported by the United States Army Signals Warfare Center.

1. Ernst Mach, *The Science of Mechanics*, Open Court, LaSalle, 1960. The first German edition appeared in 1883. See especially Chapter II on the development of the principles of dynamics.

2. Henri Poincaré, *Science and Hypothesis*, Dover Publications, New York, 1952. This book appeared in French in 1903.

3. *Ibid.*, p. 50.

4. Mach, *op. cit.*, p. 306.

5. Pierre Duhem, *The Aim and Structure of Physical Theory*, Princeton University Press, Princeton, 1954. In French, it appeared as *La Theorie Physique: Son Objet, Sa Structure*, in 1906.

6. David Lewis, *Convention*, Harvard University Press, Cambridge, 1969. It is interesting to note the similarity between the final clause quoted, and that occurring in Mach's attribution of conventionalism to Poincaré just quoted.

7. W.V.O. Quine and J. S. Ullian, *The Web of Belief*, Random House, New York, 1970.

8. W.V.O. Quine, *Mathematical Logic*, Harvard University Press, Cambridge, 1940.

9. W.V.O. Quine, *Word and Object*, MIT Press, Cambridge, 1960.

10. William Craig, "Replacement of Auxiliary Expressions," *Philosophical Review* 65, 1956, 38-55.

11. Henry E. Kyburg, Jr., "How to Make Up a Theory," *Philosophical Review* 87, 1978, pp. 84-87.

12. Adolf Grunbaum, *Geometry and Chronometry in Philosophical Perspective*, University of Minnesota Press, Minneapolis, 1968, p. 20.

13. In previous publications, for example, "Theories as Mere Conventions" in *Minnesota Studies in the Philosophy of Science*, I have called the objects with which we are concerned "languages."

14. See, for example, Stephen Toulmin, *The Uses of Argument*, Cambridge University Press, Cambridge, 1958.

15. We won't do that here. Various sources for the notion of probability we will employ are Henry E. Kyburg, Jr., *The Logical Foundations of Statistical Inference*, Reidel, Dordrecht, 1974; "Epistemological Probability," *Synthese* 23, 1971, 309-326, reprinted in *Epistemology and Inference*, University of Minnesota Press, Minneapolis, 1983; and "The Reference Class," *Philosophy of Science* 50, 1983, 374-397.

16. C. I. Lewis, *An Analysis of Knowledge and Valuation*," Open Court, LaSalle, 1949.

17. In *Theory and Measurement*, Cambridge University Press, Cambridge, 1984.

18. In the more complex version of this scheme, in which incorrigible observation statements appeared in **K***, we could get sample data in **K*** through deductive closure and thus statistical statements in **K** (now collapsed into **MK**), and thus, in the case of extreme statistical statements, predictive singular statements could appear in **K'**. We now lose this feature, but since it was a feature of a very unrealistic case, it is a small loss.

19. The second clause is new. Since, however, there is no way in which you can rationally bet against a proposition whose probability relative to your corpus of practical certainties exceeds the level of that corpus, it seems appropriate to include such statements as part of the predictive observational content of the corpus.

20. In "Knowledge and Acceptance," forthcoming, I attempt to show how context determines the levels of practical and evidential certainty.

21. Forthcoming.

7
Probability in the Theory of Knowledge

Roderick Chisholm

INTRODUCTION

In contemporary literature on the theory of knowledge, there appears to be considerable disagreement, if not confusion, about the way in which the concept of probability is to be applied to the beliefs, or to the possible beliefs, of any particular person or subject. The issues turn on "the question of how evidence is used as the basis for ordinary probability statements which omit mention of 'evidence.'"[1] This question, which seems to me to be the most important epistemological question about probability, is the topic of the present chapter.

I will first consider the most familiar use of the term "probable" — what is sometimes called its *epistemic* use. I will then consider two *relational* uses of this epistemic concept: the logical probability relation and the applied probability relation. The *logical* probability relation may be expressed in such formulae as "h is probable in relation to e," "e confirms h," and "e tends to make h probable." The *applied* probability relation may be expressed in such formulae as "h is probable *for* S in relation to e," "e confirms h *for* S," and "e tends to make h probable *for* S."

THE EPISTEMIC SENSE OF PROBABILITY

The epistemic sense of the term "probable" is that sense in which we ordinarily understand the term — whether or not we know anything about epistemology or statistics or inductive logic. It is the sense we have in mind when we ask ourselves such questions as: "Is it probable that I will be alive a year from now?" and "In relation to what I now know, is it probable that it will rain tomorrow?" This fundamental sense of "probability" has been the concern of epistemologists since at least the time of the Greek 'skeptics.'[2] Carnap suggests that it is "the primary and simplest meaning" of 'probability.'[3]

To say that a belief is probable in this epistemic sense is to say something about the nature of its justification. I would define the concept this way:

D1 p is probable for S =Df S is more justified in believing p than in believing the negation of p.

If it is probable for you, in this sense, that you will be taking a trip tomorrow, then you are more justified in believing you will be taking a trip tomorrow than in believing you will not be taking a trip tomorrow.

Propositions which are thus probable for a subject S and which are *merely* probable for S may yet be such that some are *more* justified for S than others. Perhaps it is probable for you (merely probable for you) that it is now raining in the western quarter of the United States; and perhaps it is also probable — merely probable — for you that it is raining in the western third of the United States. The latter proposition is *more justified* for you than the former. In such a case, two propositions, each of which is merely probable for you, are such that that one of them is "*more probable*" for you than the other.

A further way of elucidating this concept is to show how it is related to concepts pertaining to *other* levels of epistemic justification. All such concepts may be reduced to a single comparative concept, one that we may express by means of the locution, "So-and-so is at least as justified for S as is such-and-such." In the formulae listed on the accompanying diagram, the following abbreviations are used: "—P..." for "— is more justified for S than is ..."; "—A..." for "— is at least as justified for S as is ..."; "—S..." for "S's justification for — is equal to his justification for ..."; "Bp" for "Believing p"; "Kp" for "Knowing p"; "Wp" for "Withholding p"; "~p" for "not-p"; and "(p)" for "For every proposition p."

Definitions

xPy =Df ~(yAx)
xSy =Df (xAy & yAx)
Wp =Df (~Bp & ~B~p) [Note: Wp = W~p]

Axioms

(A1)   The A-relation is asymmetrical
(A2)   The A-relation is transitive
(A3)   (Bp A Wp) -> (Bp P B~p)
(A4)   [(Bp P Wp) & (Bq P Wq)] -> [(B(p&q) P (Bp & Wq)]

Epistemic Level of p

6.	(q)(Bp A Bq)	Certain
5.	(q)(Bp P Wq)	Obvious
4.	(q)(Bp A Wq)	Evident
3.	(Bp P Wp)	Beyond Reasonable Doubt
2.	(Bp A Wp)	Epistemically in the Clear
1.	(Bp P B~p)	Probable
0.	(B~p S Bp)	Counterbalanced
-1.	(B~p P Bp)	Has a Negative Probability
-2.	(B~p A Wp)	Has a Negation in the Clear
-3.	(B~p P Wp)	Preposterous
-4.	(q)(B~p A Wq)	Evidently False
-5.	(q)(B~p P Wq)	Obviously False
-6.	(q)(B~p A Bq)	Certainly False

The corresponding thirteen categories for not-p may be obtained by listing the thirteen formulae in reverse order. The first five categories listed are such that each implies but is not implied by the category listed immediately below it. The last five categories listed are such that each implies but is not implied by the category listed immediately above it. Category zero is inconsistent with every other category.

Every proposition is such that either (i) it has a positive probability for S or (ii) it has a negative probability for S or (iii) it is counterbalanced for S.

We must take care to distinguish this fundamental epistemic sense of "probable" from the sense that "probable" has in statistics and in inductive logic. In those disciplines "probable" is *defined* in terms of frequency of occurrence — sometimes in terms of "the limit of relative frequency in the long run." But the epistemic concept of probability, although it it is closely connected with the concept of frequency, is a concept of a very different 'sort.'[4]

Statements in which "probable" is taken *statistically* are normally rewordings of statements about statistical frequencies; they state what proportion of the members of one class are also members of another class. For example, "The probability that any given A is a B is n" might be interpreted as telling: "n percent of the members of the class of A's are also members of the class of B's." (Statisticians and inductive logicians make use of interpretations that are considerably more complex, but the added complexity does not affect the points that are here at issue.)

TENDING-TO-MAKE-PROBABLE

The relation of tending-to-make-probable is one that holds necessarily between propositions. As we have said, it may be expressed in a number of ways. For example: "e tends to make h probable"; "h is probable in relation to e" and "e confirms h."[5]

To illustrate the logic of this relation, we consider the proposition

(h) John is a Democrat

and note the probability-relations that it bears to the following propositions:

(e) 26 of the 50 people in this room are Democrats, and John is in this room
(f) 26 of the 50 people who were in this room yesterday are not Democrats, and John was in this room yesterday
(g) 45 of the 50 people who arrived on time are Democrats, and John arrived on time
(i) 99 of the 100 people who voted for the measure are not Democrats, and John voted for the measure.

We may say that: (1) e tends to make h probable; (2) e&f does not tend to make h probable; (3) e&f&g tends to make h probable; and (4) e&f&g&i tends to make not-h probable.

If a proposition e tends to make a proposition h probable, and if e&i does not tend to make h probable, then the proposition e&i may be said to *defeat* the confirmation that e tends to provide for h.'[6] The relevant concept of defeat will be defined below.

What is intended by the locution "e tends to make h probable" may be put somewhat loosely by saying: "If e were the only relevant evidence you had, then you would also have some justification for accepting h." Thus one could say of our example above: "If e were the only evidence you had, then you would have some justification for accepting h; but if, in addition to e, f were also a part of your evidence, and if e and f were the only evidence you had, then you would not have any justification for accepting h; . . . ."

We could say that, if e tends to make h probable, and if e is the only evidence you have that is *relevant* to the probability of h, then h is probable for you. But we must not expect to *define* "e tends to make h probable" by reference to the concept of relevance. We should rather define "relevance" in terms of such epistemic relations as tending to make probable.

Let us introduce this definition of the concept of a person's *total evidence*:

D2 e is the total evidence of S =Df e is the set of propositions that
are evident for S.

What we have been saying may suggest that we could now define
tending-to-make-probable this way:

e tends to make h probable =Df h is necessarily such that it is
probable for anyone for whom e is the total evidence.

But there is a theoretical difficulty involved in this type of 'definition.'[7]
Most familiar propositions are such that it is problematic whether they *can*
constitute anyone's total evidence. Consider our example once again. Is it
possible for there to be anyone whose *total evidence* could be expressed by
saying: "Most of the people in this room are Democrats and John is in this
room"? Surely anyone for whom such a proposition is evident would *also*
know something about his own sensory experiences and about his thoughts;
moreover, he would have additional knowledge about John and about
rooms and Democrats. If there *cannot* be anyone for whom that proposition
is the total evidence, then the proposed definition would require us to say
that the proposition tends to make *every* proposition probable. (If e cannot
be anyone's total evidence and if h is any proposition you like, then e is
necessarily such that: for every S, either e is not the total evidence of S, or
h is probable for S.) Our definition will not be of use to us if it requires us
to say, of the proposition, "Most of the people in this room are Democrats
and John is in this room," that it tends to make it probable that there are
unicorns and round squares on the other side of the moon. Hence we must
formulate our definition in another way.

Our proposition e ("Most of the people in this room . . .") may not be
capable of being anyone's total evidence. But it has a further feature that
gives us what we need for our definition: it is necessarily such that, *if* it is
evident for a person S, then there is *another* proposition which is evident for
S and which is such that it *could* be someone's total evidence; and this other
proposition is necessarily such that anyone for whom it *is* the total evidence
is someone for whom h is probable. And so we may modify the proposed
definition of tending-to-make-probable this way:

D3 e tends to make h probable (e confirms h) =Df e is necessarily
such that, for every x, if e is evident for x, then there is a w such
that (i) w is evident for x, (ii) w&e could be someone's total
evidence, and (iii) h is probable for anyone for whom w&e is
the total evidence.

The relevant concept of defeat is this:

> D4 d defeats e's tendency to make h probable =Df e tends to make
> h probable; and d&e does not tend to make h probable.

APPLYING THE LOGICAL RELATION

We now consider the *applied* probability relation expressed by "e makes h probable for S." The *logical* locution, "e tends to make h probable," as we have said, expresses a relation that holds necessarily between propositions. But the *applied* locution expresses a contingent proposition: it applies the necessary relation to the beliefs of a particular person.

In considering the application of probability, we must take care not to be misled by writings about so-called "subjective probability." Some writers are interested in applying the probability relation to the *set of beliefs* that a person happens to have. But the theory of knowledge is concerned with applying the relation to the person's *total evidence* and not with what it is that the person may happen to *believe*. The set of propositions that are *evident* for a given person may have members that the person does not believe; and the set of propositions that the person believes may have members that are not evident.

If one proposition *makes* another proposition probable *for* a subject S, then the second proposition may be said to *derive* the probability it has for S from the first proposition. Hence one may also put the applied probability relation by saying, "e *transmits* probability to h for S," or, as Bolzano said, "h's probability for S *accrues* from e." If we understand the making-probable relation this way, then we must say that no proposition makes *itself* probable for S (even though we *may* say that every proposition *tends* to make itself probable). How could a proposition *transmit* probability to itself? James Van Cleve has written: "The project sounds circular at best (like a witness testifying in behalf of his own credibility), impossible at worst (like a man trying to improve his own net worth by borrowing money from 'himself.'"[8] No proposition is included in its own probability-makers. Hence if one proposition makes another probable for a given subject S, then the first proposition will be such that it does *not imply* the second.

Since we are concerned with the epistemic sense of probability and therefore with the probability that a proposition may have *for* a given subject, our conception should be adequate to the following. Most of us are such that: (i) there are *necessary* statements that are *merely probable* for us; (ii) there are necessary statements that are neither probable nor improbable for us; and (iii) there may well be *impossible* statements that are *probable* for us. These facts, although they are overlooked by many writers on probability, should not be surprising. For there are some mathematical propositions that most of us are justified in accepting on *authority*. Such propositions are made probable for us by the evidence we happen to have about the authorities involved. And, if this is so, then such evidence could even transmit probability for us to propositions that are impossible.

I have said that, if e makes h probable for S, then e does not *imply* h. We may also make a further point. If one proposition makes another probable for a given subject S, then the first proposition does not *entail* the second. The relevant sense of entailment is this:

D5 e *entails* h =D e is necessarily such that whoever accepts it
    accepts h.

Thus e may imply h without entailing h. But we may assume that, if e entails h, then e also implies h.

Now we may complete our account of what it is for one proposition to make another probable *for* a particular subject:

D6 e makes h probable for S (e confirms h for S) =Df (1) e is
    evident for S; (2) e tends to make h probable; (3) there is no d
    such that d is evident for S and d defeats e's tendency to make
    h probable; and (4) e does not entail h.

Since the above definition contains the expression "any proposition that is evident for S," the definition may be said to apply the *logical* probability relation to the *total evidence* of a particular 'subject.'[9]

This definition allows us to say that some but not all necessary propositions that are evident for S are such that something makes them probable for S. And it also allows us to say that impossible propositions may be made probable for S. As we have noted, these consequences, however questionable they may seem at first, are actually desiderata for the theory of epistemic probability.

Some propositions may be said to be *epistemically necessary*: they are necessarily such that they are evident to anyone to whom anything is 'evident.'[10] These include the propositions one might express by saying "I am thinking," "I exist," "Someone exists." Our definition of "e makes h probable for S" requires us to say, perhaps counter-intuitively, that if it is evident to me that there are dogs, then the proposition that there are dogs makes probable for me the proposition that I am thinking. If we wish to avoid this consequence, we have only to add this clause to the definiens: "h is not necessarily such that it is evident for anyone for whom anything is evident." But for simplicity we will forego this complication.

We have noted that propositions that are merely probable for a subject S may yet be such that S is *more justified* in accepting some of them than in accepting others. In such cases we say that one of two merely probable propositions is *"more probable"* than the other for S. May we also assign numerical *degrees* to the probability that a proposition may have *for* a subject S?

A proposition may have a numerical probability other than 0 or 1 in relation to a *statistical* proposition — a proposition about what proportion of members of one class are members of another class. The following proposition h has a probability of .9 in relation to the statistical proposition e:

(h) John is a Democrat

(e) 45 out of the 50 people in this room are Democrats, and John is in this room.

If a proposition is thus to have a numerical probability (other than 0 or 1) *for* a subject S, then some statistical proposition must be evident for S. But the only statistical propositions that can be *evident* for an ordinary human being are *perceptual* propositions — such propositions as "4 out of 5 of the people that I see are standing." Except, then, in those cases where the basis of numerical assignment is perceptual, it seems highly problematic whether a merely probable proposition can be said to have any numerical degree for persons such as you and me. My own belief is that much work remains to be done in theory of knowledge before we are ready to deal with this important question. In any case, we cannot answer the question until we are clear about what it is for one proposition to make another proposition probable *for* a given subject.

AN OBJECTION CONSIDERED

We are now in a position to answer a familiar objection to the use of the concept of total evidence in the application of the probability relation. The objection has been put clearly by A. J. Ayer:

> But why *have* we to take as evidence the total evidence available to us, whatever that may mean? What sort of principle is this? It can hardly be a *moral* principle. So far as morality goes, we might equally well choose to rely on the evidence which yielded the highest degree of confirmation for the hypothesis in which we were interested, or on that which yielded the lowest, or on whatever evidence we found most pleasing. Unless we miscalculate, the result at which we arrive will in each case be a necessary truth; and there can surely be no moral reason for preferring one of these necessary truths to any 'other.'[11]

The supposed difficulty stems from failure to distinguish between formal probability statements and applied probability statements. Formal probability statements are necessary truths. But the need to refer to one's total evidence concerns only probability statements. Applied probability statements are contingent; every such statement is a function of the total evidence that the person in question happens to have. And the total evidence that one has at one time need not be the same as the total evidence that one has at another time.

Why, then, should we refer to a person's total evidence when we want to know what probability a certain hypothesis happens to have for that person? The answer is simple. The probability that a hypothesis has for a given person at a given time is that probability that the person's total evidence *confers upon* that proposition.

A MORAL ANALOGY

It may be that a moral analogy will throw light upon the probability relation and its 'application.'[12] Let us consider briefly the logic of *moral requirement*. Examples of moral requirement, as here understood, are: making a promise requires keeping the promise; wronging a person requires making up for the wrong; virtue (if Kant is right) requires being rewarded; and performing a sinful act requires punishment and repentance. The analogy between requirement and confirmation may be seen by constructing an example which parallels our illustration above of confirmation. For requirement may be defeated in just the ways in which confirmation may be defeated.

Consider the proposition

(h) The doctor should administer medical treatment to John

and note the requirement-relations that it bears to the following propositions:

(k) John is seriously ill; and the doctor is in a position to treat him
(f) John's wife is seriously ill; the doctor is in a position to treat her; but the doctor is in a position to treat only one of them
(g) The doctor is himself seriously ill and his treating John would aggravate John's illness
(i) If the doctor were to treat John, the treatment would temporarily aggravate John's illness but would subsequently cure the illness; and the illness of Jones' wife cannot be treated or relieved.

We may say that: (1) k requires h; (2) k&f does not require h; (3) k&f&g requires not-h; and (4) k&f&g&i requires h.

The relevant concept of *defeat* is this:

D7   s defeats p's requirement for q   =Df   (i) p requires q, (ii) p&s does not require q, and (iii) p&s is logically compatible with q.

The example enables us to understand W. D. Ross's distinction between *prima facie* duties (something *requires* one to act in a certain way) and absolute duties (one *ought* to act in a certain way).[13] And thus they enable us to say in what sense there *can* be said to be a conflict of duties (there can be conflicts of *prima facie* duties) and in what sense there can *not* be said to be a conflict of duties (there cannot be conflicts of absolute duties).

Thus we could say:

D8   S has an absolute duty to perform A   =Df   There occurs an x such that x requires S to perform A, and there occurs no y such that y defeats x's requirement that S perform A.

This absolute sense of duty is analogous, then, to the absolute sense of the probability relation.[14]

NOTES

1. The quotation is from F. C. Benenson, *Probability, Objectivity and Evidence* (London: Routledge & Kegan Paul, 1984), p. 14.

2. Cicero uses *probabilitas* in setting forth the views of the skeptics in his *Academica*, Loeb Classical Library edition, *De Natura Deorum, Academica* (New York: G. P. Putnam's Sons, 1933); see, for example, II, xxxix (pp. 588, 600).

3. "To say that the probability of *h* on *e* is high means that *e* gives strong support to the assumption of *h*, that *h* is highly confirmed by *e*, or, in terms of application to a knowledge situation: if an observer *X* knows *e*, say, on the basis of direct observations, and nothing else, then he has good reasons for expecting the unknown facts described by *h*. . . . [T]his explanation [probability as a measure of evidential support] may be said to outline the primary and simplest meaning of probability$_1$." Rudolf Carnap, *Logical Foundations of Probability* (Chicago: The University of Chicago Press, 1950), p. 164.

4. There is a clear discussion of the significance of this distinction in John Pollock, *Contemporary Theories of Knowledge* (Totowa: Rowman and Littlefield, 1986), p. 96ff.

5. The mathematical theory of probability investigates a somewhat more complex relation. One version of this more complex relation may be put as: "h is

more probable than i in relation to e." The simpler relation with which we are here concerned may be defined in terms of the more complex relation as: "h is more probable than not-h in relation to e." This more complex relation is taken as primitive by Harold Jeffries, in *Theory of Probability* (Oxford: The Clarendon Press, 1939). Jeffries uses the expression: "Given p, q is more probable than r" (see p. 16).

6. I discussed the generic concept of defeat in detail in "The Ethics of Requirement," *American Philosophical Quarterly*, Vol. I (1964), pp. 147-153. An improved and expanded version is in "Practical Reason and the Logic of Requirement," in Stephan Körner, ed., *Practical Reason* (Oxford: Basil Blackwell, 1974), pp. 1-17; see also "Reply to Comments," pp. 40-53. Compare the distinction between two types of defeat in John Pollock, *Knowledge and Justification* (Princeton: Princeton University Press, 1974), pp. 42-43; and Ernest Sosa, "The Foundations of Foundationalism," *Nous*, Vol. 14 (1980), pp. 547-564; esp. pp. 563-564.

7. Such a definition was suggested by Rudolf Carnap: "To say that the hypothesis *h* has the probability *p* (say 3/5) with respect to the evidence *e*, means that for anyone to whom this evidence but no other relevant evidence is available, it would be reasonable to believe in *h* to the degree *p*, or, more exactly, it would be unreasonable for him to bet on *h* at odds higher than p:(1-p) (in the example, 3:2)." R. Carnap, "Statistical and Inductive Probability," in E. Madden, ed., *The Structure of Scientific Thought* (Boston: Houghton Mifflin Company, 1960), pp. 269-284; the quotation is from p. 270.

8. James Van Cleve, "Epistemic Supervenience and the Circle of Belief," *The Monist*, Vol. 58 (1984), pp. 90-101; the quotation appears on page 100. It should be noted that Van Cleve is here talking about the applied relation of making-evident rather than about that of making-probable.

9. Bernard Bolzano seems to have been the first to be clear about this point. More recent philosophers who have stressed the concept of total evidence in applying the logical probability relation are John Maynard Keynes, Rudolf Carnap, and William Kneale. See Bernard Bolzano, *Theory of Science*, ed., Rolf George (Oxford: Basil Blackwell, 1972), p. 238; compare also pp. 238-245 and 359-365. Bolzano's work was first published in 1837. Compare John Maynard Keynes, *A Treatise on Probability* (London: Macmillan and Co., Ltd., 1921), p. 4; Rudolf Carnap, *Logical Foundations of Probability*, pp. 246-252, and "Statistical and Inductive Probability," p. 270; and William Kneale, *Probability and Induction* (Oxford: The Clarendon Press, 1949), esp. pp. 9-13.

10. Compare the discussion of this concept by Keith Lehrer and Keith Quillan, in "Chisholm on Certainty," in Radu J. Bogdan, ed., *Profiles: Roderick M. Chisholm* (Dordrecht: D. Reidel, 1986), pp. 157-168.

11. A. J. Ayer, "The Conception of Probability as a Logical Relation," in Stephan Körner, ed., *Observation and Interpretation* (London: Butterworths Publications Ltd., 1957), pp. 12-17; the quotation appears on page 14. Ayer's paper is reprinted in Edward Madden, ed., *The Structure of Scientific Thought* (Boston: Houghton Mifflin Company, 1960), pp. 279-284.

12. I have discussed this analogy in more detail in "Epistemic Reasoning and the Logic of Epistemic Concepts," in G. H. von Wright, ed., *Logic and Philosophy* (The Hague: Martinus Nijhoff, 1980), pp. 71-78.

13. See W. D. Ross, *The Right and the Good* (Oxford: The Clarendon Press, 1930), p. 18.

14. There are other ethical situations that throw light upon the concept of defeat. Within the theory of intrinsic value, we may say of certain states of affairs not only that they are, say, good, but also that they are *indefeasibly good* — where an indefeasibly good state of affairs is a good state of affairs which is such that there is *no* state of affairs that would defeat its goodness. We have left open here the question of whether this concept is applicable in epistemology. I have discussed indefeasible good and evil in *Brentano and Intrinsic Value* (Cambridge: Cambridge University Press, 1986), Chapter VIII.

8
Knowledge Reconsidered

Keith Lehrer

I have been grateful to the philosophical world for the attention *Knowledge* received in the periodical literature.[1] After fourteen years, I should be surprised and disappointed if I still believed exactly what I wrote then. My recent reflections and writings on the theory of knowledge developed out of the many important and useful criticisms of my earlier effort and seem to me to be consistent with the theory of *Knowledge.* I have, however, changed my mind in various respects. This chapter represents the state of my art.

The earlier work sought to define justification in terms of probability relative to a background system. I no longer think that is tenable. Justification may be defined in terms of reasonableness which contains probability as a factor, a critically important factor, but there are other factors that are not reducible to probability. The subjective account of complete justification in *Knowledge* was supplemented with an account of justification not being defeated by the correction of errors in the justifying background system. I, like Pollock, still defend the notion that undefeated justification is the basis of knowledge, but I would offer a more objective account of complete justification.[2] The requirement in *Knowledge* that justification be undefeated incorporated a condition similar to what Goldman has called *reliabilism.*[3] An objective probability of truth greater than competitors relative to the background system was required for undefeated justification. My sort of probabilism was systematic rather than historical, however. I do not think it is a necessary condition of knowledge or justification that a belief have some specified causal history.

Coherence remains for me the central notion in epistemology, though I insist with Cohen that there must be some connection between the justification of a belief and the truth of the belief.[4] In this, I differ from pure internalists. The dispute between externalism and internalism is not so clear cut as the defenders of each position think, however. Enlightened internalists, those maintaining the justification of a belief can be completely determined by reflection, Chisholm for example, are left with the need to deal with the Gettier problem.[5] In so doing, they naturally require that justification not be connected with falsity, and this requirement imposes an external condition. The purest internalists who bar external conditions from entering into an account of justification find externalism creeping in through Gettier's back door. Enlightened externalists, Goldman, for example, find it necessary to require that a person not believe anything which would undermine beliefs arising from external processes, thus introducing reference to background beliefs, that is, to internal conditions. As a rough and ready aid to the classification of theories, I have no objection to the distinction between externalism and internalism, but the dispute over the matter is more useful for igniting dialectic passion than for reaching the truth in the matter. Knowledge arises when there is the appropriate sort of match between all of what a person believes and external reality. The object of epistemology is to find the right mix of internal factors and external relationships to explicate what is required.

I shall, instead of attempting to refine distinctions between one kind of theory and another for the purpose of proceeding to bash the category of my adversary, help myself to what insights I find in the work of others and see whether this strategy might yield better results. I shall, accordingly, combine aspects of theories advocated by foundation theorists, causal theorists, faculty theorists, and what have you, to articulate the sort of coherence theory I wish to defend. If the resulting theory seems to be more of some other sort of theory than a coherence theory, I would not protest against another label. A critic of another theory of mine, a theory of consensus, once dubbed it a monster theory. Since the theory I shall present contains what may seem an unnatural combination of ingredients, I propose to call it the *monster* theory. I hope to convince you the monster is an admirable one, deserving of friendly treatment, though requiring some discipline to render it domestically acceptable.

THE MONSTER THEORY

The theory has two components. One is definitional or formal. This constitutes an analysis or explication of knowledge. It leaves open substantive issues. The formal analysis of knowledge I shall offer is compatible with a wide variety of epistemologies, among them some foundation theories for example. I think it advisable to distinguish this part of the theory from those parts that should be more controversial, though there is no dearth of philosophers inclined to controvert what follows next. I shall present the key definitions and explain them.

DK. S knows that p at t if and only if (i) p, (ii) S accepts that p at t, (iii) S is justified in accepting that p at t, and (iv) there is nothing that defeats the justification that S for accepting p at t.

This definition is intended to be a definition schema of the open sentence to the left of the "if and only if" rather than one implicitly quantified over some domain of entities for the variable p. That is a nicety, but I wish to leave open the question of whether knowing is a relation between a subject and a class of entities, propositions for example. The definition is traditional and is correct as far as it goes. It is insufficiently articulate to meet objections or to provide the sort of illumination philosophers demand of theories, or at least of the theories of others, however. One can reasonably request explication of the key terms, "justified" and "undefeated" for example, but this in no way implies the definition is incorrect or otherwise unsatisfactory.

A word of comment about the nature of analysis may be useful before proceeding to define the so far undefined notions. Analysis rests on an equivalence relation. I do not claim an analysis is an equivalence holding for all conceivable cases. Some examples, though conceivable, are not really consistent. Reid made the point long ago that conceivability is not an adequate test of logical possibility.[6] I do not claim the analysis holds even for all logically possible cases. The definition should be thought of more like a definition of "force" in physics. It is a nomological equivalence. Thus, I would rule out as irrelevant any test case that was inconsistent with the laws of nature even if it was logically possible. For the most part, discussion proceeds in terms of such cases and so I do not think this restriction is really novel. Another respect in which the intended definition is like the definition of "force" in physics is that, once the primitive terms are themselves defined, the defined notion should be more precise than the ordinary notion. As a result, some borderline cases of knowledge as the term is ordinarily applied may be excluded as not being cases of knowledge in the more precise defined sense. Such borderline cases like logical possibilities that are nomologically impossible may be of interest, but they do not constitute test cases for the definition, that is, they cannot serve as counterexamples.

Finally, I make no assumption that the notions used to define "know" are ordinary notions. They are technical. As will become clear, some of them are my creations, or so I believe. A colleague remarked he could find no reason to believe the ordinary conception of knowledge, assuming there to be such a thing, must be such that there would be other ordinary conceptions constituting necessary and sufficient conditions. That may be true, but it is irrelevant, I think, to a philosophical and historically adequate conception of analysis. Philosophers have not for the most part tried to define ordinary terms or concepts in terms of other ordinary terms or concepts, though they sometimes have said and more often thought they were doing so. They have created new terms and conceptions to use to analyze some target term or concept. I think this is obvious from the history of science and philosophy. A more controversial claim is that we create new terms and concepts that cannot be defined in terms of the old ones. That I also hold, but this is not the place to argue for it.

With those remarks on behalf of DK, let me explain my intentions in attempting to analyze the conditions employed in DK. It is not my attempt to finally arrive at some ultimate conceptual primitives used to define all the rest. I shall, in fact, begin by taking a locution as primitive, but I do not wish to be taken as an advocate of a compositional theory of concept formation. According to such a theory, all concepts that we understand are understood by us because they reduce by definition to some primitive concepts we initially understand. I doubt the compositional theory of concept formation is true. There is an intelligible notion of a term or concept being primitive relative to some system we develop. What is primitive relative to one system, however, may be defined in another system containing the same total set of terms or concepts as the first. I shall take some terms as primitive relative to the system I develop, but I do not claim what I take as primitive is metaphysically or psychologically primitive. Anything taken as primitive in one system may be defined in another system or in an expansion of the original. Nothing is ultimately undefinable.

What we can achieve in philosophy is the articulation of principles, among them definitions or equivalence principles, compatible with the laws of nature, including the laws of human nature. If, therefore, my analysis yields the result that subhuman, superhuman, diminished human, or nonhuman beings do not know anything, that is consistent with my purposes. I am concerned with human knowledge. There are, I am sure, states very like human knowledge which other beings possess, but that is not my concern here.

ACCEPTANCE

I shall take the term "accept" as primitive, but my use of it requires some explanation. Reflection on various cases of knowledge have convinced me that, though there is some common positive propositional attitude toward the content known, that is, that p, there is no ordinary use of any term exactly coinciding with the required propositional attitude. I use the expression 'propositional attitude' for the sake of tradition to describe such mental attitudes as believing, thinking, and accepting such and such without committing myself to the doctrine that these attitudes are relations to a proposition. I use the term "content" in the theory-neutral sense to refer to what the person believes, thinks, or accepts. It is a special use of the term "accepts" I employ. When I say a person accepts that p at t, I mean the person accepts that p for the specific purpose of obtaining truth and avoiding error with respect to p. The point of these qualifications is that a person may accept something for a variety of purposes, to increase felicity by accepting what one would like to be true, or to please someone else who is keen on having one accept what they say, but these purposes are not the ones germane to knowledge. The purposes of obtaining truth and avoiding error are the relevant ones. Even accepting p for these general purposes is not sufficient, however, in that one might think accepting p is useful for the purpose of accepting other things that are true and avoiding accepting other things that are false, while having no idea whether p is true. Such acceptance for these general purposes is not what is required for knowledge either. What is required is a certain kind of acceptance of p specifically aimed at being correct about p and avoiding being mistaken about p.

My reasons for preferring acceptance to belief as a condition of knowledge are partly theoretical and partly linguistic. The term "accept" in one of its uses seems to me to be a relative term in which there is some implicit reference to some purpose or aim, while the term "believe" does not have this feature. Of course, belief like acceptance may arise from a variety of causes, some being related to the truth of the content, such as vision, and others being unrelated, such as wishful thinking, as Goldman has insisted.[7] But believing something, however caused, is not a relative conception in the way accepting something is. To accept something is to accept something for a purpose, to please another, to make one happy, to concede something for the sake of argument, or, finally, to obtain truth. What one accepts for one purpose, moreover, one may reject for another. This aspect of acceptance or "acceptance" is a useful feature of the notion or term in the analysis. The required propositional attitude in the analysis of knowledge is one having truth seeking as its purpose. In *Knowledge*, where I used the notion of belief, it was necessary to select a subclass of beliefs, those the person would retain if solely interested in obtaining truth and avoiding error, which introduced a counterfactual element unnecessarily. The notion of acceptance allows us to build in the purpose of truth seeking without introducing any counterfactual element.

There is another more theoretical and psychological reason for preferring acceptance to belief. Belief sometimes arises in an individual against his or her better judgment. It also sometimes fails to arise when one's better judgment tells one it should. The point is not that acceptance is voluntary, though some kinds of acceptance are voluntary in some instances, but that belief and rational judgment may sometimes conflict. When, on the basis of the evidence one rationally affirms p, one accepts that p whether or not this produces belief. Such acceptance plays a determinate role in inference and further acceptance without necessarily yielding belief. A student of a certain sort, one lacking confidence, may always feel he will fail each examination before taking it, though, being, in fact, a brilliant and a thorough scholar, he knows he will pass the typical midterm graded by a generous instructor. His feeling he will fail deters us from saying he believes he will pass, though, on the basis of evidence about his abilities, preparation, past successes, and dispositions of the instructor, he, when seeking to accept what is true, accepts he will pass. He knows he will pass. The problem is that the rational intellect, or, in more modern terms, the central system, does not always determine belief. We may know something is the case before we believe it; indeed, our knowing it to be the case may result in our coming to believe it. In short, there may be conflict between a lower-level unreflective system and a higher-level reflective one. Acceptance without belief may result when there is an absence of belief corresponding to what one accepts in the interests of obtaining truth and avoiding error.

The foregoing remarks should not be taken as implying that acceptance of the required sort must always be reflective. In receiving information, we have need of a system that is virtually automatic in responding to sensory evidence. So belief carries over into acceptance unless there is conflict with background information. When there is conflict, belief and acceptance may diverge. Thus a person accepts that p exactly when the person either believes that p without conflict with background information or reflectively judges that p on the basis of background information. When there is no conflict between belief and background information, there is a kind of routine positive evaluation by something like a central cognitive system, but that is psychological speculation only and no part of my account of acceptance.

Perhaps the simplest account of acceptance may be put as follows. When a person considers and judges that p, the person comes into a mental state that has a certain sort of functional role in thought and inference. A person may come to be in a similar mental state having a similar functional role in thought and inference without the state having arisen from such consideration and judgment. A mental state having the appropriate sort of functional role with respect to the content that p is what I have referred to as accepting that p. It is not essential to such a mental state having such a functional role that a person have considered and judged that p, though it may arise in that way. Of course, if the state of accepting that p does not arise from consideration and judgment, the person will not think or infer that he or she did consider and judge that p, but he or she may otherwise use the content that p in the same manner as one who did so judge. Thus, accepting that p is a mental state assigning a similar functional role to the content that p in truth seeking inference and thought as a mental state arising from considering and judging that p. Accepting that p is a sort of positive attitude toward a content, that p, resulting in employment of the content, that p, as background information in thought and inference.

The notion of acceptance gives rise to the notion of an acceptance system, a system articulating what a person accepts, which replaces the notion of a corrected doxastic system in *Knowledge* as the justification-generating system. The acceptance system is defined as follows:

D1. A system X is an acceptance system of S if and only if X contains just statements of the form — S accepts that p — attributing to S just those things that S accepts with the objective of obtaining truth and avoiding error with respect to the specific thing accepted.

JUSTIFICATION

Justification arises, as I have argued and continue to aver, from coherence with a background system. This proposal is expressed in the following schema:

D2. S is justified in accepting that p at t on the basis of system X of S at t if and only if p coheres with the system X of S at t.

I shall first give a formal rather than a material account of justification by defining justification in terms of a comparative notion of reasonableness. The account is formal in the sense that epistemologists advocating diverse theories of justification could, consistent with their substantive differences, accept the definition in question. A foundation theorist could claim that what makes one thing more reasonable than another is some relation to a foundation whose reasonableness is not derived from anything else. A reliabilist could maintain that what makes one thing more reasonable than another is that the first is the result of a more reliable process, and so forth. Thus, the sort of definition I shall offer, if not theory neutral, is compatible with most current theories of justification.

I shall eventually offer some account of the notion of reasonableness. Here, however, I shall, following Chisholm, take as primitive the notion of one thing being more reasonable for a person than another. I shall sometimes apply this notion in a relativized extended manner and speak of it being more reasonable for a person to accept p than q on one assumption than on another on the basis of some system X at some time t. For the sake of formal elegance, the latter relativized expression might be taken as primitive and the notions that are not relativized to any assumptions or systems could be defined in terms of the relativized expression by treating the assumptions as vacuous and the system as empty.

It has been my contention that a person is justified in accepting something just in case either any skeptical hypothesis a skeptic might raise to shed doubt on what the person accepts is less reasonable for the person to accept than what is called in question, or it is no less reasonable for the person to accept the skeptical hypothesis conjoined with some consideration neutralizing the skeptical impact than to accept the skeptical hypothesis alone. In *Knowledge,* I assumed such skeptical hypotheses must be less probable than what they call into question, but the requirement now seems to me too restrictive. My claim that I see my hand before me is more probable and more reasonable than the skeptical hypothesis that my senses are deceiving me. My claim is, however, no more probable or reasonable than the skeptical observation that our senses sometimes deceive us. This observation, which sheds doubt on my claim that I see my hand before me, is, however, neutralized by the observation that my senses are not now deceiving me.

Treating skeptical hypotheses as competitors we may, therefore, define notions of a competitor, of beating a competitor, and of neutralizing a competitor as follows.

D3. S is justified in accepting p at t on the basis of system X of S at t if and only if all competitors of p are beaten or neutralized for S on X at t.

D4. c competes with p for S on X at t if and only if it is more reasonable for S to accept that p on the assumption that c is false than on the assumption that c is true on the basis of X at t.

D5. p beats c for S on X at t if and only if c competes with p for S on X at t, and it is more reasonable for S to accept p than to accept c on X at t.

D6. n neutralizes c as a competitor of p for S on X at t if and only if c competes with p for S on X at t, the conjunction of c and n does not compete with p for S on X at t, and it is as reasonable for S to accept the conjunction of c and n as to accept c alone on X at t.

This formal definition of justification does not presuppose a coherence theory of justification and is, as I have noted, consistent with competing theories of knowledge and justification.

A comment on my use of the skeptic and her hypotheses is essential. I am not supposing that a person who is justified in accepting something has considered any skeptical hypotheses. I have never before considered the hypothesis that there is a submicroscopic beetle, the brain beetle, that lives in all our brains and, when actively moving about among the cerebral passageways during procreation, disturbs the connections in the occipital lobes producing visual hallucination. But it is and was, even prior to my imagining the existence of the brain beetle, more reasonable for me to believe I see my hand than that such a hypothesis is true. I would explain the greater reasonableness of the one belief than the other in terms of background beliefs about hands and beetles, but the fact of the greater reasonableness of one than the other is, I contend, more obvious than any philosophical explanation of the fact. I do not suggest a skeptic would be moved by this claim or that it is an adequate reply to a philosophical skeptic. My use of the skeptic and her skeptical machinations is merely a heuristic device to focus attention on competitors of a given claim.

These definitions may also be consistent with an approach that might seem quite at odds with them, namely, the proposal of Dretske that skeptical alternatives are irrelevant to whether one knows.[8] It would be possible to interpret him as maintaining that, even though the skeptical hypotheses compete with other claims and cannot be beaten or neutralized, they are nevertheless irrelevant to whether a person knows. Of course, Dretske has denied justification is a condition of knowledge, but I think it would be implausible to interpret him as claiming irrelevant alternatives are unbeaten and unneutralized competitors. On the contrary, it seems more reasonable to interpret his claims as implying the irrelevant skeptical alternatives are not really competitors, though they might seem to be. I would find that claim philosophically odd, but it seems to me in the spirit of Dretske's position to claim skeptical alternatives do not count, epistemically speaking. I, on the contrary, think skeptical alternatives do count, that is, are competitors, because the usual perceptual claims seem to me to be less reasonable on the assumption that the skeptical hypotheses are true than on the assumption that they are false. Another possible interpretation of the relevant alternatives approach within the present framework is to admit the skeptical alternatives are competitors but to contend they are beaten as a consequence of their irrelevance. The definitions are, I propose, logically consistent with the relevant alternatives approach.

It is now, however, time to turn to the more substantiative issue of what makes a person justified in accepting something. My answer is that what makes a person justified in accepting something is coherence with a background system, but I contend there is more than one sort of system and, consequently, more than one sort of justification required for knowledge. It would be possible to define one sort of justification, undefeated justification, that logically implies all the others, but it is more illuminating intuitively to break down this notion of justification into components. The first sort of justification is relative to the acceptance system of a person specified above. We may define it as follows:

D7. S is personally justified in accepting that p at t if and only if S is justified in accepting that p on the basis of the acceptance system of S at t.

Notice this definition does not employ the notion of coherence. Coherence enters into the determination of justification by determining whether one thing is more or less reasonable to accept than another. Thus,

D2. S is justified in accepting that p at t on the basis of the system X of S at t if and only if p coheres with the system X of S at t

is a substantiative claim about justification. The substantiative issues in epistemology depend on what makes something justified and, hence, on my view of the matter, on what makes something cohere with some system.

What makes something cohere in the relevant sense with the acceptance system of a person to yield personal justification? The objectives of justification are to obtain truth and avoid error with respect to the thing accepted. So coherence in the relevant sense depends on what the acceptance system tells us about our chances of obtaining those objectives. Hence, in *Knowledge* I argued coherence was a matter of probability, subjective or personal probability. Probability still strikes as a determinant, but the story is more complicated for familiar reasons. Explanatory power, which Sellars and Harman consider a a central determinant, may be reflected, I have argued, in high prior probability assignments.[9] There is nothing to preclude us from assigning a higher prior probability to explanatory hypotheses. At some point, however, explanatory power requires explanatory comprehensiveness, and, given the conjunction principles concerning probability, a reduction in probability. In seeking to obtain truth and avoid error, we are interested in obtaining the whole truth, as well as in obtaining nothing but the truth, and the acceptance of the whole truth would involve greater risk of error than accepting only a part. Something must make the risk reasonable, and what makes it reasonable cannot be probability. For the probability diminishes as truth becomes more comprehensive. To take the example above, it is just as reasonable for me to accept the conjunction that our senses sometimes deceive us *and* that my eyes do not deceive me when I now see my hand as to accept simply that our senses sometimes deceive us, but the conjunction is not as probable. What makes the conjunction as reasonable is the fuller description and removal of the false innuendo that my eyes might be deceiving me.

One principal determinant of what makes it more reasonable to accept one thing than another on the basis of my acceptance system is what I accept about the conditions under which some source, method, or state is trustworthy in the quest for truth and the avoidance of error. I accept that the testimony of others is, under various circumstances, a trustworthy guide to truth, just as I accept that my eyes are, under various circumstances, a trustworthy guide. In some instances, it is some state of myself, a distinct memory of something, of my telephone number for example, I accept as a trustworthy guide to truth. What I accept about the trustworthiness of states of acceptance themselves provides a doxastic connection between acceptance and truth. I accept that certain states of acceptance are trustworthy guides to truth, and, since justification aims at truth, those states of acceptance are justified for me on the basis of my acceptance system. In this way, to use a metaphor from Glymour, my acceptance system bootstraps what I accept to justified acceptance.[10]

The preceding remarks indicate the truth in reliabilism and other causal, nomological, and counterfactual theories of knowledge. The truth is a doxastic truth. It is the result of doxastic ascent. We not only accept things about the external world, we also accept things about the connection between ourselves, about what we judge and believe, and the external world. I do not, of course, suggest the doxastic connection is the result of deliberation, though few escape the burden of reflecting on when their internal states are trustworthy, and those few suffer a disability. As I noted above, however, we accept things we have never thought about, and everyone trusts their senses and draws inferences on the assumption that they are to be trusted. For that reason, I maintain people accept things about the trustworthiness of their mental states, acceptance included, because their thoughts and inferences exhibit a state functionally similar to one arising from conscious consideration of the matter.

THE TRILEMMA

The foregoing remarks raise a problem the solution of which provides the solution to a traditional epistemological problem. The new problem and the old are closely connected. The new problem is that if justified acceptance that p requires, as I allege, accepting the acceptance of p as a trustworthy guide to truth, the question naturally arises as to whether this higher-order acceptance must itself be justified. If so, this would require further doxastic ascent, acceptance that the higher-order acceptance was trustworthy, and a regress threatens. Before turning to the solution to the problem, we will find it useful to notice a similarity between this problem and a traditional trilemma. The trilemma was formulated by Sextus Empiricus by contending justification must either proceed in a circle, lead to a regress, or be ended by some mere assumption.[11] The third alternative has been described by a modern author as an artificial breaking off of inquiry.[12]

The traditional problem might be formulated as follows. The sort of justification required for knowledge must be justification for accepting that p for the purpose of obtaining truth and avoiding error with respect to the claim that p. To have this sort of justification one must at least accept that accepting p is a trustworthy means to the purpose in question. But merely accepting this is insufficient. One must be justified in accepting it. Such justification would lead either to a circle, to a regress, or to the mere assumption that something is justified. Foundation theories have traditionally embraced the third alternative. They affirm something is immediately, directly, or intrinsically self-justified and have been favored by many for that reason. Externalist and reliabilist solutions have either denied justification is necessary for knowledge or affirmed that some beliefs are justified because of the causal, nomological, counterfactual, or statistical relationship to truth. Denying knowledge requires justification does not, of course, solve the trilemma with respect to justification, and the other solution is like the solution of the foundationalist.

There is a correct insight in these solutions, but, in my opinion, there is something philosophically unsatisfying in them. The dissatisfaction with the foundationalist is that it abrogates the connection between justification and truth. Justification has as its purpose the attainment of truth and the avoidance of error, and, as a result, the mere postulation or assumption that something is justified, even if it is, leaves one with an unanswered question. What reason have we for thinking such intrinsic justification serves the purpose of attaining truth and avoiding error? The reliabilist and his externalist cohorts supply an answer to the question, namely, that there is some specified connection between justification and truth, for example, that the belief-forming process instantiates some truth productive rule or method. Their solution leaves us with a residual dissatisfaction. If their account is correct, then, though we can see the justified beliefs of another serve the purpose of attaining truth and avoiding error, the person having the belief might have no idea his or her beliefs serve the purpose in question. To see the point, suppose a person is justified in some belief solely on reliabilist grounds but has no idea of these grounds at all. Imagine she asks herself the following question: "What reason have I for thinking this belief is justified for the purpose of attaining truth or avoiding error?" Her answer must be, "None whatever." Hence the dissatisfaction with this solution to the trilemma. Both solutions have something to offer, but what they omit is the doxastic connection supplying a person with a reason, whether appealed to or not, for thinking accepting what one does serves the interests of truth. On the other hand, the attempt to supply such a reason in every case appears to lead to a circle or a regress the avoidance of which is an attraction of the views considered.

There is a solution to the trilemma which, at the same time, solves the problem of doxastic ascent. The first step in the solution is to recall once again that a person may accept something she has not considered. Such acceptance is a mental state having a functional role in thought and inference similar to a mental state arising from conscious consideration and judgment except for those thoughts and inferences pertaining to the process of consideration and judgment. This step allows me to contend people accept they are trustworthy evaluators of truth and error, though they have not consciously considered the matter in these terms. When I say people accept they are trustworthy evaluators of truth and error, I mean this plays a role in their thought and inference. A person who sees her black hair thinks of herself as black haired, draws inferences in accord with this, for example, that her hair is darker than blond and that she should check *black* next to hair color on her military identification papers. All this shows she accepts that she can tell the color of her hair when she sees it, that is, that she can determine the truth of the matter. When, however, I say a person accepts that she is a trustworthy evaluator of truth, I do not mean to suggest she accepts that she can tell whether every claim is true or false. What I mean by saying a person is a trustworthy evaluator of truth and error is that when she accepts something as true for the purpose of accepting what is true and avoiding accepting what is false, her accepting what she does is a trustworthy guide to truth in the matter. It is to say she has the capacity to accept what is true and avoid accepting what is false. To say someone has such a capacity is not to say she is an infallible guide to truth. A person may be trustworthy, though fallible, in the quest for truth as in other matters. A trustworthy bookkeeper may be paid richly for her trustworthiness, though her work is not entirely free from error.

With these preliminary remarks before us, let us consider how to solve the problems in question. It is clear that the claim

T. I am a trustworthy evaluator of truth

has a special potency for supplying me with a reason for regarding acceptance as serving the purpose of attaining truth and avoiding error. For, whatever I accept for this purpose, principle T supplies me with a reason for thinking what I accept is true, to wit, that my accepting something is a trustworthy guide to truth. A person could reason, though he need not, that I accept that p in the interests of attaining truth and avoiding error, and, since I am a trustworthy evaluator of truth, my accepting p indicates that p is true. So every regress is ended and every circle avoided by appeal to T, except, of course, when T itself comes into question.

What are we to say with respect to T itself? Am I intrinsically justified in accepting T? Does the attempt to justify T take us to an ever higher level of doxastic ascent generating a regress? Or does the attempt to justify T lead us in a short circle in which T provides us with a reason for accepting itself? There is a sense in which the answer to all of these questions is positive. Let us begin with the last. Thomas Reid articulated a similar principle, though he put the matter in a negative form, affirming our faculties are not fallacious.[13] He went on to say that as evidence resembles light in many respects, so it resembles light in that as light reveals the illuminated object it also reveals itself. The obvious point is that just as principle T has the capacity to provide a reason for accepting the other things we do, so it provides us with a reason for accepting itself. The argument is short and neat. If I accept p, whatever p might be, in the quest for truth, principle T provides me with a reason for thinking my acceptance is a guide to truth, for that is what T tells me. But then, let principle T be what I accept. If I accept T in the interests of obtaining truth and avoiding error, principle T provides me with a reason for thinking my acceptance of T is a guide to truth, for principle T is perfectly general in application.

It is easy to explain how a person becomes justified in accepting T when the person, in fact, accepts that T. The following is a true principle:

> TR   If S accepts that T at t, then it is more reasonable for S to accept that T than to accept the denial of T on the basis of the acceptance system of S at t.

TR appears to me, unless the acceptance system of S is quite peculiar, to imply

> If S accepts T at t, then all competitors of T are either beaten or neutralized on the basis of the acceptance system of S at t,

which in turn implies

> If S accepts that T at t, then S is personally justified in accepting that T at t.

I do not think that it is necessarily true that it is more reasonable for a person to accept what he or she does than to accept its denial. If, for example, a person were to accept the denial of T, then the person might accept many other things even though it was no more reasonable for the person to accept those things than their denials. Indeed, any acceptance system not containing the acceptance of T, or something having similar consequences, seems likely to be a system in which it is no more reasonable for a person to accept what he or she does than to accept the denial. In the absence of any views about whether one's accepting something is a guide to truth, the mere fact that one accepts it is no reason for one to suppose it to be true. So, T has the following peculiarity. For a person to be justified in accepting anything, the person must accept T or something having similar consequences, and if the person does accept T, then the person is justified in accepting T as well as other things, though not necessarily all other things, the person accepts. Thus, principle T is surely a bootstrapping principle, pulling itself up by its own bootstraps, but it is also a make-or-break principle for the justification of other things as well.

Given the correctness of TR and what it implies, one might be inclined to argue, as did Reid, that TR is a first principle, the foundation or the root of justification and knowledge. Acceptance of T has many of the features of a basic belief in foundational epistemology, and I have no objection to the suggestion that either T or TR is a first principle. I would, however, note that principle T may be confirmed and established through experience. Someone accepting that principle would as the result of experience learn to modify and qualify what they subsequently accept about the world, but that principle would be supported rather than undermined by such experience. So T is not beyond confirmation, though, to be sure, such confirmation presupposes acceptance of it. More important, however, principle TR has an important feature other proposed foundational principles lack. The content of T provides an explanation of why one is justified in accepting TR. Principle T tells me my accepting something is a guide to truth. The purpose of justification is to obtain truth and avoid error in what I accept. Therefore, the content of principle T explains why I am justified in accepting it, namely, that my accepting it is a means to fulfilling the purpose of justification.

Other principles proposed as first principles, ones affirming that when a person accepts something about his present mental states or distinctly perceived objects, the person is justified in accepting what he accepts, leave us without any explanation of why someone interested in truth should be justified in accepting those things. It may be implicitly assumed that a person will accept that what one accepts about one's present mental states or objects one distinctly perceives are very unlikely to be in error, that is, are a trustworthy guide to truth, and is justified in so doing. If that is explicitly assumed, however, the alleged first principle concerning present mental states and distinct perceptions can be justified by appeal to a more general principle telling us when what we accept is a trustworthy guide to truth. Principle TR is not simply postulated or merely assumed to be a first principle. On the contrary, the content of principle T combined with the objectives of justification provides a reason for considering acceptance of it to be justified. Other proposed first principles, on the other hand, are simply postulated or merely assumed. Thus, we have avoided the alternatives of the trilemma by arguing that accepting T can personally justify a person in accepting T for the purpose of obtaining truth and avoiding error.

A detractor might, of course, object that what we have done is to use principle T to justify itself and, therefore, have fallen into the smallest possible circle of justification rather than having avoided it. Similarly, such a detractor might object that, to be strictly accurate, we are not appealing to principle T to justify itself but to a higher-order principle referring to truths of a lower level to which T belongs, and, therefore, we are falling into an infinite regress proceeding from each level to the next higher level in order to justify versions of T indexed to the various levels in the truth hierarchy. This detractor is not one with which I should care to dispute but one which I would seek to mollify. I suggest there is nothing vicious in the regress or the circle mentioned, and I have no objection to principle TR being represented as a circular or regressive principle of justification. Rather, I contend there is no logical defect involved. The regress does not commit us to carrying out an infinite series of acts. On the contrary, it simply shows us that an infinite series of T principles at various levels are each such that, when accepted, one is justified in accepting them. The circle shows the peculiar but significant way in which the content of T explains why one who accepts it is personally justified in doing so.

If the circular element seems pernicious, this might result from skeptical reflection on TR. A skeptic might retort to the claim that someone accepting T is justified in accepting it that the person has assumed that T is true in order to justify accepting T. Assuming the very thing one must justify is, the skeptic might continue, to argue in a pernicious circle. My reply is that appeal to principle TR is dialectically unsatisfactory as a premise for replying to a skeptic challenging the acceptance of T, but that does not show that TR is false or that a person lacks a reason for regarding his or her acceptance of T as justified when he or she accepts T. The reason is not the sort of reason for replying to a skeptical challenge. It is, nevertheless, a reason that explains the truth of TR. To understand the point, suppose a skeptic were simply to deny the truth of T when I assert it. I have no reply to his denial that would not gratuitously beg the question. If T is false, then I am not a trustworthy evaluator of truth, and it would be pointless for me to attempt to show the truth lies on my side. On the other hand, if I proceed to offer argument, I have assumed I am a trustworthy evaluator of truth and gratuitously begged the question. In this dispute, a wise person would do as Reid said he would, hold his hand over his mouth in silence.[14] Yet, accepting T as I do, I am justified in so doing, whether I say so or remain silent.

UNDEFEATED JUSTIFICATION

A skeptic might remain undaunted by the foregoing considerations and argue that if T is, in fact, false, then, though a person accepting T as true may be personally justified in accepting T and the common sense claims supported by T on the basis of what the person accepts, the person is not objectively justified in accepting T or the other claims supported thereby.

For, she might continue, the only reason the person has to justify accepting T is T itself, or something depending on T, and T is false. If the justification a person has for what she accepts depends essentially on some reason or premise that is false, then the justification is defeated by the error on which it rests. Suppose the evil demon hypothesis of Descartes or the brain-in-vat hypothesis of Putnam is true, she might suggest, then T would be false, we would lack one sort of justification we require for knowledge, and we would be ignorant.[15]

I agree with such a skeptic. There is some ambiguity in the notion of justification, however, that can lead to perplexity. Cohen noted a person in an evil demon universe is justified in accepting what he does because the person accepts what he or she does in an epistemically impeccable manner.[16] When such a person accepts that he sees his hand before him, he has exactly the same reasons for thinking what he accepts is true as any person in the actual world. He cannot be faulted in any way and is, therefore, justified in what he accepts. I agree that the person is, in one sense, justified in what he accepts, but I agree with the skeptic who says that if T is false, then the justification the person has for accepting what he does is defeated by an error on which it rests. I would put this by saying the person is personally justified, perhaps epistemically virtuous as well, but the justification is defeated. The point is of critical importance in epistemology. Gettier noted the importance originally, arguing that justified true belief was not sufficient for knowledge, but the implications extend far beyond the problem he originally raised to the truth contained in externalism, reliabilism, and probabilism.[17] Undefeated objective justification that does not rest on any error depends on the truth of T, that is, on our actually being trustworthy evaluators of truth.

The view I am defending might be described as doxastic reliabilism, a doxastic cousin of historical reliabilism of Goldman. Goldman has proposed that whether a belief is justified in the requisite sense depends on whether or not it is the result of a reliable belief-forming process, where the notion of resulting from a process is broadly construed to cover both origination and sustenance of a belief.[18] I have argued that acceptance rather than belief is the key notion and that the sort of origination and sustenance Goldman, Swain, and others appeal to are not necessary to justification.[19] I agree with him that reliability or probability is central. But it is the state of accepting something that must be a reliable or trustworthy guide to truth rather than the process that originates or sustains acceptance. I can imagine a person accepting something out of prejudice who acquires information giving him knowledge that his prejudice was true. So the acceptance leading to knowledge need not originate from the information that yields knowledge. It need not be causally or counterfactually sustained by it either. In the normal case, someone would, of course, be causally influenced by information received. In the odd and perhaps not very important case, however, a person might, if the originating prejudice lost its influence, be mentally shattered by the experience or, less catastrophically, might fall under the influence of some other prejudice which sustains his belief. The role of information in acceptance is to render acceptance a trustworthy guide to truth. Any causal influence of the information upon acceptance is coincidental to justification or knowledge in all cases except those in which the content of what is accepted is itself causal. It is the state of acceptance itself rather than the process from which it results that must be a trustworthy guide to truth in order to yield objective or undefeated justification.

The notion of undefeated justification is, intuitively put, justification based on an acceptance system that is, in a special sense, beyond criticism. The sense in which the justification based on the acceptance system must be beyond criticism is simply that no consistent elimination of acceptance when the content of what one accepts is false, or consistent replacement of acceptance in such cases by acceptance of the denial of the false content, would destroy the justification. This might be explained by the heuristic of a justification game. The question is whether my justification for accepting p is undefeated. Imagine my acceptance system A is as follows:

$$A = \begin{matrix} \text{L accepts that } p_1 \\ \text{L accepts that } p_2 \\ \text{L accepts that } p_3 \\ \\ \text{L accepts that } p_n \end{matrix}$$

Now imagine the following game with an omniscient critic. She is allowed to eliminate any member from A when p_i is false, or replace it with

L accepts that not-p_i,

or leave it unchanged. Let us call these *allowed* changes. She may make as many allowed changes as she wishes with one constraint. If she eliminates a member of A because p_i is false and p_i logically entails p_k and p_k is also false, then acceptance of p_k by L must also be eliminated if originally included in A. Similarly, if she replaces a member of A with the acceptance of the denial of p_i because p_i is false and p_i logically entails p_k and k is false, then she must replace acceptance of p_k with acceptance of the denial of p_k if originally included in A. Such elimination or replacement of things falsely accepted is in this way *deductively closed* in the acceptance system of S. The intuitive justification for such a constraint of deductive closure is that if p_i logically entails p_k and p_k is false, then accepting p_i is an error because accepting p_k is an error. Therefore, correcting errors of acceptance requires that if the error of accepting p_i is corrected, then the error of accepting p_k which guarantees that accepting p_i is an error must also be corrected. Let us call the result of such changes system M. Suppose I am personally justified in accepting that p at t. If the critic can form a system M with the result that I am not justified in accepting p on the basis of M at t, then the critic wins the game, and my justification is defeated. If, on the other hand, my acceptance is such that no such system M has the result that I am not justified in accepting p on the basis of M at t, then I win, and my justification is undefeated.

There is obviously a set of systems, M, resulting from different allowed changes the critic might make in the acceptance system given her omniscience of truth and error. Let us call the set of such systems the ultrasystem of S at t. We may then define undefeated justification as follows:

D8. S is justified in accepting that p at t in a way that is undefeated if and only if S is justified in accepting p at t on the basis of every system that is a member of the ultrasystem of S at t.

Similarly, we may define what it means to say that a system M defeats a personal justification of S for accepting that p at t as follows:

D9. M defeats the personal justification of S for accepting p at t if and only if S is personally justified in accepting p at t, but S is not justified in accepting p at t on system M at t where M is member of the ultrasystem of S at t.

The notion of something being a member of an ultrasystem explained above may be defined as follows:

D10. A system M is a member of the ultrasystem of S at t if and only if either M is the acceptance system of S at t or results from eliminating one or more statements of the form — S accepts that q — when q is false, replacing one or more statements of the form — S accepts that q — with a statement of the form — S accepts that not-q — when q is false, or any combination of such eliminations and replacements in the acceptance system of S at t with the constraint that if q logically entails r which is false and also accepted, then — S accepts that r — must be also be eliminated or replaced in the same way as — S accepts that q — was.

In *Knowledge*, I defined undefeated justification in terms of just one member of the ultrasystem in which all cases of error in the acceptance system were replaced with acceptance of the denial of the false system. Carter pointed out, correctly I think, that such replacement might inadvertently manufacture some new justification for accepting p other than the justification resulting from the acceptance system and that S, having no conception of such a justification, is not entitled to the epistemic benefits of such manufacture.[20] He then proposed another system be used to define undefeated justification, one in which all cases of error were simply eliminated. For some time that seemed to me correct, but it then occurred to me that just as replacement might inadvertently manufacture justification to which S was not entitled, so elimination might unblock some justification to which S was equally unentitled. The solution to the problem proposed above, based on a suggestion by Kuys, is that for justification to be undefeated it must survive under any elimination or replacement of error in the acceptance system generating the justification.[21]

It does seem to me, however, that an important notion of justification results from Carter's proposal. If we adopt the technical term *verific system* to describe the system resulting from elimination of all error, the verific system may be defined as follows:

D11. A system V is a verific system of S at t if and only if V is a subsystem of the acceptance system of S at t resulting from eliminating all statements of the form — S accepts that p — when p is false. (V is a member of the ultrasystem of S.)

Similarly, a technical notion of justification, verific justification, may be defined in terms of such a system as follows:

D12. S is verifically justified in accepting that p at t if and only if S is justified in accepting that p on the basis of the verific system of S at t.

We are in a position to define a kind of justification, *complete* justification, which, though entailed by undefeated justification, is a more natural and intuitive notion of justification. When a person is justified on the basis of what she accepts and would remain so even if she eliminated all errors in what she accepts, I think it is appropriate to say she is *completely* justified. We may, therefore, define complete justification as follows:

D13. S is completely justified in accepting that p at t if and only if S is personally justified in accepting p at t and S is verifically justified in accepting p at t.

If the personal justification a person has for accepting p is undefeated, then the person is completely justified as well. Thus, complete justification, if added to the definition of knowledge, would not be an independent condition. It does, however, capture an important notion of justification. There were a number of philosophers, Pailthorp and Thalberg among them, who were inclined to deny one is completely justified in accepting a conclusion one has deduced from a false premise one was justified in accepting, contrary to Gettier's contention.[22] I do not think this observation provides a solution to the Gettier problem, but I do think there is a sense in which it is correct to say that a person who has deduced a conclusion from a false premise is not really completely justified in accepting the conclusion on the basis of the deduction even if, as luck would have it, the person would have been completely justified had the premise been true. In short, then, there is a sense in which the person is justified, personally justified, in accepting what the person does in the Gettier examples, though there are other senses in which the person is not justified. The person is not completely justified, for example. The word "completely" is here used grammatically as an intensifier, and, consequently, people will differ in their intuitions regarding whether a person deducing a true conclusion from a false but justified premise is completely justified depending on how important he or she considers the falsity of the premise to be. The notion of complete justification does, however, capture the sense in which we feel that a person proceeding from false premises has not completely justified his or her conclusion.

With these definitions and observations before us, let us return to principle T, to wit, that I am a trustworthy evaluator of truth. If T is true, the justification a person has for accepting T based on accepting T would, in normal circumstance, be undefeated. Thus, what is crucial to knowledge is the following principle:

> TRU. If T is true, and S accepts that T at t as a result, then it is more reasonable for S to accept that T than to accept the denial of T on the basis of the ultrasystem of S at t.

Again, unless the acceptance system of S is peculiar, one would expect all competitors of T to be beaten or neutralized on the basis of the verific system and the ultrasystem of S, and, therefore, expect the following principles to be true:

> If T is true, and S accepts that T at t as a result, then S is completely justified in accepting that T at t.

If T is true, and S accepts that T at t as a result, then S is justified in accepting that T in a way that is undefeated at t.

Thus, the acceptance of T, if T is true, may be expected to yield knowledge of the truth of T. We may not be able to refute the skeptic who denies the truth of T or who advances some skeptical hypotheses implying the falsity of T. If, however, we are correct in thinking the skeptic is in error and in accepting the truth of T, then, skeptical machinations not withstanding, we know that T is true and know many other things as a result of this knowledge. We may not have the satisfaction of being able to dialectically refute the skeptic without begging the question, but we may, nevertheless, know that the skeptical hypotheses are false. This knowledge does not result from the irrelevance of the skeptical alternatives as some allege but from our being personally justified in accepting that we are not dreaming, hallucinating, deceived by an evil demon, brains in vats, and, assuming we are right in this, from our justification being complete and undefeated.

KNOWLEDGE REDUCED

The foregoing complicated set of definitions reduces to a simple formula for the definition of knowledge. Knowledge is undefeated justified acceptance. That is a formal feature of the theory. The substantive part is a coherence theory of justification in which personal justification results from a special relationship between the things one accepts, a wholly internal matter. One is personally justified in accepting something because the things one accepts inform one that such acceptance is a trustworthy guide to truth. The attainment of truth and avoidance of error are the objectives of justification. To obtain knowledge, however, such subjective justification does not suffice. An external connection is required. There must be a match between what one accepts as a trustworthy guide to truth and what really is a trustworthy guide to truth sufficient to sustain justification as error is corrected by elimination or replacement. Given the importance I attach to the trustworthiness of acceptance in yielding undefeated justification and knowledge, the substantive part of my theory might be called doxastic reliabilism, but, given that the acceptance of our trustworthiness yields, in the normal case, justification of its own acceptance, the theory might as well be called foundational coherentism. To obtain knowledge we need the right mix of internal coherence, reliability, and self-justification. The monster theory may appear dialectically promiscuous, but fidelity to a single approach strikes me as epistemic puritanism. The simple theory, though ever seductive, is usually the mistress of error. The queen of truth is a more complicated woman but of better philosophical parts.

NOTES

Research on this paper was supported by a grant from the National Science Foundation and a fellowship from the John Simon Guggenheim Memorial Foundation. I am indebted to John Pollock, Alvin Goldman, Peter Klein, Scott Sturgeon, and Marian David for comments on early drafts.

1. K. Lehrer, *Knowledge*, Clarendon Press, Oxford, 1974. I have since written a number of articles in the process of arriving at an improved account. The most recent and complete is "The Coherence Theory of Knowledge," *Philosophical Topics*, Vol. 14, No. 1, pp. 5-15.

2. Cf. K. Lehrer, and T. Paxson, Jr., "Knowledge: Undefeated Justified True Belief," *The Journal of Philosophy*, Vol. 66, 1969, pp. 225-237. J. Pollock developed the notion of undefeated justification in *Knowledge and Justification*, Princeton University Press, Princeton, 1974, and refined it further in *Contemporary Theories of Knowledge*, Rowman and Allanheld, New York, 1987.

3. A. I. Goldman, *Epistemology and Cognition*, Harvard University, Cambridge, 1986.

4. K. Lehrer, and S. Cohen, "Justification, Truth and Coherence," *Synthese*, Vol. 55, 1983, pp. 191-207.

5. R. M. Chisholm, *Theory of Knowledge*, second edition, Prentice-Hall, Englewood Cliffs, 1967.

6. Cf. Thomas Reid's *Inquiry and Essays*, edited by R. E. Beanblossom, and K. Lehrer, Hackett, Indianapolis, 1983, pp. 87-103.

7. Goldman, *op. cit.*

8. F. I. Dretske, *Knowledge and the Flow of Information*, Basil Blackwell, Oxford, 1981.

9. W. S. Sellars, *Science, Perception, and Reality*, Humanities, New York, 1963, and G. Harman, *Thought*, Princeton University, Princeton, 1973.

10. C. N. Glymour, *Theory and Evidence*, Princeton University Press, Princeton, 1980.

11. S. Empiricus, *Outlines of Pyrrhonism*, Vol. 1 of *Sextus Empiricus*, Bury, R. G., translator, Harvard University Press, Cambridge, 1933.

12. H. Albert, *Traktat Über Kritische Vernunft*, originally published in Tübingen, 1968, reprinted, Princeton University Press, Princeton, 1985.

13. Reid, T., *The Philosophical Works*, eighth edition, edited by W. Hamilton, James Thin, Edinburgh, 1895, p. 447.

14. *Ibid.*, p. 130.

15. H. Putnam, *Reason, Truth and History*, Cambridge University, Cambridge, 1984, Chapter One.

16. Lehrer and Cohen, *op. cit.*

17. E. L. Gettier, Jr., "Is Justified True Belief Knowledge?," *Analysis*, Vol. 23, No. 6, 1963, pp. 35-38. Cf. K. Lehrer, "The Gettier Problem and the Analysis of Knowledge," in *Justification and Knowledge*, edited by G. Pappas, Reidel, Dordrecht, 1981.

18. Goldman, *op. cit.*

19. Goldman, *op. cit.* The best explication of sustenance remains M. Swain, "Justification and the Basis of Belief," in *Justification*, pp. 25-49.

20. R. Carter, "Lehrer's Fourth Condition for Knowing," *Philosophical Studies,* Vol. 31, 1971, pp. 327-336.

21. This was suggested to me by a similar proposal by T. Kuys, in "Coherentism, Fallibilism, and Skepticism," unpublished. See also M. Swain, *Reasons and Knowledge*, Cornell University Press, Ithaca, 1981, for an account of justification that is similar to that offered here.

22. C. Pailthorp, "Knowledge as Undetected Justified True Belief," *Review of Metaphysics,* Vol. 23, 1967, pp. 25-47, and I. Thalberg, "In Defense of Justified True Belief," *Journal of Philosophy*, Vol. 66, No. 22, 1969, pp. 795-803.

9
Knowledge Representation and the Interrogative Model of Inquiry

Jaakko Hintikka

1. EPISTEMIC LOGIC AS A MEDIUM OF KNOWLEDGE REPRESENTATION

The problem of knowledge representation arises in many different ways. Philosophers know it best as a problem concerning the nature of knowledge, especially its logic and semantics. It is also a problem in computer science (information science), especially perhaps in database theory.

One earlier attempt to deal with this problem was epistemic logic.[1] Epistemic logic is based on the simple idea that to know that S is to be able to omit from one's attention all propositional alternatives (scenarios, possible situations, courses of events, possible worlds, or whatever you choose to call them) in which it is not true that S.[2] Knowledge (information), in brief, means elimination of uncertainty, not to coin a new phrase. From this idea, most of the ideas incorporated in the usual formulations of epistemic logic flow naturally.

Epistemic logic has been by and large successful. It has nevertheless led to several further problems. Among them there are the following:

(i) A satisfactory model-theoretical treatment of epistemic logic seems hard to reconcile with the fact that one frequently fails to know the logical consequences of what one knows. As philosophers often put it, we must not assume "logical omniscience."

In fact, the difficulty in avoiding the paradox of logical omniscience seems to have been in some quarters the standard objection to any serious model-theoretic treatment of epistemic logic.[3]

(ii) A full analysis of reflexive knowledge ("knowing that one knows") is difficult to achieve on the basis of the usual epistemic logic.[4]

(iii) It is not obvious how to build an explicit model theory for constructions of the form *knowing* + indirect question.

(iv) Besides an analysis of *knowing that* and of *knowing* + indirect question, an analysis of various kinds of apparently nonpropositional knowledge (e.g., *knowledge* + direct object, "knowledge by acquaintance") is also needed.

Of these problems, (iii) will be definitively solved in a forthcoming work of mine. The key to a solution is to understand the behavior of lines of cross-identification between different propositional alternatives ("scenarios"), especially the different ways such "world lines" can break down.[5]

Attending to such "world lines" solves also the problem (iv). For it can be seen that those lines of identification can be "drawn" in two fundamentally different ways, either descriptively or perspectively.[6] The main complicating factor is that the difference between the two overall methods of cross-identification is not indicated systematically in natural language. It nevertheless shows up occasionally in ways a linguist can put his or her pen on, especially in the contrast between the two constructions

  (i) *knows* + objectival construction and
  (ii) *knows* + indirect question;

and in certain apparent exceptions to restrictions on coreference. Because the distinction between the two modes of cross-identification is not reflected systematically in the overt features of natural language, it has been largely neglected by linguists and philosophers alike. Its great psychological and linguistic significance is nevertheless beginning to emerge.[7]

Partial treatments of problems (i) and (ii) have also been presented. Notwithstanding a widespread prejudice, it is easy to give a fully explicit, realistically interpretable epistemic logic which does not incorporate the assumption of "logical omniscience."[8] This can even be done in such a way that the restrictions on logical omniscience are closely connected with important logical and philosophical problems.[9]

Likewise, a number of relevant observations concerning the problem of "knowing that one knows" can be elicited from the current treatments of epistemic logic. It is becoming clear, however, that the first two problems (i)-(ii), unlike (iii)-(iv), cannot be definitively disposed of by means of the existing epistemic logic, or by means of minor improvements thereof.

The two difficulties (i)-(ii) can be considered different aspects of a more general problem. This is the problem of tacit knowledge. The basic reason for these two difficulties is that in the usual kind of epistemic logic, only active knowledge is in effect being considered. It is assumed, in other words, that all the information that a knower has access to is already explicit, ready to be used. There is no room for any distinction between actual and tacit knowledge. This is, among other things, the ultimate reason why in the existing treatments of epistemic logic it is so natural to assume that knowing implies knowing that one knows. This assumption is simply a reflection of an unspoken decision to deal with all knowledge as active knowledge.

Treating all kinds of knowledge on one and the same level is not only unrealistic psychologically. Whether one's information is stored in one's memory or in a computerized database, some process is needed to bring it to bear on the task at hand. The structure of these processes obviously presents interesting logical and conceptual problems. Of these problems, traditional epistemic logic is bound to remain silent. For instance, a computer scientist's work is not done if he or she merely designs better ways of storing information. It is also vital to devise ways of accessing this information in an efficient way. What is crucial here is that this optimal way of activating information depends on what is known about the structure and contents of the database and not just on the hardware where it is stored. Thus in a sense the crucial question here is knowing what information there is in a given database, i.e., what the database "knows." Computers, like humans, don't automatically know what they know.

2. THE INTERROGATIVE MODEL OF INQUIRY

The basic idea of this paper is to use the interrogative model of inquiry which I have developed and outlined elsewhere to model tacit knowledge and its activation.[10] This model, in its main features, is simplicity itself. It can be cast in the form of a two-person game. Earlier, I have called the players "the Inquirer" and "Nature." In the present paper, I shall occasionally call the former player also "the Knower" and the latter "the Oracle." The basic idea is as simple as you can imagine: The Inquirer is trying to deduce a given conclusion C from a set of premises T. The only difference as compared with this purely deductive task is that the Inquirer may put questions to the Oracle (Nature) and use the answers (when available) as additional premises.

This simple idea can be spelled out explicitly by the following characterization of the interrogative games:

(1) The interrogative process is conducted in a fixed first-order language L. It is assumed for simplicity that there are no function symbols in L.
(2) The interrogative process is relative to a model M of L. Usually all members of T are assumed to be true in M.
     The language L is assumed to contain names of all the members of the domain do(M) of M.
(3) There are two players, the *Inquirer* (also known as "the Knower") and *Nature* (or "the Oracle").

(4) There are two kinds of moves, *deductive* and *interrogative* moves. At each stage of the game, the Inquirer has a choice between these two types of moves. Each move is relative to the state of a *subtableau* at the time.

(5) As a scorekeeping device, a Beth *tableau* (semantical *tableau*) is used, modified as indicated below.[11] I shall accordingly use the usual *tableau* concepts in the following, including the concepts of right column, left column, *subtableau*, closure, etc.

It is by inverting a closed *tableau* that a Gentzen type of representation of the resulting deductive argument is obtained.[12]

(6) In a deductive move, the Inquirer carries out a step of *tableau* construction.

It is assumed that a suitable complete set of *tableau* rules are observed, but with the following additional stipulations:

(i) No movement of formulas between the two columns is allowed. (This prohibition can sometimes be relaxed. The details do not matter for the purposes of this paper, however.)

(ii) A *subtableau* is closed if S and ~S occur in the same column in it.

(iii) Only rules satisfying the subformula principle are used.[13]

(7) In an interrogative move, the Inquirer addresses a question to the Oracle. If the question is answerable, the Oracle's answer is added to the left column of the *subtableau* in question.

Further specifications are of course needed to indicate which questions are answerable. It turns out that the character of the interrogative game depends essentially on restraints on answers to questions.[14]

(8) There are two kinds of questions, propositional questions and *wh*-questions.[15] In the case of either question, its presupposition has to be present in the left column before the question may be asked.

(i) The presupposition of a propositional question is of the form
$$(2.1) \ S_1 \ v \ S_2 \ v \ ... \ v \ S_i$$
and its possible answers are
$$(2.2) \ S_i \ (i = 1, 2, ..., i).$$

(ii) The presupposition of a *wh*-question is of the form
    (2.3) $(\exists x)S[x]$
    and its several answers are of the form
    (2.4) S[b],
    where "b" is a name of a member of the domain do(M)
    of M.

(9) If the presupposition of a question is true in M, then the answer must also be true in M.[16]

There are no other restrictions to Nature's (the Oracle's) answers.

(10) In the beginning of the process, there are in the left column two sets of formulas, *T* and *RA*.

(i) *T* consists of the theoretical premises $T_1, T_2, ..., T_k$.

(ii) The members of *RA* are of the form $(S_i \lor {\sim}S_i)$ $(i \in ra)$.

(11) There are two variant forms of the interrogative process.

(i) In the first, called categorical questioning, there is a single sentence C, called the conclusion, initially in the right column.

(ii) In the second, called dialectical questioning, the Inquirer uses two *tableaux* which are initially identical, except one has C in its right column and the other ~C in its right column.

In other words, in categorical questioning, the Inquirer is trying to prove a given predetermined conclusion, whereas in dialectical questioning the Inquirer is trying to answer a "big" or principal question by putting a number of "small" questions to Nature (the Oracle).

In order not to trivialize the process, the rules of the interrogative games must normally make it impossible for the Inquirer to ask ("petition") the principal question and have it answered. In brief, the so-called fallacy of *petitio principii* must be ruled out.[17] In my interrogative games, this happens partly through the requirement that the presupposition of a "small" question must have been established before the question is asked, partly through the various limitations which may be imposed on the answers that the Oracle will yield in the different applications of my general schema.

Unless otherwise specified, I shall assume that we are dealing with categorical questioning.

(12) In a variant form of the process, a third kind of move is allowed to the Inquirer (at the Inquirer's discretion). This

move consists in moving a premise of the form $(S_i \vee \sim S_i)$ from *RA* to the left column.

This kind of move is called a question-backing move, for reasons to be explained later.

(13) Another variant form of the interrogative games is obtained by allowing the Inquirer the option of introducing an explicit definition into the game, instead of making any of the other kinds of moves (interrogative, deductive, or question-backing moves). Such a step is called a definitory move. In order to be able to make such a move, the presuppositions of the definition (in the usual sense of the word) must be present in the left column of the relevant *subtableau*.[18]

3. TACIT VS. ACTIVE KNOWLEDGE

How can the interrogative model be used to explicate the notion of knowledge and to distinguish its several varieties from each other?

Let us begin from the idea of *tacit knowledge*.[19] It was said earlier that one of the major problems with existing epistemic logics is that all knowledge in them is treated in effect as if it were active, no room being left for tacit knowledge. Yet it is clear that much of the information one has access to is not being put to use at any given moment of time. What is even more important, the selection of what knowledge is actually activated plays an important role in one's reasoning and, hence, has somehow to find a niche in a satisfactory model of knowing.

One first task is thus to incorporate the notion of tacit knowledge in the interrogative model. For the reasons indicated, tacit knowledge cannot be identified with the set of premises the Inquirer has available for the interrogative process or has established through the process. It is much more naturally represented as the "database" within the help of which the Inquirer is carrying out the interrogative process. In other words, tacit knowledge should be thought of as a source of answers to the questions which the Inquirer addresses to it. This source cannot of course in this case be thought of literally as Nature, but must rather be thought of as the Inquirer's own store of information. Hence I shall call it "the Oracle" rather than "Nature" whenever the activation of tacit knowledge is being discussed.

We can — and we shall in fact — amplify the entire model by making it possible for the Inquirer to address his or her questions to either one of two sources of information. One represents the Inquirer's tacit knowledge and is called the Oracle. The other is to be thought of as the source of the information which the Inquirer can extract from his or her environment. For some purposes, the distinction between the two sources of answers matters.

This will be indicated by specifying the source (the Oracle or Nature). Sometimes, the distinction is without difference. This, too, will be indicated in some way or other.

The concept of tacit knowledge can now be defined as follows:

Def. 1. The Inquirer's *tacit knowledge* is represented by a set of *TK* of propositions S_i (i $\in$ tk). This set defines what questions the Oracle will answer. It will answer only such questions as have an answer in *TK*.

But why should the kind of tacit knowledge thus defined differ significantly from active knowledge? The sole role of the items S_i (i $\in$ tk) available as Oracle's answers is after all that they may become additional active premises of the Inquirer's questioning process. Hence it may seem that the distinction between tacit and active knowledge does not matter very much.

What makes a crucial difference here is the role of the two kinds of knowledge in the Inquirer's strategy selection. The items of active knowledge, e.g., the different initial premises T_i in the left column of the Inquirer's *tableau*, are by definition known to the Inquirer. The Inquirer knows which premises are available to be used in the rest of the questioning. The Inquirer can accordingly use this knowledge of what he or she actively knows in selecting his or her further moves.

In contrast, it has of course to be assumed that the Inquirer does not know (or knows only partially) what items there are in the set *TK*. The Inquirer often cannot use any such knowledge in choosing his or her strategy. Thus, even though the tree structure of the interrogative game, represented in its extensive form, is essentially the same in the two cases, the information sets associated with the elements (nodes) of the tree are different in the two cases. On the contrary, an important interim aim of the Inquirer's questions to the Oracle may be to find out what the Oracle (so to speak) knows and doesn't know, i.e., what questions the Oracle will answer, so as to be able to use this knowledge in the rest of the interrogative game.

The possibility of doing this presupposes that the Inquirer has some partial idea of what is included in *TK* and what is not. This partial knowledge of *TK* can be of many different kinds. For instance, the following restrictions are possible (and of some interest):

(i) The Oracle answers all and only questions couched in some sublanguage L of the basic first-order language L that is being used.

(ii) The Oracle answers a yes-or-no question concerning the truth or falsity of an atomic proposition A iff all the individual constants of A occur in a certain list *LI* of members of do(M). The Oracle answers no other questions.

As an example of an Oracle like (ii), something like an ideal encyclopedia may be thought of.

Thus completely tacit knowledge is only a limiting case of a spectrum of many different kinds of partly tacit knowledge. The different kinds of partly tacit knowledge have not been investigated adequately, at least not by logicians and philosophers. I don't even have a good taxonomy to offer to you. They nevertheless offer a fascinating subject matter for further investigation, especially in relation to the effects of various kinds of partial knowledge of *TK* on the Inquirer's optimal strategies. I shall return to some questions in this direction later.

This attempt to find out what there is in *TK* gives rise to logical and other conceptual problems that are closely related to various theories in computer science, including theories of databases, frames (Minsky), and scripts (Schank).[20]

Thus the definition of tacit knowledge as distinguished from active knowledge depends essentially on the strategies the Inquirer can employ and not just on the moves the Inquirer can carry out, as they appear on the game *tableau*. This dependence of the concept of tacit knowledge on the strategic aspects (information sets) of the interrogative procedures shows the usefulness of conceptualizing them as games against Nature in the way I have done.

As distinguished from completely or incompletely tacit knowledge, I can also define *active knowledge*.

Def. 2. The Inquirer's *active knowledge* is represented by the set *AK* of propositions in the left column of the game *tableau*.

These are, of course, the propositions the Inquirer is already employing as potential premises for further deductive moves.

A further distinction is nevertheless needed here. Suppose a proposition S_i occurs in the left column of one *subtableau* but not in another one. Suppose, moreover, that S_i is true in the model M in which the questioning game is conducted. Then it will be most unnatural to try to deny that the Inquirer knows that S_i, for the Inquirer is, at least for the purposes of the *subtableau* in whose left column S_i occurs, treating it as if it were true and established. (The Inquirer is thus certainly *aware* that S_i is the case.) Moreover, the Inquirer has arrived at S_i by means of a rule-governed method of inquiry. Furthermore, S_i was assumed to be true. In such circumstances, S_i surely must be said to be known to the Inquirer in some sufficiently weak sense of knowledge.

For instance, the Inquirer may be thought of as having arrived by means of one line of questioning at a true conclusion, but as not having been able to exclude certain competing possibilities. This sense of knowing is quite frequent in ordinary use. Here's an example:

> He was pretty sure by now that he knew the identity of the murderer, but he had arrived at the answer by a combination of small clues and the instinct he called his 'nose.' This did not give him anything like the solid proof he needed. (Patricia Moyes, *Murder à la Mode*, Holt, Rinehart and Winston, New York, 1983, p. 162.)

Thus we must distinguish from each other two different kinds of active knowledge:

> Def. 3. The Inquirer's *active knowledge in the absolute sense* or, as I shall express myself in the following, simply the Inquirer's *active knowledge* is represented by the set *AK* of propositions S_i ($i \in$ ak) such that occurs in the left column of each *subtableau*.

> Def. 4. The Inquirer's *active knowledge in the relative sense* (relative to some given *subtableau*, henceforth also called the Inquirer's *range of awareness*) is represented by the set *AW* or propositions S_i ($i \in$ aw) such that (i) S_i occurs in the left column of the given *subtableau* and (ii) S_i is true in the model M in which the interrogative process takes place.

Active knowledge in the relative sense may change when the Inquirer moves from considering one *subtableau* to considering another. There is nothing unnatural about this variability of the Inquirer's range of awareness, however.

Active knowledge (in the strong sense) includes of course all the initial premises T_i which the Inquirer has available for the interrogative process. It also includes each proposition which has been established by the interrogative process in the sense that it would have been so established if it had been the initial entry in the right column of the Inquirer's closed *tableau*.

4. THE RATIONALE OF THE CONCEPT OF KNOWLEDGE

The same observations as helped us to appreciate the difference between tacit and active knowledge serve to bring out the rationale for bringing in the concept of knowledge explicitly into the language to be used. In brief, they bring out the real reason for constructing an epistemic logic. It is of considerable importance to see what precisely this rationale is. We have been able to formulate the rules for the interrogative "games" without going beyond ordinary first-order languages without any explicit epistemic operators. In this sense, epistemic concepts are not needed in executing a process of knowledge-seeking by questioning. However, what we have seen shows that it is impossible to formulate explicitly the principles of strategy selection in questioning without being able to express in one's language what questions the Oracle might answer, i.e., without being able to say (and hence actively know) what one tacitly knows.

Even though this observation deserves a fuller discussion than I can devote to it here, it immediately yields a number of interesting suggestions:

(i) The primary importance of an explicit epistemic logic does not lie merely in its ability to allow us to reason about what someone knows or does not know. The main interest (at least one main interest) of epistemic logic lies in the fact that it allows us to formulate principles of strategy selection in our processes of gaining further information. Since there are relatively few studies of this kind of strategy selection in the literature, one of the principal uses of epistemic logic largely remains to be developed.

(ii) The main interest of epistemic logic pertains to questions as to what the Inquirer knows tacitly and, more generally, to what answers might be forthcoming from the Oracle or from Nature. It is not clear what kind of concept of knowledge existing treatments of epistemic logic are supposed to be applicable to, but in at least some formulations of epistemic logic, active knowledge is being considered. If so, a reconsideration of the current formulations of epistemic logic may be in order.

For instance, we have not assumed that all tautological premises $(S_i \text{ v} \sim S_i)$ are available as presuppositions of the Inquirer's questions. (Later, it will be seen what the reasons for this procedure are.) What this means is in effect that the Inquirer does not tacitly know all such tautologies. Yet in most systems of epistemic logic, all propositional tautologies can be proved to be known.

(iii) Since the main function of introducing the concept of knowledge explicitly is to be able to discuss what questions are answerable by the Oracle, the quality of these answers is of lesser importance. The Inquirer will be faced with the problem of strategy selection and hence with the problem of which questions are answerable by the Oracle even if the answers are true only with a certain probability. (If anything, the problem of strategy selection becomes keener in that case.) Therefore, nothing crucially important in epistemic logic should hang on the reliability of the Oracle's answers. By the same token, the question as to what one's standards of knowing are will play little role in epistemic logic, rightly understood and rightly developed.

5. POTENTIAL VS. TACIT KNOWLEDGE

After this digression, we can return to our examination of the different senses of knowing. Tacit knowledge in the sense defined in section 3 is of course miles apart from the kind of *potential knowledge* one has, e.g., of the logical consequences of what one knows. One variety of such potential knowledge can be defined as follows:

Def. 5. The Inquirer's *potential knowledge* is represented by the set *PK* of propositions S_i which the Inquirer can establish (prove) by means of the interrogative process (against the Oracle, of course, not against Nature!).

Once again, further distinctions are in order. The potentiality of merely potential knowledge can be deeper or closer to realization.

One's knowledge of Euclidean plane geometry can serve as an example of differences between tacit knowledge and potential knowledge. I am likely to give the right answer to each question concerning the truth or falsity of an axiom of elementary geometry. In other words, I know them tacitly. In contrast, I often cannot answer without further inquiry a question concerning the theoremhood of some complicated geometrical proposition, even if it follows logically from the axioms. Such propositions are known to me potentially but not tacitly. What makes the difference is the complexity of the interrogative process that is needed to establish a given conclusion C. Among the observations that can be made here there is the following:

Some conclusions C can be established by purely deductive means. They will be called *deductively known* propositions.

Among the purely deductive means, I am including here the addition of tautological premises of the form $(S_i \vee \sim S_i)$ in the left column of a (*sub*)*tableau*, over and above the steps of *tableau* construction mandated by the game rules. (The former, unlike the latter, sometimes fail to satisfy the subformula principle.) Later, I shall discuss the limitations that might be put on the use of such tautological extra premises of the form $(S_i \vee \sim S_i)$.

6. VIRTUAL KNOWLEDGE

Another distinction can be made between interrogative processes of different complexity. Some conclusions C (deductive or not) can be established without introducing new auxiliary individuals into the argument, in a sense that can be spelled out in full detail. Then in an obvious sense C can be obtained by analyzing the configuration of individuals given to the Inquirer at the outset of the interrogative process (or, alternatively, in C itself). In the purely deductive case, such conclusions have variously been called analytic consequences (Kant), corollarial consequences (Peirce), or trivial ones (Hintikka).[21] As none of these terms seems entirely happy, however, I shall call them here *virtual* consequences. This motivates the following definition:

> Def. 6. The Inquirer's *virtual knowledge* is represented by the set *VK* of all the propositions S_i ($i \in$ vk) which the Inquirer can establish by means of the interrogative process without introducing auxiliary individuals into the questioning process.

This definition of virtual knowledge is calculated to capture the idea of an *analytic* consequence in something not unlike the traditional sense of the term.[22] By the same token, we can speak also of *virtual deductive* consequences. They are those deductive consequences that can be established by a deduction not involving new auxiliary individuals.

The notion of virtual knowledge deserves some additional comments:

(i) Even though I will not try to give here an explicit formal definition as to when a move in the questioning game introduces a new individual, it is readily seen that such an individual can be introduced in two different ways, either by the introduction of a dummy name instantiating an existential formula in the left column, or by the Oracle's or Nature's answer to a *wh*-question.

What needs to be specified further is merely the question as to when the instantiating individual is genuinely a new one and not already referred to, however obliquely, at the earlier stages of the process, including the premises *T*.

(ii) Both in deductive and interrogative inquiry, the Inquirer's greatest skill typically consists in introducing suitable auxiliary individuals. In deductive argumentation, this simply amounts to the well-known observation that in deductive heuristics the crucial question is which existential formula to instantiate first. As far as interrogative processes are concerned, essentially the same point is illustrated, among many other things, by the "curious incident of the dog in night-time" in Sherlock Holmes which I have used elsewhere as an example of a successful question process. In that story, everybody had been trying to figure out the identities of and/or the roles played in the nocturnal mystery by its principals: the stolen horse (i.e., the famous racing-horse *Silver Blaze*), the slain trainer of the horse, and the unknown killer. Nobody made any progress until Holmes introduced an "auxiliary individual" into the configuration: the watch-dog. "But the dog did not do anything!" "That is the curious incident," says Holmes, thereby calling attention to the fact that it must have been the trainer himself who stole *Silver Blaze*.

(iii) In the case of a nonvirtual consequence C, the number of auxiliary individuals necessary to reach C can serve as a measure of the difficulty or, rather, one kind of difficulty in establishing C.

(iv) The distinction between virtual and nonvirtual knowledge is connected with a number of important traditional problems in philosophy. This lends the distinction additional interest.

(v) Because of the purely analytic nature of the virtual consequence relation, it is tempting to think that in some sense a rational agent must know all the virtual consequences or at least all virtual deduction consequences of what he or she knows, provided that the knower fully understands what that known information is. I used to maintain this myself. Subsequently, I have become better attuned to the objective (structural, logical) factors that may prevent the Inquirer from perceiving even a virtual consequence. They are eminently worth a much closer study than has been devoted to them. It turns out that there are several essentially different types of obstacles to grasping a virtual consequence. The task of weighting these different dimensions of logical difficulty relative to each other and relative to the difficulty caused by the need of introducing auxiliary individuals is as fascinating as any open problem in systematic logical theory.[23]

One interesting thing about these definitions is that, within them, I have been able to treat deductive and interrogative moves on a par. For instance, consider the definition of virtual knowledge in which an item of knowledge is the variant of virtual knowledge iff it can be elicited by means of the questioning procedure without introducing new individuals into the argument. It does not matter in this definition whether the new individuals are imported by deductive or by interrogative moves. Thus, if we want to consider the interrogative model as a model of knowledge-seeking in general, the definition of virtual knowledge belongs to the general theory of knowledge, not just to the theory of deductive or inductive or abductive knowledge. For the definition does not distinguish from each other different kinds of moves.

7. POTENTIAL KNOWLEDGE IN ARISTOTLE'S SENSE

There are still other senses of potential knowledge. One of them is discussed by Aristotle.[24] One may know that everything has a certain property, in brief,

$$(7.1) \ K \ (\forall x)Px,$$

where K has the force of "it is known that." This does not imply, however, that one knows, of each individual, that *it* has this property. In short, (7.1) does not logically imply

$$(7.2) \quad (\forall x)(\exists z)(x = z \ \& \ KPz).$$

In such circumstances, it is not unnatural to say that the person in question knows of a given individual, say b, that Pb only potentially, but not actively or actually. Indeed, this is precisely what Aristotle does. I have no objection to this term as long as it is realized that potential knowledge in this sense is something quite different from all the senses of potential knowledge defined in this chapter, even though Aristotle apparently tries to assimilate the two kinds of merely potential knowledge to each other.

I will not in this chapter heed the Aristotelian sense as an independent sense of potential knowledge. The Aristotelian sense can be explicated as a derived distinction that can be spelled out in terms of the interplay between scopes of quantifiers and the scopes of epistemic operators.

8. THE ROLE OF TAUTOLOGICAL PREMISES IN DEDUCTION

So far I have offered definitions of various kinds of knowledge. The crucial questions concerning the use of the interrogative model in epistemology and in the cognitive psychology of knowing and reasoning nevertheless pertain to the process of actualizing tacit knowledge rather than to the input or the output of this process. Hence the question becomes: What can we say of this process? More specifically, what can we say of the Inquirer's role in it? Is there some characteristic of the knower in question (the Inquirer), either absolutely or at the time of the interrogative process, that accounts for his or her better or worse success in this enterprise? What makes Sherlock Holmes a better reasoner than his rivals?

At first sight, there is little room for such parameters characteristic of the inquirer in question. Activation of tacit knowledge seems a perfect Gertrude Stein concept: it is interrogation and deduction and interrogation and deduction and. . . . Where is there any room in the process for better or worse inquirers here, as distinguished from better or worse strategies available to any old inquirer?

An answer is yielded by a closer examination of the "logic" of the interrogative process. I am using the word "logic" advisedly here. I am calling attention to the logical properties of the interrogative process in the everyday sense of "logic" pertaining to what logicians study. One thing they may well study are the global properties of the processes involved —

in the case at hand, of the interrogative processes. One of the most central results concerning the global properties of deductive arguments carried out in first-order logic is Gentzen's first *Hauptsatz*.[25] It says, roughly, that in first-order logic every logical truth can be proved using only such rules as satisfy the subformula principle. What this means is especially clear in terms of a *tableau*-like procedure. There it means that each new formula introduced in the course of the tableau construction is a proper subformula of some older formula already in the *tableau*. (It can even be required that this parent formula occurs in the same column.)

For instance, *modus ponens* does not satisfy the subformula principle, for in *tableau* terms it says that, for any sentence S_1 in the left column of a *subtableau*, the *subtableau* can be divided into two *sub-subtableaux* whose additional sentences are, in their left columns, $(S_1 \& S_2)$ and $\sim S_2$, respectively. Here S_2 is an arbitrary new sentence, which of course need not be a subformula of any previously present formula in the *tableau*. Indeed, it can be arbitrarily more complex than any formula already in the *tableau*. The most general form of the usual violations of the subformula principle (yielding deductively valid *tableau*-building rules) is a rule which allows the Inquirer to insert, at any move, an arbitrary formula of the form $(S_2 \lor \sim S_2)$ into the left column of a *subtableau*. Here S_2 can be arbitrarily complex, and need not be a subformula of any formula previously present in the *tableau*.

Hauptsatz-type results show that such rules are always dispensable, as far as purely deductive arguments are concerned. (Actually, the meat of such results lies in showing how to transform an argument using the offending rules into an argument which uses only such rules as satisfy the subformula principle.) It is because of the possibility of *Hauptsatz*-type results that I was able to restrict the deductive (*tableau*-building) rules so as to make them conform to the subformula principle.

Even though tautological extra premises of the form $(S_i \lor \sim S_i)$ can always be eliminated from a purely deductive argument, they can nevertheless serve a useful function in logical proofs. They can serve to shorten proofs and to make them simpler. The underlying reason why they can do this is also easy to appreciate. As was noted above, one of the factors which can make a deductive argument difficult is that more individuals must be considered in it than in the premises or in the conclusion. Hence new auxiliary individuals have to be introduced in the course of the argument. Now one way in which individuals are introduced into an argument is by means of quantifiers. Hence the main way in which a tautological premise $(S_i \lor \sim S_i)$ can facilitate a deductive argument is by adding to the number of individuals considered in relation to each other. This they can do by containing long chains of nested quantifiers.

9. THE ROLE OF TAUTOLOGICAL PREMISES IN INTERROGATIVE INQUIRY

Now an interesting fact about the logic of the interrogative process is that it does not obey the subformula principle. In fact, additional tautological premises of the form $(S_i \text{ v} \sim S_i)$, inserted in the left column of a (*sub*)*tableau,* can make a difference, and frequently do. The difference in question is of course a greater power, in providing (establishing) consequences. This phenomenon is easily documented.

Formally speaking, one of the simplest cases in which tautological premises will increase the power of the interrogative process can be characterized as follows:

The only questions the Oracle or Nature answers are yes-or-no questions concerning atomic propositions (in a given model M) plus such *wh*-questions whose presupposition is in the left column of the *tableau*.

Suppose now that the proposition $(\forall x) A(x)$ is true in M. Can the Inquirer establish it (without some set of theoretical premises T)? Obviously not without the extra premise

$$(9.1)\ (\forall x)A(x) \text{ v } (\exists x)\sim A(x)$$

or something equivalent. For without suitable existence statements serving as presuppositions of *wh*-questions, the Inquirer can establish only truth-functions of atomic propositions.

The premise (9.1) does the trick, however. For in one of the two disjunctive *subtableaux* , $(\forall x)A(x)$ is immediately established. In the other, the Inquirer can ask: Which individual x satisfies $\sim A(x)$? Suppose the Oracle or Nature answers "b." Then the Inquirer can close this *subtableau* by asking: $(A(b)$ or $\sim A(b))$? Since $(\forall x)A(x)$ is true in M, the Oracle or Nature will answer "$\sim A(b)$," which contradicts the earlier answer "$A(b)$" to a different question.

Now where does the additional force come from that tautological premises of the form $(S_i \text{ v} \sim S_i)$ can lend to the interrogative process? Why aren't tautologies behaving like tautologies? The intuitive answer is clear. (It is illustrated by the special case outlined in the last few paragraphs.) Tautological premises can contribute something new because they open up the possibility for the Inquirer to ask new questions, by providing him with presuppositions of questions which the Inquirer could not otherwise have asked. In particular, they may be needed to activate the Inquirer's tacit knowledge. For there must be questions available to the Inquirer whose answers allow the items of the Inquirer's tacit knowledge to make their entry into the interrogative process.

Furthermore, tautological premises of the form $(S_i \lor {\sim}S_i)$ can open new lines of interrogative inquiry by providing (after an application of the deductive rule which splits the *subtableau* construction into two disjunctive branches, one with S_i in its left column and the other with ${\sim}S_i$ in its left column) by providing presuppositions for *wh*-questions.

It can also be seen that one of the ways in which tautological premises $(S_i \lor {\sim}S_i)$ can help an interrogative argument is in the same way as it helps a deductive argument, viz., by introducing new auxiliary individuals.

Because of the crucial role of tautological extra premises in interrogative inquiry, it behooves us to make explicit the dependence of the questioning game on the set of such tautological premises available to the Inquirer. In earlier definitions, this set has in effect been assumed to be empty. This assumption is highly unnatural, for surely the Inquirer can put any questions whatsoever to the Oracle, if this Oracle is thought of as the Inquirer's memory or tacit knowledge. (Whether an answer is available is another matter.) Equally obvious, no real inquirer can be assumed to have all tautological premises of the form $(S_i \lor {\sim}S_i)$ available to be inserted into the left column of a *subtableau*. (For further reasons for such limitations, see below.) This motivates the definition of *RA* (section 2 above), which is worth repeating here:

Def. 7. The Inquirer's set of available extra premises is a set *RA* of tautologies $(S_i \lor {\sim}S_i)$ $(i \in \mathrm{ra})$.

This definition goes together with the following rule for the interrogative games:

At each stage of the game, the Inquirer may choose to make *a question-backing move* instead of an interrogative or a deductive one. Such a rule consists in inserting a member of *RA* into the left column of the *subtableau* in question.

Instead of modifying the game rules in this way, we may allow the Inquirer to use members of *RA* as initial premises on a par with the members of *T*. It seems to me slightly more natural to use an additional rule and not an additional set of premises. This is the course I shall assume we are following in the rest of this chapter.

In either case, the notion of potential knowledge becomes relative to the set *RA*. Even though this may be unobjectionable, there is some special interest in the special case of potential knowledge where the set *RA* is maximal. This motivates the following definition:

Def. 8. The Inquirer's *available knowledge* is represented by the set LKi (i $\in$ lk) of sentences which can be established by the interrogative game against the Oracle with RA equalling the set of all disjunctions (S_i v ~S_i), where S_i is in the underlying language L plus names of members of do(M).

Many of the same things can be said of available knowledge as were said above of potential knowledge.

10. RANGE OF ATTENTION

But what is the cash value of the notion of RA? How does this notion show up in the applications of the interrogative model? I have argued on earlier occasions — in case the point is not obvious enough — that in the interrogative process the Inquirer's skill is manifested principally in his or her choice of the right questions to put to the Oracle (or to Nature). Better strategies are in other words distinguished from worse ones by a different selection of queries the Inquirer addresses to the Oracle. Now it was seen that the main role of the set RA is to delimit the set of yes-or-no questions the Inquirer is prepared to raise. Hence the set RA is very important in determining the choice of optimal strategies available to the Inquirer and, hence, in determining the overall character of interrogative inquiry. This motivates picking it out for special attention in the way I have done.

A concrete example of the use of tautological presuppositions (S_i v ~S_i) might be the following mystery-story scenario: John Doe is suspected of a murder, and there is in fact solid circumstantial evidence for his guilt. However, the DA's investigations have produced what looks like an unbreakable alibi for John Doe. A man with his precise description and behavior was spotted by reliable witnesses in a restaurant ten miles from the scene of the crime at the time. In most circumstances, the evidence provided by these eyewitnesses would constitute sufficient grounds for assuming the innocence of John Doe. The investigation suddenly takes a new turn, however, when a clever sleuth raises the yes-or-no question: Does John Doe perhaps have an identical twin? It is easy to imagine circumstances in the story in which this question can be answered as soon as it is raised, say, by consulting birth records. The existence of such an identical twin, of course, immediately puts into a new light the eyewitnesses' reports, for now they could pertain to John's look-alike twin without impugning their accuracy in the least. This will also invalidate John Doe's *prima facie* alibi, and may thereby lead to the solution of the mystery.

Note, in particular, that what makes the difference is speaking in general terms, that the new question makes possible (if the answer is affirmative) the introduction of a new individual into the argument, viz., John Doe's twin.

All this is likely only to deepen the mystery. How can mere tautologies be so useful in material, *a posteriori* inquiry if they have themselves no empirical content? A reference to their power to introduce new individuals into the argument does not suffice as an explanation. An answer lies in the intuitive meaning of the tautological premises. Indeed, the commonsense import of the set *RA* is not hard to fathom. What does it mean for the Inquirer's yes-or-no questions to be restricted to the set

(10.1) $\{S_i \lor \sim S_i?\}$ $(i \in ra)$?

What this clearly means is very close to what we normally express by saying that the Inquirer's *attention* is limited to these questions. For what a restriction on the scope of one's attention does is not to limit the inferences one draws from what one already knows, but to limit the questions one is prepared to raise. I shall accordingly call the set *RA* in the rest of this work the Inquirer's *range of attention*. Membership in *RA* in effect defines the subject matters which the Inquirer is prepared to inquire into.

This is especially clear when we consider the activation of tacit knowledge by means of yes-or-no questions. In this process, the role of the members of *RA* is to serve as the presuppositions of these yes-or-no questions. The answers to the questions whose presupposition is no *RA* thus characterizes (approximately) that part of the Inquirer's tacit knowledge which can be put to the service of an interrogative process. Here we can see especially clearly how close *RA* comes to our intuitive idea of the range of attention.

I am of course not claiming that the role of the set *RA* in an interrogative process captures precisely what we mean in ordinary discourse by the range of one's attention. There seem nevertheless to be good reasons to think that my notion does capture some relevant aspects of the role of attention in human reasoning and inquiry.

For one thing, there is nothing new in the idea that one's powers of reasoning are to a considerable extent determined by the power of sustained attention one can command. I cannot think of a better witness here than that past master of introspective psychology, William James:

> And now we can see why it is that what is called sustained attention is the easier, the richer in acquisitions and the fresher and more original the mind. In such minds, subjects bud and sprout and grow. . . . Geniuses are commonly believed to excel other men in their power of sustained attention. . . . But it is their genius making them attentive, not their attention making geniuses of them.[26]

And this keener attention means, according to James, wider scope of attention:

> Genius, in truth, means little more than the faculty of perceiving in an unnatural way.[27] (*op. cit.*, p. 110)

In contrast to geniuses,

> Most of us grow more and more enslaved to the stock conceptions with which we have once become familiar . . . . (*ibid.*)

William James does not in so many words connect genius or "sagacity," as he also calls it, as manifesting itself in powers of sustained attention, with the propensity to raise questions of a certain kind. Such a connection seems to lurk just below the surface of what James says, however, and is made explicit by John Dewey.

As illustration rather than evidence, we may also recall how an inquirer's range of attention manifests itself in Sherlock Holmes' "deductions," interpreted (as I have proposed to interpret them) as interrogative processes. In them, the answerer is Nature (the Inquirer's environment) rather than one's own tacit knowledge.

In Sherlock Holmes' lines of thought, attention comes in (among other ways) as determining one's powers of *observation*. Indeed, Holmes' "Science of Deduction and Analysis" relies, *prima facie* somewhat surprisingly, on observation. Even though the applier of this "Science" is called "a logician," its aim is to reveal "how much an observant man might learn by an accurate and systematic examination of all that came in his way."

My main suggestion in the past has been to view Holmesian observations as answers to questions he is putting to Nature (or whatever his source of answers may naturally be called). Now I am amplifying this suggestion and pointing out the corollary that, in terms of the interrogative model, the skill in ("turn for," as Sherlock puts it) observation is measured by the range of questions he can thus put to his environment and, hence, by what I have here called the range of one's attention.

This Holmesian "Science of Deduction and Analysis" is seen in operation when Holmes "deduces" or "perceives" Dr. Watson's recent whereabouts on being first introduced to him.

> "... You appeared to be surprised when I told you ... that you had come from Afghanistan."
> "You were told, no doubt."
> "Nothing of the sort. I *knew* you came from Afghanistan.

From long habit the train of thoughts ran so swiftly through my mind that I arrived at the conclusion without being conscious of intermediate steps. There were such steps, however. The train of reasoning ran, 'Here is a gentleman of a medical type, but with the air of a military man. Clearly an army doctor, then. He has just come from the tropics, for his face is dark, and that is not the natural tint of his skin, for his wrists are fair. He has undergone hardship and sickness, as his haggard face says clearly. His left arm has been injured. He holds it in a stiff and unnatural manner. Where in the tropics could an English army doctor have seen much hardship and got his arm wounded? Clearly in Afghanistan.' The whole train of thought did not occupy a second. . . . "

What distinguishes Holmes' observational power from those of his inferiors is not that he is better able to discern the tint of the good doctor's wrists or the haggard look on his face than the next man. What is distinctive is the way Holmes chooses the right observations to make, because he is choosing the right questions to ask. He pays attention to the military air of his future friend, because he is raising the question about Watson's profession. He notes the color of Dr. Watson's wrists because that helps him answer a question about the good doctor's recent whereabouts; and so on. Hence the range of the questions Holmes asks comes in fact very close to being literally the range of his attention, insofar as Dr. Watson is concerned. The observations themselves are not especially remarkable. "It is simple enough as you explain it," we might say with the inimitable Dr. Watson.

Thus the use of the notion of a range of attention as a factor in an interrogative inquiry is seen to be both natural and apt to bring out an important feature of interrogative processes in general. The interrogative model is really doing some work here, it seems to me. For instance, the need of taking into account, in analyzing notions like knowledge and belief, what people attend to or are aware of has been emphasized by Ronald Fagin and Joseph Y. Halpern.[28] In a traditional deductive account, however, there is a difficulty in distinguishing satisfactorily between propositions that the knower attends to (or is "aware of" in Fagin and Halpern's sense) and those that the knower knows in the sense of using them as premises. This distinction can be made in an almost natural and theoretically motivated way in an interrogative approach.

Notwithstanding the connection between RA and the concept of attention, it might nevertheless seem that my assumption of a *constant* range of attention RA is unrealistic. Isn't it precisely the possibility of extending one's range of attention in a suitable way that is often the key to successful inquiry?

To this, I can give a twofold answer. It is, first, in any case an interesting task to study the process of interrogative inquiry given a constant range of attention. Second, for a large class of interrogative processes, the assumption of a constant range of attention is clearly a realistic one. Essentially, *RA* defines what questions the Inquirer is in a position to ask and to have answered. Now you don't program a computer to raise a certain class of questions as a part of its query process and then change this class in the midst of the computation, even though I may change the program for the next query process.

Likewise, for relatively short human reasoning processes ("deductions" in the Sherlock Holmes sense), the range of attention is best thought of as constant. It consists in everything that the Inquirer is prepared to "take in" concerning the situation in question. The Sherlock Holmes "deduction" quoted above illustrates this vividly.

Of course, this example instantiates empirical inquiry where Nature (one's environment) is the answerer, rather than one's own tacit knowledge base ("the Oracle"). This does not make any difference to the operative point, however.

11. FURTHER OBSERVATIONS

The analyses and definitions presented so far open the door for further observations.

First, it is of interest to recall what the different kinds of knowledge I have defined depend on. The following is a summary of the dependencies:

    (i)   Tacit knowledge does not depend on anything else.

    (ii) Active knowledge in the strong sense depends on the state of the questioning game (*tableau* construction). What is possible for such a state depends of course on the same factors as potential knowledge (see below).

    (iii) Active knowledge in the weak sense (awareness) depends on the state of the questioning game, the particular line of thought (*subtableau*) in question, plus the model M in which the inquiry takes place. (The last dependence is due to the truth requirement.)

    (iv) One's potential knowledge depends on one's tacit knowledge and on one's range of attention.

    (v) One's virtual knowledge depends on the same factors plus the limitations that are placed on the deductive steps.

    (vi) One's available knowledge depends only on one's tacit knowledge.

(vii) One's deductive knowledge depends on the stage of the questioning game, for the obvious reason that more premises may become available for deduction.

Less obviously, one's deductive knowledge does not depend on one's range of attention. Indeed, as a moment's reflection shows, this is in effect what Gentzen's first *Hauptsatz* establishes. It does not follow, however, that the range of one's attention does not make a difference to purely deductive arguments. For even though tautological premises of the form (S_i v ~S_i) do not affect the range of what one can prove purely deductively, they can affect the ease with which one proves what one proves, in that the extra premises can greatly shorten even a purely deductive argument.

This observation highlights interesting differences between purely deductive and interrogative (empirical) arguments.

Of all the different types of knowledge I have defined, potential and virtual knowledge are closed with respect to logical consequences. Moreover, virtual knowledge is closed with respect to a subset of the usual rules of inference. Hence it is a relevant question as to how the notion of virtual knowledge can be captured by means of a suitable axiomatization. I shall not discuss this problem here, however.

It might first seem that the dependence of active knowledge on the state of the game (stage of *tableau* construction) is an unwanted feature of a concept. On a closer examination, however, it can be seen to be just what we want. One indication is what happens in reasoning about different persons' interdependent knowledge, for instance, in the kind of reasoning exemplified by the famous case of the cheating husbands.[29] There one knower's line of thought depends essentially on what others know or don't know at different stages of their respective inquiries. Hence a notion of active knowledge is positively needed there that depends on the stage which one's interrogative process has reached.

Another example is offered by medieval *obligationes* games, which were one of the mainstays of the logical techniques of later scholastics but which are only now beginning to be understood.[30] These games were not couched in terms of what is known, but rather in terms of what is to be "granted." Many of the problems which the medievals ran into, and many of the problems which recent commentators have encountered, are due to the fact that "what is to be granted" in their intended sense depends on the stage which the game has reached. What is "not to be granted" at some stage of the game may turn out "to be granted" at a later stage. One reason why *obligationes* dialogues have been so hard to understand is that epistemic concepts exhibiting such dependence have not been studied very much in recent logic and logical semantics.

From the remarks just made, it is seen that logical omniscience is no longer a problem in the logical analysis of knowledge. The fact that potential knowledge and available knowledge are closed with respect to logical consequence is only to be expected, and does not present any interpretational problem whatsoever.

Other obvious connections between the different kinds of knowledge can likewise be noted. All tacit knowledge is available knowledge. However, not all tacit knowledge is potential knowledge, for it also requires the right range of attention to be capable of being activated. All potential knowledge is not virtual knowledge, either, for it may depend for its actualization on more complicated deductive moves than is allowed for virtual knowledge. All these observations help to clarify further the nature of the notions I defined above.

We can thus see that the interrogative model performs a valuable service to the study of knowledge representation, to cognitive science, and to epistemology by enabling us to separate from each other a variety of different senses and kinds of knowledge which in fact are seen to differ from each other in our cognitive practice.

12. KNOWING THAT ONE KNOWS

One of the most interesting problems on which the interrogative model and the conceptualizations based on it can throw light is the correlated notions of knowing that one knows and implicit knowledge. (By implicit knowledge, I mean knowledge of which the person in question fails to know that he or she knows.)

The most important observation that can be made concerns a failure on the part of the Inquirer to know actively what is an item of knowledge available to the Inquirer, in the sense of being an element of *AK*. The following are among the factors that can occasion such a failure:

    (i)   Limitations of the Inquirer's range of attention *RA*. Such a limitation may imply that an item of tacit knowledge is not activated because the presuppositions of the right questions are not available.

    (ii)   The Inquirer may fail to have any idea what there is in his or her tacit knowledge.

   (iii) An explicit, actively known conclusion can be elicited from the Inquirer's tacit knowledge only by means of complicated interrogative and deductive steps and is therefore not actively or even virtually known by the Inquirer.

All these senses of not knowing what one knows have to be distinguished from the purely psychological sense in which a reasoner can fail to pay attention to what he or she is doing.

As was pointed out above, the sense (ii) of not knowing what one knows does not show up directly in the moves that the Inquirer can or cannot make. It will show up in the repertoire of strategies which the Inquirer has available to him or her in deciding. The extensive form of the game may in other words sport the same game tree, but the information sets are different.

In fact, the task of using partial knowledge of what then is in the Inquirer's tacit knowledge for the purpose of using this tacit knowledge effectively is similar to the problems one encounters in computer science and artificial intelligence in trying to make optimal use of a database (or its equivalent). In some cases, part of the Inquirer's early strategy may in fact aim at finding out, by means of suitable questions, what questions the Oracle can answer, i.e., what information there is in the Inquirer's tacit knowledge, in order to use this information in the best possible manner. We might call questions of the former type (especially when the Oracle is another human being, as in a teaching situation) diagnostic questions and those of the latter type question information-seeking questions in a narrow sense of the expression.

As was pointed out in section 4 above, success in this subsidiary enterprise of diagnosing the extent of the Oracle's knowledge will enhance the Inquirer's chances of accomplishing his or her main purpose of information-seeking. Hence it normally is advantageous for the Inquirer to know the limits of his or her knowledge, even to know what he or she does not know. Thus we reach an explanation and justification of the old emphasis on the importance of knowing one's ignorance, which goes back all the way to Socrates.

One of the most characteristic features of the earlier discussions of knowing that one knows is that in it the different senses (i)-(iii) — especially perhaps (ii) and (iii) — are assimilated to each other. As an example, consider the slaveboy scene of Plato's *Meno*.[31] There Plato lets Socrates show how the slaveboy knew a certain geometrical truth without knowing that he knew, in the sense of knowing it deductively and hence potentially but not actively. This potential knowledge and its activation through Socrates' skillful questioning (interrogative game) is all the more impressive as it is not virtual knowledge but requires a construction of the fuller diagram by Socrates, i.e., the introduction of several new auxiliary geometrical objects into the argument. From this point of knowledge activation Plato lets Socrates infer that the initially unknown knowledge was remembered knowledge, thus supporting the idea of *anamnesis*. The assumption is that the geometrical knowledge in question was tacit knowledge and hence not known. This makes a difference, for the recognition of an item of information as potential (rather than tacit) knowledge would not have supported the theory of *anamnesis* in the least. Hence Plato is in effect assimilating tacit and potential knowledge to each other, which means assimilating the two different kinds of "not knowing that one knows" (ii) and (iii) to each other.

Still another — and perhaps even subtler — way of looking at what Socrates did is to think of him as extending the slaveboy's range of attention and thereby activating his so far merely available knowledge. As was noted earlier, however, this presupposes considering the slaveboy's nonactive knowledge as tacit rather than potential knowledge.

NOTES

The research reported here was facilitated by NSF Grant No. IST-8310936 (Information Science and Technology, PIs Jaakko Hintikka and C.J.B. Macmillan).

1. See Jaakko Hintikka, *Knowledge and Belief: An Introduction to the Two Notions*, Cornell University Press, Ithaca, N.Y., 1962.

2. In epistemic logic, it is obvious that the relevant alternatives to the actual state of affairs or course of events cannot normally be entire "possible worlds" in any literal sense of the term. Right from the beginning of serious epistemic logic, those alternatives could have been called, more appropriately, "scenarios" or "situations." Hence the recent emphasis on "situations" rather than "possible worlds" is no news in epistemic logic, contrary claims notwithstanding.

3. The paradox of logical omniscience is Noam Chomsky's reason for distrusting model-theoretical ("possible worlds") treatments of the logics of different propositional attitudes like knowledge; see Noam Chomsky with Riny Huybregts and Henk van Riemsdijk, *The Generative Enterprise*, Foris, Dordrecht, 1982, pp. 90-91. Chomsky nevertheless is simply wrong in saying that "there isn't any imaginable way to make" such a model-theoretical logic work. Someone ought to tell Chomsky that, imaginable or not, perfectly natural model-theoretical treatments of epistemic logic avoiding the paradox have existed since 1975; see Veikko Rantala, "Urn Models: A New Kind of Non-Standard Model for First-Order Logic," *Journal of Philosophical Logic*, vol. 4 (1975), pp. 455-474, and Jaakko Hintikka, "Impossible Possible Worlds Vindicated," *ibid.*, pp. 475-484, both reprinted in Esa Saarinen, editor, *Game-Theoretical Semantics*, D. Reidel, Dordrecht, 1979.

4. Cf. *Knowledge and Belief* (note 2 above), and the special *Synthese* edition dealing with this problem (vol. 21, no. 2, June 1970).

5. Most of the ideas needed here have been expounded in earlier works of mine, partly collected in *Models for Modalities*, D. Reidel, Dordrecht, 1969, and *The Intentions of Intentionality*, D. Reidel, Dordrecht, 1975. The one idea missing (or at least not sufficiently emphasized) so far is a sharp distinction between two different ways in which world lines can break down. Sometimes we know perfectly what it would be like for a given individual b to exist in some one world, even if it

does not do so. However, in other cases, one cannot (even in principle) know what a given individual b would be like if it existed in a certain world. Then it does not even make sense to ask whether it exists there or not. In the former case, $(\exists x)(b = x)$ fails to be true; in the latter case, $(b = b)$ is not true, either.

6. Cf. ch. 3 of *The Intentions of Intentionality* (note 5 above); ch. 11 of Jaakko Hintikka, *Knowledge and the Known* (D. Reidel, Dordrecht, 1974); and ch. 8 of *Models for Modalities* (note 5 above).

7. It turns out that the distinction between the two modes of cross-identification, suitably generalized, manifests itself in actual human cognition in the form of two cognitive systems, one public and impersonal ("what" system) and the other knower-centered ("where" system). Another form of the same contrast is Tulving's distinction between what he calls semantic memory and episodic memory; see Endel Tulving, *Elements of Episodic Memory*, Clarendon Press, Oxford, 1983. It is turning out also that the two cognitive systems are even anatomically distinguishable from each other; see Lucia Vaina, *From Perception to Cognition*, D. Reidel, Dordrecht, forthcoming.

8. Cf. note 3 above. For earlier, proof-theoretical solutions to the problem, see Jaakko Hintikka, *Logic, Language-Games, and Information*, Clarendon Press, Oxford, 1973, and "Knowledge, Belief, and Logical Consequence," in J.M.E. Moravcsik, editor, *Logic and Philosophy for Linguists*, Mouton, The Hague, 1974, pp. 165-176.

9. See *Logic, Language-Games, and Information* (note 8 above); Jaakko Hintikka, "Aristotle's Incontinent Logician," *Ajatus* , vol. 37 (1978), pp. 48-65; and "C.S. Peirce's 'First Real Discovery' and Its Contemporary Significance," in Eugene Freeman, editor, *The Relevance of Charles Peirce*, The Hegeler Institute, LaSalle, 1983, pp. 107-118. Christopher Hookway, in his book *Peirce (The Arguments of Philosophers)*, Routledge & Kegan Paul, London, 1985, pp. 199-200, notes my discovery of Peirce's awareness of the crucial distinction that helps to solve the omniscience problem. He nevertheless dismisses my reconstruction because it is a purely logical one. I find this not only strange but perverse. Hookway apparently thinks that every logical reconstruction of an interesting philosophical distinction is a matter of pure syntax, for he adduces allegedly against reconstruction of a number of interesting general consequences of Peirce's distinction and of problems it led Peirce to. Those consequences are in fact extremely closely related to my reconstruction of Peirce and hence support it. The only reason why Hookway imagines that they speak against it is obviously his blindness to any way of viewing logic except purely syntactically.

10. See my paper "What is the Logic of Experimental Inquiry?" forthcoming in *Synthese*, vol. 74 (1988), and the references listed there.

11. See E.W. Beth, "Semantic Entailment and Formal Derivability," *Mededelingen van de Koninklijke Nederlandse Akademie van Wetenschappen*, Afd. Letterkunde, N.R. vol. 18, no. 13, Amsterdam, 1955.

12. In order to reach a Gentzen-type argument from a closed semantical *tableau*, one has to reverse the direction of the procedure and list all formulas in the left column on the left side of the sequent sign and all formulas in the right column

on the right side of the sequent sign. Of course, a few additional applications of the structural rules are also needed in the Gentzen formulation.

13. Each formula newly introduced by a deductive move must be a subformula (or a substitution-instance of one) of an earlier formula in the same column.

14. Cf. my paper "What Is the Logic of Experimental Inquiry?" *op. cit.*, and the references given there.

15. For the theory of questions and answers presupposed here, see Jaakko Hintikka, *The Semantics of Questions and the Questions of Semantics (Acta Philosophica Fennica*, vol. 28, no. 4), Societas Philosophica Fennica, Helsinki, 1976.

16. This assumption that Nature's answers are always true (and known by the Inquirer to be true) must of course be relaxed in a completely realistic model of inquiry. Some comments as to what happens in that case are found in my paper, "The Interrogative Model of Inquiry and Probabilistic Inference," *Erkenntnis,* vol. 26 (1987), pp. 429-442.

17. Cf. Jaakko Hintikka, "The Fallacy of Fallacies," *Argumentation,* vol. 1 (1987), pp. 211-238.

18. For these presuppositions, see, e.g., Patrick Suppes, *Introduction to Logic*, D. Van Nostrand, Princeton, 1957, ch. 8.

19. I am not proposing to deal with all senses of tacit knowledge in this paper. What is often meant by tacit knowledge is more appropriately called tacit or unconscious reasoning, which may manifest itself as skillful performances of certain tasks. Within the interrogative approach to reasoning, such "tacit knowledge" can perhaps be dealt with by imposing suitable closure conditions on the set *TK* representing the Inquirer's tacit knowledge. We could require, e.g., that it be closed with respect to certain restricted versions of the interrogative procedure itself (another interrogative game played, as it were, by the Inquirer's unconscious mind against the Oracle). This approach looks promising but would lead immediately to the question as to what kinds of inferential (interrogative or deductive) steps are difficult for the spontaneous human information processing faculty to perform. More thought must be devoted to this task before a satisfactory model can be proposed. For instance, virtual knowledge reaches beyond such unconscious inference, for certain propositional inferences are harder for us humans to perform than others.

20. Cf., e.g., Michael L. Brodie, John Mylopoulos, and Joachim W. Schmidt, editors, *On Conceptual Modelling*, Springer-Verlag, New York & Berlin, 1984; J.F. Sowa, *Conceptual Structures*, Addison-Wesley, Reading, Mass., 1984; Marvin Minsky, "A Framework for Representing Knowledge," in P.H. Winston, editor, *The Psychology of Computer Vision*, McGraw-Hill, New York, 1975, pp. 95-128; and Roger Schank and Robert P. Abelson, *Scripts, Plans, Goals and Understanding*, Lawrence Erlbaum Associates, New York, 1977.

21. See note 9 above.

22. Cf. *Logic, Language-Games, and Information* (note 8 above), chapters 6-9; and Jaakko Hintikka and Unto Remes, "Ancient Geometrical Analysis and Modern Logic," in R.S. Cohen *et al.*, editors, *Essays in Memory of Imre Lakatos*, D. Reidel, Dordrecht, 1975, pp. 253-276.

23. Cf. my paper, "A Note on Anaphoric Pronouns and Information Processing by Humans," *Linguistic Inquiry,* vol. 18 (1987), pp. 111-118, for a few comments on some of the dimensions of this problem.

24. See Aristotle, *Analytica Posteriora* A 1, especially 71 a 17 ff.

25. See any competent introduction to proof theory or M.E. Szabo, editor, *The Collected Papers of Gerhard Gentzen,* North-Holland, Amsterdam, 1969.

26. William James, *The Principles of Psychology,* vol. 2, Dover Reprint, p. 423.

27. *Ibid.,* p. 110.

28. See R. Gagin and J.Y. Halpern, "Belief, Awareness, and Limited Reasoning," *Proceedings of the Ninth International Joint Conference on Artificial Intelligence,* 1985, pp. 491-501.

29. See, e.g., Danny Dolev, Joseph Y. Halpern, and Yoram O. Moses, "Cheating Husbands and Other Stories: A Case Study of Knowledge, Action and Communication," reprint, 1985; Yoram O. Moses, *Knowledge in a Distributed Environment,* Department of Computer Science, Stanford University, 1986, ch. 5.

30. Cf. Eleanor Stump and Paul Vincent Spade, "Obligations," in Norman Kretzmann, Anthony Kenny, and Jan Pinborg, editors, *The Cambridge History of Later Medieval Philosophy,* Cambridge University Press, Cambridge, 1982, pp. 315-341 (with further references).

31. Plato, *Meno,* 82-83.

About the Contributors

WILLIAM P. ALSTON is Professor of Philosophy at Syracuse University. He is the author of *Philosophy of Language*. Two volumes of Alston's collected essays, one in epistemology, *Epistemic Justification*, and one in philosophical theology, *Divine Nature and Human Language*, are scheduled to be published by Cornell University Press in 1989.

RODERICK CHISHOLM is Professor of Philosophy at Brown University and the University of Graz. He is the author of *Theory of Knowledge* (third edition, 1989); *Perceiving: A Philosophical Study*; *Person and Object*; *The Foundations of Knowing*; and *The First Person*.

MARJORIE CLAY is Professor of Philosophy at Bloomsburg University of Pennsylvania. She edited *Teaching Theory of Knowledge*, a curriculum guide produced by participants at the 1986 Summer Institute on the Theory of Knowledge.

FRED DRETSKE is Professor of Philosophy at the University of Wisconsin at Madison. He is the author of *Seeing and Knowing*; *Knowledge and the Flow of Information*; and *Explaining Behavior: Reasons in a World of Causes*. He is, in his own words, "an epistemologist who now thinks that to understand knowledge, one must first understand belief."

ALVIN I. GOLDMAN is Professor of Philosophy at the University of Arizona. He is the author of *A Theory of Human Action* and *Epistemology and Cognition*, as well as of numerous scholarly articles in theory of knowledge and the philosophy of cognitive science.

JAAKKO HINTIKKA is FSU Foundation Professor of Philosophy at Florida State University, after having held professorships at the University of Helsinki, Academy of Finland, and Stanford University. He has authored numerous articles and books in seven languages, including *Knowledge and*

Belief; Logic, Language-Games and Information; *The Game of Language*; and, together with the late Merrill B. Hintikka, *Investigating Wittgenstein* and *The Logic of Epistemology and the Epistemology of Logic*.

HENRY E. KYBURG, JR., is Burbank Professor of Moral and Intellectual Philosophy and Professor of Computer Science at the University of Rochester. His books include *Probability and the Logic of Rational Belief; Philosophy of Science*; *Probability and Inductive Logic*; *Epistemology and Inference*; and *Theory and Measurement*. He is currently working in the field of artificial intelligence.

KEITH LEHRER is Professor of Philosophy at the University of Arizona and the University of Graz. He is the author of *Knowledge*. He is coauthor of *Philosophical Problems and Arguments: An Introduction* and *Rational Consensus in Science and Society*. His forthcoming works include *Thomas Reid*, in the Arguments of the Philosophers Series published by Routledge; and *Metamind*, published by Clarendon Press.

ERNEST SOSA is Romeo Elton Professor in the Philosophy Department at Brown University and editor of *Philosophy and Phenomenological Research*. He has published a number of articles in epistemology, some of which will be collected in a volume to be published by Cambridge University Press.

BARRY STROUD is Professor of Philosophy at the University of California at Berkeley. He is the author of *Hume*; *The Significance of Philosophical Scepticism*; and numerous essays in epistemology and the history of modern philosophy.

ECHEANCE   *DATE DUE*

UNIVERSITY OF SUDBURY
UNIVERSITE DE SUDBURY